Human Development and Capacity Building

T0384263

Capacity building looks at developing the infrastructure, institutions and people and is critical to the development and participation of humans in the economy and society. Capacity building ranges from development of schools, roads and hospitals through to health and welfare systems, education, communication and information sharing, participation and voice, governance and opportunity.

This book aims to outline the nature and scale of the capacity-building challenges facing countries in the Asia Pacific region. *Human Development and Capacity Building* presents case studies from selected countries with an emphasis on rural development and programmes that enhance opportunity and participation in the economy. It focuses on issues arising from women development in Pakistan, indigenous union voice in the French Pacific, job creation programmes in Indonesia and the role of international aid and labour agencies in capacity building in Myanmar. The rich coverage will be of invaluable use to those interested in capacity building.

Maria Fay Rola-Rubzen is Deputy Dean of Research and Development and Associate Professor at Curtin Business School, Curtin University. Dr Rola-Rubzen is an economist with over 25 years of experience in international development in various countries in Asia, Africa and Australia.

John Burgess is Professor of Human Resource Management at Curtin Business School, Curtin University, Australia. He is also one of the authors of *Diversity Management in Australia: Theory and Practice*.

Routledge Studies in the Modern World Economy

For a complete list of titles in this series, please visit www.routledge.com.

Human Development and Capacity Building

Asia Pacific trends, challenges and prospects for the future

Edited by
Maria Fay Rola-Rubzen
and John Burgess

Routledge
Taylor & Francis Group

LONDON AND NEW YORK

First published 2016 by Routledge

2 Park Square, Milton Park, Abingdon, Oxfordshire OX14 4RN

711 Third Avenue, New York, NY 10017

Routledge is an imprint of the Taylor & Francis Group, an informa business

First issued in paperback 2018

British Library Cataloguing-in-Publication Data
A catalogue record for this book is available from the British Library

Library of Congress Cataloging-in-Publication Data
A catalog record for this book has been requested

ISBN: 978-1-138-84370-7 (hbk)
ISBN: 978-1-138-31784-0 (pbk)

Typeset in Galliard
by Apex CoVantage, LLC

Contents

Figures

Tables

Contributors

Emma Allen is an economist in labour market research at the International Labour Organization, Jakarta, Indonesia.

S. Barman is Assistant Technology Manager in Department of Agriculture, Government of West Bengal, India.

John Burgess is Professor of Human Resource Management at Curtin Business School, Curtin University, Australia.

Kalyan Kanti Das is Assistant Professor at the Department of Agricultural Economics, Uttar Banga Krishi Viswavidyalaya, West Bengal, India.

Kantha Dayaram is Associate Professor of Global Leadership and Change at Curtin Business School, Curtin University, Australia.

Vicente de Paulo Correia is Senior Lecturer at the Department of Agro-Socio Economics at Universidade Nacional de Timor Loro Sae (UNTL), East Timor.

Farveh Farivar has recently completed her PhD in Management at Curtin Business School, Curtin University, Australia.

Stéphanie Graff is an Associate at Dynamiques Européennes (DynamE) – UMR 7367, France, and an Adjunct Research Fellow at Cairns Institute, James Cook University, Australia.

Yogesh Jadeja is the Director of Arid Communities and Technologies, India.

Amjad Khan is Agriculture Officer with the Government of Khyber Pakhtunkhawa, Pakistan.

Sten Langmann has recently completed his PhD in Human Resource Management at Curtin Business School, Curtin University, Australia.

Stéphane Le Queux is Senior Lecturer in Employment Relations at James Cook University, Australia, an Adjunct Professor at Tahiti Business School, French Polynesia, and an Affiliate Researcher at the Inter-University Research Centre on Globalisation and Work, Canada.

Yi Liu is Lecturer of Management at Curtin Business School, Curtin University, Australia.

Yue Liu is a PhD candidate in Business at Curtin Business School, Curtin University, Australia.

Joyce Luis is Associate Scientist at the International Rice Research Institute, the Philippines.

Basant Maheshwari is Professor of Water Resources at the School of Science and Health, University of Western Sydney, Australia.

Alan Montague is Lecture of Management at the College of Business, Royal Melbourne Institute of Technology University, Australia.

Alan Nankervis is Professor of Human Resource Management at Curtin Business School, Curtin University, Australia.

Hakimuddin Ognawala is Senior Scientist at Farm Science Centre (ICAR), India.

Sachin Oza is the Executive Director of Development Support Centre, India.

Roger Packham is Adjunct Professor at University of Western Sydney, Australia.

Thelma R. Paris is Consultant of Climate Change, Agriculture and Food Security Regional Program for Southeast Asia (CCAFS-SEA).

Cecil Arthur Leonard Pearson recently retired and was a Senior Research Fellow of Management at Curtin Business School, Curtin University, Australia.

David Pick is Associate Professor of Management at Curtin Business School, Curtin University, Australia.

Ramesh Chandra Purohit is Professor of Soil and Water Conservation at the College of Technology and Engineering, Maharana Pratap University of Agriculture and Technology, India.

Maria Fay Rola-Rubzen is Deputy Dean of Research and Development and Associate Professor at Curtin Business School, Curtin University. Dr Rola-Rubzen is an economist with over 25 years of experience in international development in various countries in Asia, Africa and Australia.

Laxmi Thingbaijam is a PhD candidate at the Department of Agricultural Economics, Uttar Banga Krishi Vishwavidyalaya (UBKV), West Bengal, India.

Maria Estela Varua is Senior Lecturer of agricultural economy at the School of Business, University of Western Sydney, Australia.

Prikshat Verma is Lecturer of Management at the Australian Institute of Business, Australia.

John Ward is a specialist in integrated natural resource management at Mekong Region Future Institute, Laos.

1 Capacity building in the Asia Pacific

An introduction

Maria Fay Rola-Rubzen and John Burgess

Introduction

The scale of global development and relief challenges is monumental. Natural disasters are apparent on a weekly basis and devastate the poorest communities who have few resources to either prepare for or recover from floods, fires, cyclones or earthquakes. Even in the developed world, there are major economic challenges linked to the aftermath of the global financial crisis (GFC) as many economies in Europe struggle with high rates of unemployment, growing poverty, large flows of (legal and illegal) migrants in search of a better life and increasing civil unrest. In Africa, Europe and the Middle East many countries are being devastated by ongoing civil and international conflicts. There also remains the global challenge of climate change and its consequences for communities and well-being worldwide.

The news, however, is not all doom and gloom. Many parts of the developing world, in Africa, Asia and South America, are prospering. The last decade has seen many countries sustain high growth rates, improve living standards and upgrade community infrastructure. Success stories include India, China, Vietnam, Brazil and Ghana. Trade and investment has expanded in the third world, and foreign direct investment has increased into Africa, Asia and South America, especially in response to opportunities for resource development (United Nations Conference on Trade and Development [UNCTAD] 2007). Moreover, there is an emergence of multinational enterprises from developing economies, especially the BRIC economies (Brazil, Russia, India and China), and the trade and investment flows are no longer dominated by OECD economies and multinationals (UNCTAD 2012).

The Asia Pacific region has been an area of strong economic growth for the past two decades, it contains two of the largest economies in the globe (China and India), several emerging and growing economies (Indonesia, Thailand, Vietnam), and it is home to many global corporations based in Japan, South Korea, Taiwan, Hong Kong and Singapore. High standards of living can be found in Japan, Singapore, Australia and New Zealand. It is vibrant and cosmopolitan and contains a spread of culture, religions, living standards and lifestyles. Compared to Europe and the United States, the impact of the GFC on the region was minimal (Burgess and Connell 2013). Alongside development and material success, however, there remains poverty, deprivation and significant challenges within the region, such as the large numbers of poor people, especially in rural areas of Indonesia, Thailand, India, China, Papua New Guinea, Cambodia, Bangladesh, Pakistan and Laos. Many countries are regularly devastated by natural disasters (e.g. the Philippines, Nepal, Bangladesh, India and Vanuatu). There are also countries that have a short history of recent engagement with the international community (Myanmar, Timor Leste). In other nations, there is ongoing political instability and uncertainty (Myanmar, Pakistan, Thailand), and there remains ethnic and religious divisions across the region (China, Pakistan, Myanmar, India). Overall, it is a region of opportunities, challenges and diversity.

This volume explores capacity building in the Asia Pacific region. The context is on capacity building and development; we are examining situations where the process of capacity development is linked to local economic development and towards improving living standards. Invariably, the challenges of capacity building are greater in remote regions and in rural regions that lack infrastructure and resources; so these dominate the cases included in this volume. The purpose of the book is to demonstrate the many different processes and programmes linked to capacity development and examine how these programmes contribute to improving and sustaining local living standards. This is not a 'how to' collection, rather it is about indicating the range of capacity-building challenges and the responses to these challenges and about reflecting on the conditions under which capacity-building programmes can be effective in improving lives.

There are limitations in the scope of the book. It cannot represent the full range of capacity development challenges and case studies that are operating in the region. It does not include many important nations in the region such as China, Thailand and Malaysia. It is not a 'how to' book; rather, it is reflective about different challenges and a range of programmes across countries. In the introduction, the following issues are explored: What is capacity building? What are the origins of and assumptions behind capacity building? What are the examples of capacity building in action? How is a capacity-building programme developed? How is it evaluated? What then follows is an outline of the structure of the volume together with a discussion of the context and capacity programmes that are presented.

What is capacity building?

Capacity building is difficult to define since it is not a single process nor is it the same in different contexts. There are many definitions and conceptualisations of capacity building. The UK Department for International Development (Department for International Development [DFID] 2008: 3) suggests that:

> Capacity building is a complex notion – it involves individual and organisational learning which builds social capital and trust, develops knowledge, skills and attitudes and when successful creates an organisational culture

which enables organisations to set objectives, achieve results, solve problems and create adaptive procedures which enable it to survive in the long term.

The United Nations Environmental Program (United Nations Environmental Program 2006: 2) suggests that capacity building is about:

> building abilities, relationships and values that will enable organizations, groups and individuals to improve their performance and achieve their development objectives. Capacity building was also described as initiating and sustaining a process of individual and organizational change that can equally refer to change within a state, civil society or the private sector, as well as a change in processes that enhance cooperation between different groups of society. This definition puts emphasis on three aspects: (a) capacity building as the catalyst and constant fuel for a process of change, (b) the importance of building institutional capacity, and the (c) involvement of a wide range of different groups in society.

Australian Volunteers International (Australian Volunteers International [AVI] 2006: 1) suggests that:

> Capacity building is essentially about change. Change that enables individuals, organisations, networks/sectors and broader social systems, to improve their competencies and capabilities to carry out functions, and more effectively manage the development processes over time.

The report goes on to state that:

> Capacity building facilitates people and institutions to realise *their own* development objectives and recognises that recipients of aid must be empowered to manage their own development agenda. This change in paradigm from donor-driven to recipient-led agendas acknowledges that top-down approaches focusing on only the quantity rather than the quality of assistance have failed. The goals of capacity building should not result in an attempt to impose a foreign model or way of doing things, but strive to identify and use local expertise and develop a grassroots domestic model. There are a number of general principles underpinning capacity building that hold the process of *change and learning over time* as core values and need to be considered when developing initiatives and strategies.
>
> (AVI 2006: 5)

The Asian Development Bank (Asian Development Bank 2011: 1) supports this notion that capacity development is a 'change process internal to organizations and people'; hence, one cannot 'do' or impose capacity development on an organisation or an individual – it has to be internally driven and the capacity development (CD) must be desired by the entity undergoing development for it to be successful.

Capacity building is critical for growth and sustainable development in all sectors. For instance, according to Alaerts, Blair and Hartvelt (1991), capacity building is necessary for sustainable growth in the water sector. Similarly, capacity building plays an important role in the health sector and community services sector (Airhihenbuwa et al. 2011; NSW Department of Health 2001) and can be a catalyst for redressing social exclusion.

Capacity development has resonance with community development. Indeed, capacity development and community capacity development have been used for local development initiatives in developing and developed countries (Craig 2005). In cities and regions globally, there are local communities that, to different degrees, are being left behind in realising national and international standards of living. In developed economies, there is a long history of deprivation in inner city regions and rural areas, characterised by poverty, crime, high unemployment and health problems and, in general, being left behind by the rest of the economy in terms of opportunities and living standards. The discourse on community development mirrors that of capacity development, only the context differs. Chaskin (1999: 3) comments that:

> Capacity denotes both the idea of containing (holding, storing) and the notion of ability (of mind, of action). Applied to communities, the notion implies the existence within them of particular capabilities, faculties, or powers to do certain things. These capabilities may have an impact on a number of aspects of community functioning, but in the context of community building are all concerned with ways to help promote or sustain the well-being of the community and its components (individuals, informal groups, organizations, social interactions, the physical environment). Community capacity defines, in a general way, communities that 'work'; it is what makes well-functioning communities function well.

From this quotation, there are a number of key foundations and processes linked to capacity building. First, and as suggested, capacity building involves a paradigm change to development from a top-down to a bottom-up process. Communities are encouraged and supported to develop strategies and programmes that suit local conditions and capabilities. Local communities have input into and ownership of the development process. External assistance and support is required, from capital to knowledge, but the process is driven locally. Second, and following, the process is participatory; it should reach out to the community and encompass those who may previously have been marginalised in terms of participation and decision making. Third, the process supports developing local capacity that takes many forms from physical and infrastructural assets (roads, power, communications) through to human capability (training, education, skill development). Fourth, capability development is ongoing and dynamic, it is not about a one off change; rather, it is about a cumulative process of change whereby external support is assimilated into an ongoing community development process. Finally, sustainability and local ownership is inherent to the process and with it comes community building, information sharing and community learning. Effective capacity building is ongoing and cumulative; there are strong elements of not only participation but of learning and adaptation so that the 'building' process can move forward.

While the principles and intent of capacity building are appealing for their community, and for participatory and developmental foundations, the process is not straightforward or direct. Where do you start? What is the catalyst to get the process moving? Who should get it started? What resources and support does the community require? What is the role of external stakeholders? How do you evaluate capacity building? What works? Is there is a process of dissemination and evaluation that can improve the outcomes of capacity development? These are some of the basic questions linked to capacity building that will be addressed in this volume.

Capacity building represents a holistic and dynamic process of development

Capacity building embraces a framework of holistic development in that local development encompasses attitudes, opportunities, ambitions, physical and human capital, organisation and collaboration. As suggested, it is more than infrastructure and human capital improvements. The United Nations Development Programme (United Nations Development Programme 2014: 1), in its report on human development, stated that:

> Real progress on human development, then, is not only a matter of enlarging people's critical choices and their ability to be educated, be healthy, have a reasonable standard of living and feel safe. It is also a matter of how secure these achievements are and whether conditions are sufficient for sustained human development. An account of progress in human development is incomplete without exploring and assessing vulnerability.

Sources of vulnerability include natural disasters, social exclusion, corruption, political insecurity, wars and discrimination. Addressing vulnerability is linked to generating capacity to ameliorate vulnerability in its many different forms.

The ideas from knowledge development and knowledge sharing, social capital, strategic human resource development, diversity management and learning organisations extend the understanding of the development process to include ideas, processes, opportunities, technology, mentoring, leadership and management as all playing strategic roles in the development process. Moreover, the process is dynamic and sustainable. Various catalysts and support mechanisms can set in chain a process of learning and development. Through support, and trial and error, there is an ongoing process of community improvement. Sustainability is important in two senses: first in the environmental context, it suggests that local communities have to be aware of resource constraints and development must not be at the expense of water availability and quality, soil depletion or air quality. The second aspect of sustainability is that the process must provide for momentum so that communities can independently manage and monitor the development process. Recognition must be given to the fact that outside assistance, whether finance or know-how, will not be continuous and may be contingent on events and circumstances that are difficult to control. Local communities will have to manage and sustain the process.

Many of the examples in this volume demonstrate how small changes and one-off local development programmes have a cumulative and ongoing positive impact on local development and well-being. These events could include access to improved seed varieties, access to expertise in crop management, access to reliable market data, access to micro capital sources, access to a reliable water supply, access to training and skill development opportunities and improved infrastructure such as roads and satellite communications. The United Nations Environmental Program (2006: 2) emphasised that sustainable capacity development encompasses

> initiating and sustaining a process of individual and organizational change that can equally refer to change within a state, civil society or the private sector, as well as a change in processes that enhance cooperation between different groups of society. This definition puts emphasis on three aspects: (a) capacity building as the catalyst and constant fuel for a process of change, (b) the importance of building institutional capacity, and the (c) involvement of a wide range of different groups in society.

Within this holistic and cumulative process, there are a number of features that stand out. First, development processes are often hindered by small obstacles that can often be overcome with limited outside assistance, for example access to a safe water supply or to sustainable energy, such as solar panels. Second, attitudes and culture may limit development opportunities; these could include not placing children in education or limiting the participation of women in the labour market. In many cases, attitudes may limit potential development by limiting access and opportunity. There are untapped resources that are being held back by attitudes that restrict participation and access to skills, training and leadership opportunities. The third important issue is that capacity building requires embedded local institutions to sustain the development process. It has to start somewhere, and it has to be driven by local stakeholders. These institutions include leadership, ownership and inclusion. A bottom-up process requires considerable skill development around key attributes such as leadership, management, advocacy and coordination. These essential soft skills may be latent, and they may require nurturing and support in the initial stages of the process. Knowing what to do and when to do it, and having leaders to do it, is equally important as having the equipment, roads and schools.

Capacity-building programmes

Capacity building can take many forms, involve different investment and partners, be local or national and have different time horizons. The DFID (2008) plan outlined many of its capacity-building programmes. The South East Asia Community Access Programme (SEACAP) is linked to organisational learning and institutional development in supporting local infrastructure investments. The programme supports accessible research in rural communities to integrate the experience; opportunities learned are integrated into professional engineering programmes so that graduates have the knowledge to develop infrastructure programmes that are suitable for local conditions and financial capacity. Another program, based in Africa, is to support the National Research Councils of Malawi and Kenya to develop their capacity to organise and distribute health research to support improved health conditions in both countries. Another aim of the programme is to support the research infrastructure and to assist local health researchers to stay within the region. The United Nations (United Nations [UN] 2011) has a capacity-building programme for the Palestinian State that encompasses a number of distinct elements:

- Governance-Administrative development: improving public policy management process, coordination structures and mechanisms and promoting a culture of service, professionalism and efficiency in the public sector
- Health: improving access, quality, efficiency and equity of health care services
- Education: enhancing quality of education services provided to all Palestinians
- Social Protection: developing legislation and institutional capacities toward achieving social protection
- Infrastructure Outcome: improving environmental health conditions of the community
- Food Security, Livelihood and Employment: increasing sustainable food security

The UN report (2011) details specific programmes linked to these objectives. Each programme incorporates a number of partners, has specific objectives and a timeline. This highlights that despite capacity building being a broad concept that encompasses material and non-material objectives, it still requires systematic evaluation.

Measurement, evaluation and learning in capacity building

Monitoring and evaluating capacity building is also an ongoing process. How do you measure progress and success? This is difficult if the processes are linked to long-term transformation and if the changes are around non-material developments such as access to information and the development of soft skills. Nevertheless, external donors and agencies are under an obligation to monitor programmes and track outcomes against goals. From this, it follows that within these processes there is trial and error and learning through doing; some programmes will not be successful, but the experience and insights gained can be applied to other programmes and processes. Systematic valuation suggests clear objectives, a set time frame, clear responsibilities and a sequential process of development and evaluation. This is the case in many aid projects where there are donors, demonstrable outputs and assigned responsibilities. This process also applies to some capacity-building processes (for example improving physical infrastructure), but it does not apply to all, for example those linked to opportunity, information sharing and knowledge access. As Muller (2007) suggests, learning processes are important. This involves evaluating the participating organisation's ability to learn and develop in a capacity-building project: this covers leadership development to the ability to adjust in light of new developments.

Australian Volunteers International (2006: 3) discusses the issues and challenges associated with evaluation. They suggest the need for a continuous cycle of analysis, evaluation and learning involving an analysis phase and an action phase that are supported by an action plan and a change plan:

> During the analysis phase, existing abilities and competencies are assessed and opportunities for performance improvements are identified and prioritised, taking into consideration the constraints in both the internal and external environments. During the action phase, a future vision is articulated, and an implementation plan is developed and implemented. Throughout the life of the activity, periodic assessments are made against the baseline established during the initial analysis. Targets set in the action plan, and the change plan, can then be updated or modified as circumstances demand.

In the examples set out in the book, there are clear cases of discrete and measurable outcomes such as clean water and crop yield. There are other cases that are more nebulous and cover issues linked to opportunity, participation and skill acquisition. Nevertheless, in nearly all cases, there are external donors and partners, and as such, a process of evaluation is required not only to assess the individual project but to provide knowledge for other communities and donors about what works, why it works and under what conditions it works. The learning and knowledge-sharing process is as important as the success of the specific project being evaluated.

The organisation of the volume

The volume is organised into two groupings of the articles. The first section incorporates those studies that take a macro perspective and examine national and international challenges and programmes linked to capacity building. This includes improving gender equality and developing women's leadership capabilities, improving training and skill acquisition programmes and addressing the abatement of corruption. In the second grouping, the focus is on regional and local studies, examining the challenges and programmes linked to rural and remote regions, and includes human development and capacity building of Indigenous people; farmer capacity building and agricultural development and harnessing community capacity for efficient water use, job generation and improving market access. The specific details of each chapter are as follows.

Rola-Rubzen, Paris, Luis and Farivar (Chapter 2) report on a programme developed by the International Rice Research Institute based in Los Baños, Philippines, which aimed to develop the leadership skills of women in agricultural research and extension systems in Asia and Africa. This chapter reports on the evaluation of the training programme in 2012, after it had been running for ten years. The participants in the programme reported on the positive impacts of the training on their personal and professional empowerment. Improving self-confidence, leadership skills and technical skills were the main impacts of the training. Around one-half of the participants moved on to more senior positions after participation in the training program. Providing training and mentoring support is important in developing leadership skills for women, and in turn, these women act as role models and mentors to other women.

Dayaram and Liu (Chapter 3) examine the motivation of women for workforce engagement in Bhutan. This is a case where female labour force participation rates have increased from 47 to 68 per cent in less than a decade. What factors are driving this increase? Interviews with women in professional employment revealed that there was a mixture of material (improved living standards), altruistic (society development) and personal (job satisfaction) reasons driving workforce participation. Bhutan has a national goal of increasing gross national happiness that recognises the importance of well-being, community development and quality of life as being more important than having an output-driven development objective. Women's workforce participation was supported by national policies promoting gender equity and a national focus on community development. There still remain ongoing challenges including the segregation of women into low-paying jobs and unskilled occupations.

Nankervis, Verma and Montague (Chapter 4) examine professional skills in the context of the growing Vietnamese economy where annual growth has averaged about 5 per cent for the past 25 years. With growth come challenges such as meeting labour demand and skill needs. Here Vietnam faces similar challenges to India and China, that of transformation from agrarian to industrial and service economies and, in the process, transforming the skill sets of the workforce. The development of skills is a national priority, and the skills gap stretches across the workforce from services and trades, through to professionals and managers. In this chapter, the focus is on reporting on a survey of managers regarding the skills shortages and the roles, functions and capabilities of human resource managers. The findings support perceptions of both widespread labour and skill shortages, especially for the vocationally trained and for professionals. The problems identified include not only the rapid and sustained growth in labour demand but shortcomings across the entire educational system and in the disjointed links between the education and employment system. There is a perception of a widespread shortfall in professional and management capabilities, especially with respect to human resource managers who were seen as being incapable of effective workforce planning and evaluation, employee support and development and developing talent management programmes. Here, there is a public policy imperative to evaluate and reform the education and training systems so as to better match labour supply and demand and to improve longer-term employment and income opportunities. In this case, the imperative is one of national human capacity support and development.

Rola-Rubzen, Dayaram and Burgess (Chapter 5) examine the facilitators and barriers to women's leadership in Myanmar. Across the developed and developing world, women remain an underutilised source of productive employment and leadership. The untapped potential remains considerable as women are consistently underrepresented in the workforce and in economic, political and civic leadership roles. The literature illustrates the segregation of women in less developed countries (LDCs) into the informal economy, into low paid or unpaid work, and their exclusion from participation in civil governance and leadership roles. The barriers to leadership and governance roles are a mix of tradition, culture, experience, resources, support and opportunities. This article utilises in-depth interviews with women in leadership roles in business and community groups and examines the factors that have supported and hindered their leadership development.

Le Queux and Graff (Chapter 6) examine the potential for and barriers to capacity building in the French Pacific territories of New Caledonia and Polynesia. Using a political economy approach, they highlight the legacy of colonial dependency that has created divisions and elites in the territories and challenged future development. In particular, there are resource differences between nickel-rich New Caledonia and Polynesia, distinct ethnic and community differences (Melanesians and Polynesians), distinct political differences (Kanaks are a minority and Polynesians a majority), and differences in wealth and job opportunities between urban and remote island communities. In particular, the article examines the agencies for change and inclusion, notably labour unions and local communities, and the potential path towards self-determination in both territories. France, as the colonial power, remains an important presence in both territories and as such has a significant role to play in the development process. In this chapter, the political and power elements of capacity building are important (as they are in the Pearson and Liu chapter) since capacity building suggests a local voice and effective participation in the developmental process.

Allen and Burgess (Chapter 7) examine public employment programmes in Indonesia in the aftermath of the 2009 GFC. Targeted public programmes can increase local employment and income, reduce poverty, provide training and develop local infrastructure. One-off injections of funds and expertise can have longer-term consequences for living standards and capacity development. Where there is a slowdown or recession, then public employment programmes represent an important countercyclical measure against rising and long-term unemployment and growing local deprivation. The chapter examines the effectiveness of public sector employment programmes in four villages in the provinces of Banten and West Java. The focus of the examination is on the employment quality associated with the programmes, their reach to include vulnerable groups in the local community and their impact in improving social protection. A survey of the short-term fiscal stimulus packages found that over 70 per cent of the jobs created went to the poorest households; the programme constituted an important form of social protection for poor income households; the programme included those on the margins of the labour force, especially youth and those with few formal qualifications; and the programme provided opportunities for those who were previously not in the workforce. In these case studies, short-term job generation was able to target the vulnerable and provide opportunities for those on the edge of and outside of the labour market. Local and family income increased, albeit temporarily, and experience and skills acquired through employment contribute to developing local capacity.

Langmann and Pick (Chapter 8) analyse the corruption resistance process in India. They highlight the importance of combatting corruption as a means towards more effective service delivery and for maintaining public confidence in government. They evaluate three challenges for corruption resistance faced by the public sector in India. These are the need to take into account the wide variety of contexts that corruption can occur in; the second is to conceptualise the process of corruption, and the third is to identify approaches towards corruption abatement. At the core of the chapter is to develop a multi-level framework to evaluate the order for research to be conducted to identify internal dynamics and causal corruption process and to identify potential forms of corruption resistance in the public sector and develop a framework for researching, practicing and evaluating corruption resistance. To illustrate the framework in action, a case study example of an NGO operating in India is discussed. The chapter ties corruption resistance mechanisms to community capacity building.

Pearson and Liu (Chapter 9) examine the local development of the Yolngu peoples of the Gove Peninsula, Northern Australia. While Australia is a first world economy in the Asia Pacific region, Indigenous communities remain marginalised and perform poorly in terms of living standards, health, education, housing and community infrastructure. The article outlines the historical application of policies to assist local development; in the main, they were misguided, based on assumptions regarding conditions that were not present, were culturally insensitive and excluded input from local communities. Not surprisingly, they invariably failed to deliver on jobs and improvements in living standards. Within the context of clan-based kinship relationships, the absence of a market economy and meaningful work opportunities, programmes developed and managed from urban centres were always going to yield minimal outcomes in terms of local development. Citing historical precedent, the chapter demonstrates that, despite widespread views to the contrary, Indigenous communities were entrepreneurial and were active traders with Indonesian fisherman who regularly ventured south to trade in Northern Australia. Building upon this precedent, the chapter outlines a successful programme of local community skill development, business development and community participation in capacity-building programmes.

Correia and Rola-Rubzen (Chapter 10) report on a programme to improve income and living standards in a rural area of Timor Leste. Small-scale subsistence farming is the norm across the country, and despite attempts to improve agricultural productivity, one of the main challenges is that of providing farmers in remote regions reliable market access. The chapter examines a case study of a programme organised by World Vision that supported these farmers in providing access to urban markets. The building of local capacity to more effectively market the produce was achieved through external funding, training, managing crops to match market demand and more effectively integrating farmers into supply chains that are linked to markets. The case study demonstrates how relatively small changes and access to skills and knowledge can make a difference; however, challenges remain where there is poor infrastructure and a reluctance to change traditional cropping practices.

Maheshwari, Ward, Varua, Purohit, Ognawala, Oza, Jadeja and Packham's paper (Chapter 11) deals with a major global problem, that of sustaining and maintaining accessible water supply. Accessible water is important to maintain life but doubly important in rural areas where water is essential for crop and livestock management. In the Indian provinces of Rajistan and Gujarat, the problem is that the available water supply from aquifers is being depleted at a non-sustainable rate, threatening the livelihood of the villagers. The chapter reports on a programme that was designed to assist the villagers in the regions to better manage water use. The programme was designed to inform villagers of the nature of the problem, to provide training on more effective water management and to support the community in establishing a process of local regulations to effectively manage water extraction. The programme involved training to monitor water use and depletion, activities in schools and across the community to raise awareness of the problem and the development of mechanisms to support local water management. In this case, capacity building was achieved through an awareness programme and through supporting and educating the local communities to self-manage the water supply.

Khan, Rola-Rubzen and Dayaram (Chapter 12) examine the empowerment and participation of women in the potato farming sector of Pakistan. The study employs the Women Empowerment Index (WEI) developed by the International Food Policy Research Institute, and applies it to the context of potato farming in Pakistan. The research suggests that participation in crop production activities is positively related to empowerment for women, however, while women are contributing in field activities for potato production, their overall empowerment status was still much lower than that of men, especially in terms of decision making and leadership. There was a gap between workforce participation and community leadership. Building capacity through effective training and development of the women farmers would support meaningful labour and community participation.

Das, Barman and Thingbaijam (Chapter 13) investigate the possibilities of shifting to maize production in districts located in North Bengal, India. Here, there is traditional agricultural production, a village economy context, poverty and forms of exclusion, for example by the caste system. The article demonstrates how improved cropping and seed varieties can make a big difference to community living standards. Shifting to maize production has the potential to increase crop productivity and returns. However, farmers require access to seed varieties, improved cropping techniques and access to expertise and training. In this case, capacity building occurs through access to knowledge and know-how, access to technology (seed varieties) and the development of farming skills.

The final chapter by Rola-Rubzen, Burgess and Liu (Chapter 14) reflects on the themes from the volume and indicates avenues for further research.

Acknowledgements

We thank the Curtin Business School for funding a workshop held in Fremantle, Perth, that supported this book project. We thank the publishers for their support. We thank the authors for their patience and commitment. Importantly, we thank Yue Liu who supported the editing and production of the book.

References

Airhihenbuwa, C. O., Shisana, O., Zungu, N., Belue, R., Makofani, D. M., Shefer, T., Smith, E. and Simbayi, L. 2011, 'Research capacity building: a US-South African partnership', *Global Health Promotion*, vol. 18, no. 2, pp. 27–35.
Alaerts, G. J., Blair, T. L. and Hartvelt, F.J.A. 1991, 'A strategy for water sector capacity building: proceedings of the UNDP Symposium', paper presented at the International Institute for Hydraulic and Environmental Engineering, Delft, Netherlands, 3–5 June.
Asian Development Bank 2011, *Practical guide to capacity development in a sector context*, Asian Development Bank, Manila, Philippines.
Australian Volunteers International 2006, *Introduction to capacity building: information sheet*, Australian Volunteers International, Canberra, Australia.
Burgess, J. and Connell, J. 2013, 'Asia and the Pacific Region: change and workforce adjustments post GFC', *Asia Pacific Journal of Business*, vol. 19, no. 2, pp. 279–285.
Chaskin, R. 1999, *Defining community capacity: a framework and implications from a comprehensive community initiative*, The Chapin Hall Centre for Children at the University of Chicago, Chicago.
Craig, G. 2005, *Community capacity-building: definitions, scope, measurements and critiques*, Organisation for Economic Co-operation and Development (OECD) Publishing, Prague, Czech Republic.
Department for International Development 2008, *DIFD research strategy 2008–2013*, Department for International Development, London, UK.
Muller, D. 2007, 'USAID's approach to monitoring capacity building activities', paper presented at the United Nations Framework Convention on Climate Change Experts Meeting on Capacity Building, Antigua, 5 November 2007.
NSW Department of Health 2001, *A framework for building capacity to improve health Australia*, Sydney, viewed 8 August 2015, <www.health.nsw.gov.au>.
United Nations 2011, *UN strategic capacity development programmes in support of Palestinian State building*, United Nations, New York, NY.

United Nations Development Programme 2014, *Human development report 2014 – sustaining human progress: reducing vulnerabilities and building resilience*, United Nations Development Programme, New York, NY.

United Nations Conference on Trade and Development 2007, *World investment report: transnational corporations, extractive industries and development*, United Nations Conference on Trade and Development, New York, NY.

United Nations Conference on Trade and Development 2012, *World investment report 2012 overview: towards a new generation of investment policies*, United Nations Conference on Trade and Development, New York, NY, and Geneva, Switzerland.

United Nations Environmental Program 2006, *Ways to increase the effectiveness of capacity building for sustainable development*, United Nations Environmental Program, Stavenger, Norway.

2 Enhancing women's capacities in agricultural research and development in Asia and Africa

Maria Fay Rola-Rubzen, Thelma R. Paris,
Joyce Luis and Farveh Farivar

Introduction

Women from poor rice farming households in Asia contribute 50 to 80 per cent of the total labour inputs in rice production. Quite apart from their household and caregiving responsibilities to the elderly and young children, women play crucial roles in ensuring food and nutrition security as farmers, farm managers, income earners and agricultural wage labourers. In patriarchal societies, decision-making in agriculture and household matters are dominated by the male head of the household (Pandey, Paris and Bhandari 2010; Paris 2007). Traditionally, Asian women have been assigned supportive roles relative to the men in their family. A range of other social and civil society institutions in Asia have served to reinforce these traditional roles, making leadership opportunities even scarcer for some. This is especially true in the field of agricultural research and development and accompanying extension sectors.

Women scientists in Asia often have multiple challenges barring them from success. Not only do they have to compete with male colleagues to have their work heard and acknowledged in both national and international forums, but if they are younger, they face the cultural stigma of youth as well. Younger colleagues are not always supported in presenting their work. Customarily, senior scientists are accorded that honour, which is seen as the respect one should pay an elder and more venerated colleague. Far too often, these scientists (who are often male) are the only participants from Asia traveling to international scientific venues to present their work. It is only when a mentor steps in to help a younger woman scientist in this context that change begins to happen (Debeb and the Center for Gender in Organizations 2007). Goh et al. (2008) believe women researchers, research managers, extension leaders and other women professionals 'must take the lead in order to have an impact on the field overall and influence policies that affect the sector'. They also contend that the development of women's leadership skills is the key to paving the way for women in research, development (R&D) and extension as well as extension practitioners in the future.

Key to revitalizing the agricultural research, development and extension (RD&E) system is increasing the number of women involved in the system. There is a need to increase the number of female scientists at national and international agricultural research centres as well as in extension systems. We need to have more women in leadership positions, and they should be represented more in agricultural research, development and extension programmes. A persistent lack of gender balance among scientists and leaders in most agricultural institutions, as well as among agricultural policy makers in the agricultural scene the world over, continues to drive a lack of critically important diversity of insights. Insights that can feed into developing the types of agricultural innovations and women-friendly policies need to be ramped up to sustain food production (Meinzen-Dick et al. 2011). Therefore, a leadership course for women professionals in research, development and extension systems, including researchers, research managers, extension leaders and other women professionals, is needed to ensure a gender-responsive agricultural RD&E system and policies that affect the sector.

This paper presents a case study of a women leadership course organised by the International Rice Research Institute (IRRI), an international research and training organization with headquarters in Los Baños, Laguna, in the Philippines. IRRI is under the Consultative Group of International Agricultural Research Centres (CGIAR) around the world. The objective of this chapter is to examine the motivations and drivers for women attending the leadership programme and determine the benefits women participants derived from attending the program.

Women and leadership

Economic globalisation has restructured the face of the labour market, as women inevitably entered the job market in large numbers. In many countries, women find the opportunity to gain steady employment that allows them to play a key role in their economic condition and increase their control over decision-making (Luke and Munshi 2011). Although women have started coming to the forefront and tried to fulfil multiple roles to bring change in the development of societies, gender inequality in the executive ranks is still an undeniable and persistent issue. The glass ceiling in terms of the gender gap in the executive suite suggests women need specific supportive programmes to reach higher levels in the executive rank. Detecting factors that generally help leaders influence followers' behaviour and identify the barriers that hinder women leadership can lead to developing a supportive and effective programme suitable to women's specific circumstances.

Leadership theory (Kerr et al. 1974) suggests that structure and consideration are the two important factors that control the power of leaders on followers. Structure refers to how leaders manage, arrange and organise their guidelines to control the followers (Kerr et al. 1974). The structure dimension indicates the leaders' governing ability and capacity to influence the followers to increase the followers' satisfaction (Kerr et al. 1974). The consideration construct, on the other hand, refers to the manner in which leaders treat their followers and contends that the followers' satisfaction will increase if they perceive the leader as friendly and caring (Stoeberl et al. 1998). Leadership technical competence and interpersonal effectiveness are key elements in increasing leaders' power and control over followers. Gender traits can play a key role in different leadership qualities and styles; women more likely align themselves with transformational leadership styles, whereas men tend to adapt transactional leadership styles (Northouse 2007). A study conducted in four countries (Norway, USA, Australia, and Sweden) suggested that women leaders emphasise facilitation and interaction, while men leaders highlight goal setting (Gibson 1995). Transformational leadership associates with higher levels of productivity, well-being, and job satisfaction (Brandt and Laiho 2013). Fisher (2005) argues that women leaders surpass the capacities of their male counterparts in several managerial skills due to their natural feminine characteristics. This suggests organisations need to seriously look into increasing women's leadership opportunities.

A number of studies have shown that leadership training programmes lead to capacity development, improving skills and confidence and changing the practices and behaviours of women (Young and Dixon 1996; Markus 2001; Debeb and the Centre for Gender in Organizations 2007). Debeb's study for example demonstrated transformational change to women that undertook the CGIAR Women's Leadership series.

Barriers to women's leadership

As previously mentioned, several barriers obstruct women in taking up leadership roles. Women's perceived lack of capacity and confidence is one of the main reasons behind the lack of women leaders (Airini et al. 2011). In addition, the lack of family-friendly policies and the multiple demands of a modern lifestyle increase women's workload and hinder growth in the number of women leaders (Mason and Goulden 2004). Kellerman (2004) argues that it is not often about women's leadership ability and capacity but, rather, about the degree of women's willingness to pay the costs of leadership that suggests women's values differ from men's values. Women also face cultural barriers and gender-stereotypic perceptions in organisations such as that women are less productive, less capable and less competitive due to their traditional role as housewives (Heilman, Manzi and Bruan 2015).

The way organisations operate can reinforce the gendered stereotypes (Nelson, Maxfield and Kolb 2009). Briefly, research on women's leadership barriers has been classified into two groups: individual/perceptual perspective and structural perspective (Fletcher and Ely 2003; Ogden, McTavish and McKean 2006). The individual or perceptual perspective focuses on women's capacity building and willingness, which advance women's careers in corporate leadership rank, while the structural perspective concentrates on organisational culture and the behaviour of people inside the organisations that hinder women's progress (Dawn Frail 2012).

Enablers to women leadership

Maxwell and Ogden (2006) discuss three set of enablers that help women's career progression. First, a shift away from traditional management style seems necessary, as the traditional approach views management as associated with masculinity

(Maxwell and Ogden 2006). Second, organisational culture change is essential to support women's advancement, as senior management develops an anti-gender discrimination atmosphere across the organisation (Maxwell and Ogden 2006). Third, establishing family-friendly policies that enhance the level of work–family balance is necessary to provide women with sufficient time to develop their leadership skills (Maxwell and Ogden 2006). When management's mindset accepts softer skills associated with successful management, women are acknowledged to utilise feminine interpersonal skills such as persuasion, intuition and coaching to become successful leaders (Powell et al. 2002). According to Tomlinson, Brockbank and Traves (1997), women leaders have a certain advantage over men leaders, as they naturally are capable of showing empathy and their feelings toward their followers.

Another enabler to women leadership is training opportunities. Providing sufficient time and funds for training was reported as one of the most important enablers to women's career progress (Ogden, McTavish and McKean 2006). However, some evidence suggested that women are less likely to request training due to the lack of confidence and management support (Ogden, McTavish and McKean 2006). Developing training and advancement programmes that specifically target women seems helpful in encouraging women to apply for training. Cross and Armstrong (2008) implied that a women's network is an important enabler in facilitating leadership opportunities for women. However, the perception of an organisation's leadership team toward internal women's network is vital, as negative perceptions of the contribution of these networks to women's career progression can act as an obstacle as well (O'Neil, Hopkins and Sullivan 2011). Attending training programmes provides women with extra opportunity to build and strengthen women's networks.

The IRRI Leadership Course for Asian and African Women for Research and Extension (LCAAWRE): background and history

The idea for the Leadership Course emanated from the Socioeconomist-Gender Specialist of the Social Sciences Division at IRRI, after she participated in the Women's Leadership course organised by the CGIAR Gender and Diversity Program, which was hosted by IRRI at its headquarters located at Los Baños, Laguna, Philippines. After completing the Women's Leadership course, the IRRI gender specialist realised the dire need for offering the same course to Asian women, but tailored and refined to consider Asian culture. Thus, while keeping the basic leadership concepts, the Women's Leadership course for Asian women in Research and Extension added new features such as modules on gender issues in Asian agriculture, inspirational talks from successful women leaders, strategies in mainstreaming gender in rice research and technology development, Asian culture, communication skills using multi-media, field trips to rural areas to interact with women's groups, developing and presenting action plans and – most importantly – mentoring.

In 2002, the first Leadership Course for Asian and African Women for Research and Extension (LCAAWRE) was organised in collaboration with IRRI's Training Center. The training course involved participants engaged in management, research and extension and IRRI Training provided a budget to support some of the participants and the resource persons. To run the course under a limited budget from IRRI, scientists and managers at IRRI with long-term experience in their special fields were tapped as resource persons/speakers. The training received high ratings; thus, the course was given every year, and African women were also invited to participate in the course. The objectives of the course were to 1) understand the concept of leadership in general and leadership relevant to Asian and African women in particular, 2) learn strategies for developing both work-related and personality skills as prerequisites to becoming a leader; 3) develop basic leadership skills for application in their work and personal lives and 4) develop a work plan integrating gender concerns in the R&D and extension environment (International Rice Research Institute [IRRI] 2012; Paris and Cabrera 2012; IRRI 2008).

Aside from developing the leadership skills of Asian and African women in agriculture, the training course aimed to make them effective agents of change in the agriculture sector and trainers of local women on improved crop production, processing, and seed management. Consequently, the course follows the conceptual framework (see Figure 2.1), which has distinct components, namely, personal clarity, which combines technical competence (power of action) and interpersonal effectiveness (power of relationship). Personality includes understanding and developing leadership skills, self-disclosure and leadership/management/coaching. On the other hand, leadership/management roles/coaching and active listening include facilitation skills, project management and conflict resolution, scientific writing and coaching and mentoring. Other components of the course include understanding different cultures; handling difficult people, situation and conflicts; relating with people in the community and awareness and developing a concept note for action research targeting women farmers, which was presented on the last day (IRRI 2012; Rola-Rubzen 2013).

In 2012, after ten years of successfully running the training program, IRRI thought it was timely to examine how effective the programme was and examine what have been the benefits to participants. Hence, an evaluation of the impact of IRRI LCAAWRE was conducted. This chapter is based from the report of the impact of the IRRI LCAAWRE programme (Rola-Rubzen 2013).

Methodology

To evaluate the outcome of the IRRI LCAAWRE, a questionnaire was developed based on the topics covered in the training conducted from 2002 to 2011, and the questionnaire was sent to former participants. The target samples were all the participants who attended the training conducted at IRRI headquarters, with the list of participants provided by the Training Center at IRRI. The structured questionnaire was sent through email to all the participants with email addresses

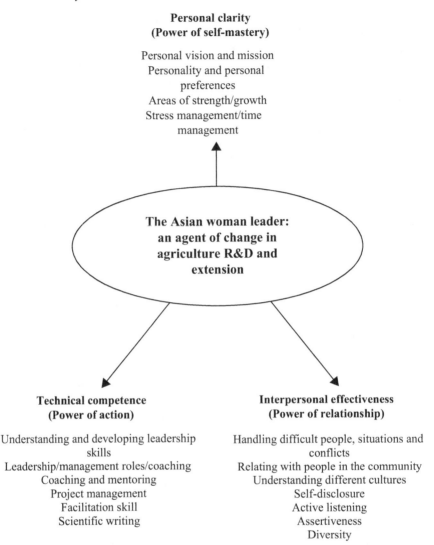

**Personal clarity
(Power of self-mastery)**

Personal vision and mission
Personality and personal
preferences
Areas of strength/growth
Stress management/time
management

The Asian woman leader:
an agent of change in
agriculture R&D and
extension

**Technical competence
(Power of action)**

Understanding and developing leadership
skills
Leadership/management roles/coaching
Coaching and mentoring
Project management
Facilitation skill
Scientific writing

**Interpersonal effectiveness
(Power of relationship)**

Handling difficult people, situations and
conflicts
Relating with people in the community
Understanding different cultures
Self-disclosure
Active listening
Assertiveness
Diversity

Figure 2.1 Conceptual framework of the IRRI Asian and African women leadership
course

Source: Adapted from Perez and Hechanova-Alampay (2005) in Avance (2010).

and snail mail to those with only a postal mailing address. The questionnaires
were sent to recipients starting on September 2011. Several follow-up emails and
calls were made, and the waiting period was also extended to December 2011.

The questionnaire covered several topics. The background information of
the respondent included the year the participant attended the training, country
of origin, type of organization and number of years employed in the current

office of employment, position before and after attending the training and year promoted if applicable. Other socio-demographic characteristics included educational attainment age, marital status, and number of household members by age group living in the house. The questionnaire included questions on the motivation to participate in the IRRI Leadership Course for Asian and African Women in Agriculture R&D. A list of factors that influenced the willingness to participate and the degree the training met participants' expectations were asked. Respondents had to reflect on the positive and negative impacts of the programme and the usefulness of the various aspects of the program. The evaluation further included statements on the impact of the training on their professional and personal life.

The information was analysed using descriptive statistical analysis for the quantitative information and narratives for the qualitative information.

Results and discussion

The findings on the motivation for participating in the IRRI leadership course, enablers for participation in the leadership course and the effectiveness/usefulness of the leadership course are outlined in this chapter. Detailed findings can be found in the full report (Rola-Rubzen 2013).

Sample and demographic data

In total, 32 employees participated in the survey. Attendees were asked to report in which year they attended the course. The majority of respondents reported that they attended the course in 2004 and 2009, 25 per cent and 22 per cent, respectively (Table 2.1). About 9 per cent attended the IRRI Leadership course in 2005, while 16 per cent attended in 2006 and in 2008, and 13 per cent attended in 2003. About 56 per cent (n = 18) of the respondents who undertook the IRRI leadership course were researchers, senior researchers or scientists. The IRRI leadership course was also popular among administrative staff, as 22 per

Table 2.1 Year participant attended the course

Year attended	No.	%
2002	5	16
2003	4	13
2004	7	22
2005	3	9
2008	5	16
2009	8	25
Total	**32**	**100**

Table 2.2 Type of organisation of attendees

Organisation	No.	%
CGIAR	14	44
Government/non-government	12	38
University/institution	6	19
Total	**32**	**100**

cent (n = 7) of attendees had administrative jobs. The rest were academic staff (n = 3) or had managerial jobs (n = 4).

The majority of attendees worked in CGIAR centres (44 per cent), followed by government/non-government organisations (38 per cent) and universities or educational institutes (19 per cent) (see Table 2.2). The attendees had a wide range of work experience from less than 5 years of work experience to more than 25 years of work experience. On average, 60 per cent of attendees (n = 19) had between 5–20 years of work experience. A comparison of the previous positions with their current positions revealed that the number of people with managerial jobs (n = 10) had increased by 19 per cent, whereas the number of people with research positions (n = 15) and administrative positions (n = 3) slightly decreased by 9 per cent and 13 per cent, respectively, indicating an improvement in leadership roles.

The respondents were from different countries in Asia (no responses were received from African participants); 44 per cent of the respondents were from the Philippines (n = 14), and 22 per cent of respondents were from China (n = 7). The rest were from Cambodia (n = 2), Indonesia (n = 2), Myanmar (n = 1), Vietnam (n = 2), Thailand (n = 1), Nepal (n = 1) and Bangladesh (n = 1). The survey also elicited the participants' level of education, and the analysis showed that more than half of them had Master's degrees (n = 17), while 34 per cent held a PhD degree (n = 11). One attendee had an MBA in HRM and Finance, and two had a Bachelor's degree as their highest level of education.

In total, 81 per cent of attendees were married (n = 26), 16 per cent were single (n = 5) and one (3 per cent) was a widower. Attendees were classified into four age categories: less than 30 years, between 31–40 years, between 41–50 years of age, and over 51 years of age. The analysis showed 91 per cent of them were more than 30 years of age, and 75 per cent were between 31–50 years of age (n = 24) (Table 2.3).

Motivation for participating in the IRRI leadership course

Attendees were asked to indicate the factors that motivated them to attend the IRRI leadership course. As Table 2.4 shows, the majority of attendees participated in the course because they believed the course would increase their leadership and managerial skills.

Table 2.3 Demographic information of the respondents

Characteristic	No.	%
Highest level of educational attainment		
Bachelor's degree	2	6
Computer technology	1	3
Master's degree	17	53
MBA in HR and finance	1	3
PhD	11	34
Total	*32*	*100*
Age		
Average age (42 years old)		
Less than 30 years old	3	9
31–40 years old	11	34
41–50 years old	13	41
More than 51 years old	5	16
Total	*32*	*100*
Marital status		
Married	26	81
Single	5	16
Widower	1	3
Total	*32*	*100*

Table 2.4 Reasons for participating in the course

Motives	No.
Enrich the technical and professional skill	5
Enhance leadership and managerial skills	13
Improve self-confidence	2
Self-improvement	3
Networking	6
Get funding	2
Promote gender perspective and gender equity in agriculture	3
The course was interesting and useful	2

Developing leadership skills was a strong motivator for women, along with skills closely related to good leaders – communication, negotiation skills, managerial skills and negotiation and conflict-resolution skills, as many participants reported:

> As a training officer of our institution, I would like to enhance further my knowledge, attitude and skills in leadership, communication, facilitation, negotiation/conflict management etc.

> I would like to understand the methods in management of human, the tips in working with the followers in a group cooperatively and happily and how to adjust ourselves to the situation of work environment, understand ourselves and others.

> It is a rare opportunity for women from the developing countries to participate in such a good course to improve their leadership ability and contribute to the agricultural development sector for the country. The course was also beneficial to all women.

> My supervisor encouraged me to understand the concept of leadership course; develop personality skills to become a good leader that I would need to apply in our work gender concerns in the R&D and extension.

Another motivation for women was to increase their technical knowledge and professional skills, according to several participants:

> The topic attracted me first as I thought it to be very much relevant as we are in agriculture R&D. I know my subject well but I thought this type of training will enrich my skill technically.

> As I was doing one project with IRRI, I thought having some kind of training on women in agriculture would be beneficial for me.

> I was asked by my Supervisor to participate. Good for me that I decided to participate because the course helped me develop more my personal and professional skills. It made me more well rounded.

Other reasons for participation included self-improvement, improving self-confidence, improving gender research, promoting gender equity, raising gender issues in agriculture R&D, and expanding networks. One participant stated:

> I am one of those who are seeking for continuous self-improvement both professionally and personally.

It appears that witnessing the impact on other women participants acted as a motivator. As one woman stated:

> I have been working closely with the other women from India who earlier attended this course. I also wanted to improve my confidence like them and when I was asked by my boss to attend this course I immediately agreed.

Some women were motivated to join the course to learn how to make a difference in gender equity and to subsequently apply the programme to improve the lot of women:

> The creation and the innovation of the program have motivated me to participate in the IRRI Leadership Course for Asian Countries, which at my period, women were treated as slave in the family of husband (if they were not educated), as handmaids who never have more knowledge than housework or have any decision on behalf of husband and never take charges of any other fields such as: Rural Development, Management (office, public relations, communication; . . . Leadership is applicable not only for rural rice field, but also for the fields of family organizing and office management too.

Networking was another strong motivator in doing the course, as several participants noted:

> [T]he chance to meet other women and learn from their experiences.

> [T]o be able to develop more friends from around the world, thus widen my network.

> To meet and interact with different nationalities and know more their culture especially on gender issues.

Along with the qualitative data, attendees were asked to present their agreement with some of the factors that encourage them to participate in the IRRI leadership skills based on a 5-point Likert scale from '1 = Very Unimportant' to '5 = Very important' (Table 2.5). In total, 91 per cent of attendees declared that 'improving leadership skills' was the main reason they participated in the course, and 87 per cent of those also reported improving their credibility as a leader was important or very important to them. In addition, 85 per cent of attendees sought to enhance their skills in integrating gender concerns into agricultural programmes and projects. To improve negotiation skills was another important factor for attendees (81 per cent), followed by enhancing technical skills (78 per cent) and meeting potential collaborators outside the organisation (75 per cent). Some other factors were also important or very important to the majority of participants, such

Table 2.5 Factors that motivated women to participate in the course

	Very unimportant		Unimportant		Neither important nor unimportant		Important		Very important		Not applicable	
	No.	%	No.	%	No.	%	No.	%	No.	%	No.	%
Availability of funding	1	3	0	0	2	6	5	16	21	66	3	9
My desire to improve leadership skills	1	3	0	0	1	3	7	22	22	69	1	3
The opportunity to travel to a new place	3	9	0	0	10	31	10	31	3	9	6	19
The desire to meet people from other cultures	2	6	0	0	2	6	11	34	0	0	17	53
The prospect of being promoted after acquiring the training	2	6	2	6	10	31	5	16	7	22	6	19
Because I was asked by my supervisor/manager to attend the training	3	9	4	13	3	9	5	16	7	22	10	31
My desire to become a better communicator	0	0	0	0	0	0	0	0	0	0	0	0
I want to improve my interpersonal skills	0	0	0	0	0	0	0	0	0	0	0	0
I want to learn how to be a better negotiator	2	6	0	0	3	9	10	31	16	50	1	3
I want to increase my self-confidence	0	0	0	0	0	0	0	0	0	0	0	0
I want to expand my network	0	0	0	0	0	0	0	0	0	0	0	0
Desire to improve my credibility as a leader	1	3	1	3	1	3	9	28	19	59	1	3
Desire to improve my scientific and technical abilities	1	3	0	0	1	3	9	28	16	50	5	16

Prospect of meeting potential collaborators outside my organisation	1	3	1	3	4	13	10	31	14	44	2	6
Desire to learn new technologies and methods to enhance agricultural productivity and food security	2	6	1	3	5	16	9	28	11	34	4	13
Desire to improve my skills in integrating gender concerns into projects and programmes	1	3	0	0	2	6	12	38	15	47	2	6
To improve my ability to find solutions to technical or scientific problems	1	3	0	0	3	9	12	38	13	41	3	9

as learning new skills and methods to improve agricultural productivity (62 per cent) and/or finding solution to technical issues (78 per cent).

Two important factors that enabled attendees to participate in the course were the availability of funds for the training and their supervisors' support (84 per cent and 26 per cent, respectively). Although all the attendees reported that their supervisors supported their participation in the course, the level of support varied, as 44 per cent reported their supervisors supported them to a great extent; whereas around 13 per cent declared that their supervisors supported their participation in the course to some extent. Supervisors supported the attendees through recommending the course to them, approving their participation in the course, providing sufficient funds and organizing the trip. IRRI-led collaborative projects provided small funds for women who were members of the team.

Colleagues' support was another factor that enabled attendees' participate in the course. About 90 per cent of respondents (n = 29) reported their colleagues supported their participation in the training program. Qualitative data provided some examples of colleagues' support, according to several participants:

> My colleagues have been very supportive of my services to our people.

> They encourage to have more women as head and vice head of department in the institute to balance the gender of leadership in the institute.

> They want me to improve professionally and personally.

Effectiveness and usefulness of the leadership course

In terms of the effectiveness and usefulness of the leadership course, findings revealed that 75 per cent (n = 24) of respondents thought the course was very relevant to their needs and the rest reported the course was somewhat relevant to what they needed. Attendees were asked to report as to what degree the leadership course for Asian and African women in agriculture R&D matched their expectations. Around 47 per cent reported that the leadership course provided them with more than what they expected (n = 15), while 3 per cent stated the course was less than what they imagined (n = 1). The rest believed the leadership course was exactly what they thought before the participation in the course (n = 9) or was somewhat more than their expectation (n = 7) (Table 2.6).

In general, all attendees reported that the course was useful, as 25 per cent indicated the course was useful to a great extent, while 44 per cent stated the course was useful to some extent and the rest believed the course was useful to a significant extent. Attendees were also asked how useful the different aspects of the training were. Aspects respondents found very useful are shown in Table 2.7.

As shown in Table 2.7, 81 per cent of respondents (n = 26) believed the course helped them to develop effective communication skills and 75 per cent

Table 2.6 Degree IRRI LCAAWRE met participants' expectations

Q13	No.	%
Less than expected	1	3
What you expected	9	28
Somewhat more than expected	7	22
More than expected	15	47
Total	**32**	**100**

Table 2.7 Usefulness of training aspects

Aspect of training	Very useful (%)
Effective communication	81
Self-improvement	75
Developing leadership skills	69
Developing work-related knowledge/skills	69
Development of action plans	69
Project management	66
Gender analysis (including gender assessment)	63
Understanding the concept of leadership	59
Integrating gender concerns into projects/programmes	56
Case studies of women leaders	47
Knowledge on rice technologies	47

(n = 24) thought the course was very useful and helped them to improve themselves. In addition, 69 per cent of attendees (n = 22) found the course very useful in developing work-related skills and knowledge and 69 per cent declared the course was very useful in improving leadership skills and developing an action plan (n = 22). Furthermore, 66 per cent (n = 21) suggested the IRRI leadership course was very useful in gaining project management skills while 63 per cent (n = 20) found the course very useful for understanding gender analysis techniques. Finally, 56 per cent believed the IRRI leadership course was very useful in learning how to integrate gender concerns into a project.

Respondents were also asked if they were able to apply the knowledge and/or skills acquired through their participation in the IRRI leadership course and which skills they actually used in the workplace. As shown in Table 2.8, the majority of respondents reported that the course improved their communication and negotiation skills (32 per cent). In addition, 21 per cent of attendees declared that the course improved their training skills. More than 18 per cent of attendees

Table 2.8 Outcome of the IRRI LCAAWRE course in the workplace

Skills	No.	%
Leadership/managerial skills	5	15
Communication and negotiation skills	10	32
Confidence and assertiveness	6	18
Conflict-resolution skills	5	15
Training skills	7	21
Gender knowledge	2	6
Facilitator's skill	1	3

believed the course generally enhanced their confidence, and more than 15 per cent of attendees reported the course helped them to deal with work conflict more effectively. A majority of attendees indicated that they were able to implement the action plan developed during the training.

Impacts and outcomes of the training

The analysis found that participation in the course had some immediate positive effects on the attendees. In total, 46 per cent of attendees (n = 15) reported the course positively influenced their levels of confidence and helped them become proactive and productive (see Table 2.9). In addition, the course enhanced some of their specific skills, such as leadership skills (16 per cent), communication skills (12 per cent), negotiating skills (6 per cent) and presentation skills (12 per cent). Furthermore, the course provided the attendees with a better understanding of cultural aspects and differences. Although the attendees reported a wide range of positive impact of the course, some of them also reported some negative impacts of the training programme on their jobs. For example the course increased attendees' expectation from their subordinates and increased their supervisors' expectation to perform better after the training, which resulted in higher level of work pressure. Nonetheless, 43 per cent of attendees (n = 14) reported the course had no specific negative effect on them so far.

Overall, 81 per cent of attendees (n = 26) were very satisfied with the quality of the IRRI leadership course, and only one attendee was unsatisfied. Finally, attendees rated the training course's overall impact to 66 per cent as excellent, 33 per cent as good and 1 per cent as average. Finally, attendees were asked whether IRRI should continue this kind of training course, and the responses showed attendees believed this kind of training is necessary. As one participant stated,

> Yes, to change the preconceived ideas that women are 'second class' citizens, which means that women could not be good leaders especially in society.

Table 2.9 Impacts of the training programme

Impacts	Agreement	
	No.	%
Given a clearer vision of what attendees want to be in their profession	23	71.8
Improved leadership	32	100
Improved skills in strategic planning	27	84.3
Improved decision making	29	90.6
Improved communication skills	31	96.8
Improved interpersonal skills	31	96.8
Improved negotiation skills	30	93.7
Improved self confidence	31	96.8
Strengthened confidence in dealing with difficult situations at work	32	100
Improved skills in dealing with difficult situations at work	31	96.8
Improved networking with others	31	96.8
Improved skills in managing conflict and conflict resolution	25	78.1
Helped overcome some of the main constraints posed by work environment	25	78.1
Enhanced abilities to deal with social and cultural constraints attendees face as women	27	84.3
Improved credibility as a leader	28	87.5
Improved scientific and technical abilities	22	68.7
Helped to work smoothly with men	22	68.7
Helped to work smoothly with people from other cultures	27	84.3
Enhanced abilities to guide and mentor other people	29	90.6
Improved abilities to collaborate or participate in R&D activities within the organisation	28	87.5
Improved abilities to collaborate or participate in R&D projects with other organisation	26	86.6
Improved abilities to carry out research projects	25	78.1
Led to institutions providing more support and recognition for attends' performance	23	71.8
Exposed attendees to new technologies and methods	21	65.6
Improved skills in integrating gender concerns into projects and programmes	27	84.3
Improved the understanding on how to apply new methods or technologies to current research	22	68.7

(*Continued*)

Table 2.9 (Continued)

Impacts	Agreement	
	No.	%
Improved abilities to find solutions to technical or scientific problems that attendees would not have been able to solve before	21	65.6
Increased the understanding of the situation of the target beneficiaries of work/project research	27	84.3
Helped to identify barriers/constraints to the adoption of new agricultural technologies and methods	24	75.0

Conclusions and policy implications

This chapter investigated how the IRRI leadership programme has contributed in enhancing women's capacities in agricultural research and development organisations using qualitative and quantitative data gathered from 32 women who attended the programme in its ten years in operation. Respondents reported a wide range of positive impacts of the training on their personal and professional empowerment. Improving self-confidence, leadership skills and technical skills were the main impacts of the training on the attendees that facilitated their progress in their institute, as almost half of them got higher positions and promotions after the participation in the training program. This suggests the importance and contribution of women's leadership training in reducing the gender gap in executive positions in Asia.

Leadership theory suggests that technical competence and interpersonal effectiveness are leaders' sources in influencing their followers' behaviour. The results in this chapter showed that the training programme provided attendees with opportunities to improve their skills in both areas. For example attendees declared that their ability to deal with conflicts and complicated situations, their understanding of different cultures and their self-confidence and exposure to the professional community have been increased after participating in the training program. These factors enhance interpersonal effectiveness. Furthermore, the majority of attendees reported their leadership/managerial skills, technical skills and communication skills were improved during the course showing improvement in technical competency, building their capacity to be better leaders.

This study also suggests that supervisors and colleagues play an important role in supporting the capacity development of women, particularly in developing countries. The support of colleagues particularly of people of influence in the organisation cannot be downplayed as literature on enablers suggests. In many cases, the workforce in developing countries in national RD&E organisations is quite small, and employees' workloads are high. Hence, time to attend trainings and capacity-building activities is limited. The support of the supervisors and often the head of the organisation are critical, particularly in giving women time to attend the trainings and funding support to attend the training. But support is not limited to providing funds and sufficient time; as some attendees emphasised, their supervisors' encouragement and understanding were also very important enablers. However, while formal training had a positive impact on the development of women's leadership, this is not enough. There is a need for their respective institutions to allocate adequate support to enable those trained women to implement the actions plans they have developed or to conduct high-quality research on gender issues for policy development. Moreover, systemic change efforts are necessary to achieve a transformation of organisational culture and practices so as to create the conditions in which the leadership potential of all its members, men and women, can be fully unleashed (Debeb and the Centre for Gender in Organizations 2007).

Acknowledgements

We wish to thank the staff members of the International Rice Research Institute (IRRI), namely, Dr Noel Magor (Head), Maria Socorro Arboleda, Ma. Angelina Maghuyop and Ma. Teresa Clabita of the IRRI Training Center, Gina Zarsadias and Elannie Cabrera of the Social Sciences Division (SSD), Sylvia Avance (Host Country and Community Relations Office) and Mario Movillon (Philippine Rice Research Institute).

References

Airini, Collings, S., Conner, L., McPherson, K., Midson, B. and Wilson, C. 2011, 'Learning to be leaders in higher education: what helps or hinders women's advancement as leaders in Universities', *Educational Management Administration & Leadership*, vol. 39, no. 1, pp. 44–62.

Avance, S. 2010, *Understanding leadership lecture notes: leadership course for Asian and African women for research and extension*, International Rice Research Institute (IRRI), Los Baños, Philippines.

Brandt, T. and Laiho, M. 2013, 'Gender and personality in transformational leadership context', *Leadership & Organization Development Journal*, vol. 34, no. 1, pp. 44–66.

Cross, C. and Armstrong, C. 2008, 'Understanding the role of networks in collective learning processes: the experience of women', *Advances in Developing Human Resources*, vol. 10, no. 4, pp. 600–613.

Dawn Frail, C. 2012, 'Keeping more women in the leadership pipeline: drivers, facilitators, and enablers to women's advancement', Master of Arts in Leadership thesis, The University of Guelph, viewed 1 July 2015, <www.dawnfrail.com/wp-content/uploads/2012/07/Keeping-More-Women-in-the-Leadership-Pipeline.pdf>.

Debeb, G. and The Centre for Gender in Organizations 2007, 'Inspiring transformation: lessons for the CGIAR women's leadership series', *Working Paper*, no. 47, CGIAR Gender Diversity, Washington, DC.

Fisher, H.E. 2005, 'The natural leadership talents of women', in L. Coughlin, E. Wingard and K. Hollihan (eds.), *Enlightened power: how women are transforming the practice of leadership*, Jossey Bass, San Francisco, CA, pp. 133–140.

Fletcher, J. and Ely, R. 2003, 'Introducing gender: overview', in R. Ely, E. Foldy and M. Scully (eds.), *Reader in gender, work, and organization*, Blackwell Publishing, Malden, MA, pp. 3–9.

Gibson, C.A. 1995, 'An investigation of gender differences in leadership across four countries', *Journal of International Business Studies*, vol. 26, no. 2, pp. 255–279.

Goh, A., Recke, H., Hahn-Rollins, D. and Guyer-Miller, L. 2008, 'Successful women, successful science', *Working Paper*, no. 48, CGIAR Gender Diversity, Washington, DC.

Heilman, M.E., Manzi, F. and Bruan, S. 2015, 'Presumed incompetent: perceived lack of fit and gender bias in recruitment and selection', in M.A. Broadbridge and S.L. Fielden (eds.), *Handbook of gender careers in management: getting in, getting on, getting out*, Edward Elgar Publishing, Northampton, UK, pp. 90–104.

International Rice Research Institute 2012, 'Leadership Course for Asian and African Women for Research and Extension', The International Rice Research Institute (IRRI), viewed 7 December 2014, <www.training.irri.org/short-courses/2012-list-of-short-courses/leadership-course-for-asian-and-african-women-for-research-and-extension>.

International Rice Research Institute 2008, Leadership Course for Asian and African Women for Research and Extension Course Brochure, International Rice Research Institute, Los Baños, Philippines.

Kellerman, B. 2004, *Bad leadership: what it is, how it happens, why it matters*, Harvard Business School Press, Boston, MA.

Kerr, S., Schriesheim, C.A., Murphy, C.J. and Stogdiall, R.M. 1974, 'Towards a contingency theory of leadership based upon the consideration and initiating structure literature', *Organizational Behaviour and Human Performance*, vol. 12, no. 1, pp. 62–82.

Luke, N. and Munshi, K. 2011, 'Women as agents of change: female income and mobility in India', *Journal of Development Economics*, vol. 94, no. 1, pp. 1–17.

Markus, G.B. 2001, *Building leadership: findings from a longitudinal evaluation of the Kellogg Fellowship Program*, W.K. Kellogg Foundation, Battle Creek, MI.

Mason, M.A. and Goulden, M. 2004, 'Do babies matter (Part II)? closing the baby gap', *Academe*, vol. 90, no. 6, pp. 10–15.

Maxwell, G. and Ogden, S. 2006, 'Career development of female managers in retailing: inhibitors and enablers', *Journal of Retailing and Consumer Services*, vol. 13, no. 2, pp. 111–120.

Meinzen-Dick, R., Quisumbing, A., Behrman, J., Biermayr-Jenzano, P., Wilde V. and Noordeloos, M., Ragasa, C. and Beintema, N. 2011, *Engendering agricultural research, development and extension*, International Food Policy Research Institute, Washington, DC.

Nelson, T., Maxfield, S. and Kolb, D. 2009, 'Women entrepreneurs and venture capital: managing the shadow negotiation', *International Journal of Gender and Entrepreneurship*, vol. 1, no. 1, pp. 57–76.

Northouse, P.G. 2007, *Leadership: theory and practice*, Sage Publications, Thousand Oaks, CA.

Ogden, S.M., McTavish, D. and McKean, L. 2006, 'Clearing the way for gender balance in the management of the UK financial services industry', *Women in Management Review*, vol. 21, no. 1, pp. 40–53.

O'Neil, D.A., Hopkins, M.M. and Sullivan, S.E. 2011. 'Do women's networks help advance women's careers?', *Career Development International*, vol. 16, no. 7, pp. 733–754.

Pandey, S., Paris, T. and Bhandari, H. 2010, 'Household income dynamics and changes in gender roles in rice farming', in S. Pandey, D. Byerlee, D. Dawe, A. Dobermann, S. Mohanty, S. Rozelle, and B. Hardy (eds.), *Rice in the global economic; strategy research and policy issues for food security*, International Rice Research Institute (IRRI), Manila, Philippines, pp. 93–111.

Paris, T. R. 2007, *Women's roles and needs in changing rural Asia with emphasis on rice-based agriculture*, Food and Fertilizer Technology Centre, Taipei, Taiwan.

Paris, T. R. and Cabrera, E. 2012, *Leadership course for Asian and African women in agricultural R&D (2002–10)*, International Rice Research Institute (IRRI) Technical Report, Los Baños, Philippines.

Perez, J. and Hechanova-Alampay, R. 2005, *Strategic training certification course*, Ateneo Center for Organizational Research and Development (CORD), Ateneo University, Manila, Philippines.

Powell, G. N., Anthony Butterfield, D. and Parent, J. D. 2002, 'Gender and managerial stereotypes: have the times changed?', *Journal of Management*, vol. 28, no. 2, pp. 177–193.

Rola-Rubzen, M. F. 2013, *Strengthening women's leadership capability in Asia and Africa: the impact of the IRRI leadership course for Asian and African women for research and extension*, Asian and African Women Leadership in Research and Development Course, (Draft report).

Stoeberl, P. A., Kwon, I.W.G., Han, D. and Bae, M. 1998, 'Leadership and power relationships based on culture and gender', *Women in Management Review*, vol. 13, no. 6, pp. 208–216.

Tomlinson, F., Brockbank, A. and Traves, J. 1997, 'The "feminization" of management? issues of "sameness" and "difference" in the roles and experiences of female and male retail managers', *Gender, Work & Organization*, vol. 4, no. 4, pp. 218–229.

Young, D. P. and Dixon, N. M. 1996, *Helping leaders take effective action: a program evaluation*, Centre for Creative Leadership, Greensboro, NC.

3 Women's work motivation and the influence on human capital development in Bhutan

Kantha Dayaram and Yue Liu

Introduction

A plethora of studies focusing on the issues of society, women and work have largely centred around developed nations in western socio-economic contexts (Crompton 2006; Gregory and Milner 2009; Pocock 2003). Various other studies have focused around the experiences of women in the more developed regions of Asia where policy is largely driven around neo-liberal trends (Mat Zin 2006; Samad 2006; Tsui 2008). This paper explores the social, political and cultural specificity of concepts such as, women, work, social norms and cultural traditions within Bhutan, which is unique in both its geography and national policy focus. Unlike its Southeast Asian counterparts where economic measures largely focus on gross domestic product (GDP) and wealth accumulation (Tsui 2008), Bhutan has come into the forefront of global attention with the conception of its national focus on improving the happiness index of the nation whilst simultaneously building its economic importance within the region. Bhutan has implemented specific interventions such as the empowerment of women and formal policies aimed at removing workplace gender bias and improving gender equity (Royal Government of Bhutan [RGB] 2003; UNDP Bhutan Country Office 2007). This study further explores the way that women approach the work terrain (Emslie and Hunt 2009; Van Daalen, Willemsen and Sanders 2006) within the context of the experiences of women in a newly emerging formal workplace setting. It has been noted that country case studies 'offer valuable lessons about the relationship between policy and organisational practice, as well as the cultural attitudes that underpin both' (Gregory and Milner 2009: 3). Indeed, studies that offer alternative perspectives on varying cultural approaches adopted to improve human development and labour participation rates enrich the existing body of literature (Greenhaus and Powell 2006; Marcinkus, Whelan-Berry and Gordon 2007). This study argues that social norms and cultural traditions in less developed countries (LDCs) and mainly agrarian economies, such as Bhutan (United Nations Conference on Trade and Development 2013) possess unique identities; for instance Bhutan influences women's working experiences in different ways as compared to their counterparts in developed contexts. This paper attempts to highlight issues surrounding the entry of Bhutanese women in the formal work sector.

The study examines the following research questions:

1) How do Bhutanese women perceive their work motivation?
2) What are the roles of social norms and cultural traditions, and how have these impacted women's work lives?
3) What types of support do Bhutanese women receive to help them transition into the formal work sector?

Model construction

Women's work motivation and labour force participation

From 1990 to 2010, women's participation in the labour market remained stable at around 52 per cent globally, while different sub-regions showed various changes in women's labour force participation (LFP) rates (United Nations [UN] 2010). Even with the recent increases in women's LFP rates, some sub-regions' rates in the world still fell below 50 per cent in 2010. The women's LFP rates were the lowest in the areas of Northern Africa and Western Asia, which were less than 30 per cent. It was relatively higher in Southern Asia at 40 per cent, and it reached 50 per cent in the Caribbean and Central America. In the rest of the sub-regions, women's participation rates were between 50 and 70 per cent (UN 2010).

In most developing countries, in addition to working in the agrarian sector, a large percentage of women are employed in the informal sector, which provides the main source of work for women outside of agriculture (UN 2010). Prior to 2000, there were various definitions of the informal sector, and it was common to consider it as composed of non-wage earners as opposed to wage and salary workers in the formal sector (Beneria and Roldan 1987; Castells and Portes 1989; Charmes 2012; Chaudhuri and Mukhopadhyay 2009; Fields 1990; Henley, Arabsheibani and Carneiro 2009).

The informal work sector is seen as self-reliant workers and employers in their own informal businesses, family workers, members of informal producers' cooperatives and employees occupying informal jobs (Hussmanns 2004). The definition and measurement of informality differs across countries. For example, in Brazil, workers without a labour card or not contributing to a social security fund are considered informal employees. In India, informality is defined as the lack of employers' and workers' organisations (Saget 2006). In South Africa, the formal sector consists of registered businesses, while the informal sector does not (van Klaveren and Tijdens 2012).

Traditional dual labour market theories suggest that the informal sector is unregulated, has an absence of minimum wages and employment rights and offers easier access to employment than in the formal sector (Fields 1990; Harris and Todaro 1970; Heintz and Posel 2008; Lewis 1954; Stiglitz 1976). The empirical study by Günther and Launov (2006) determined that the informal sector included individuals who are voluntarily involved in informal work and individuals for whom the informal sector is their last option to avoid involuntary unemployment. Workers in the informal sector earn lower wages than workers in the formal sector with similar jobs. It is also argued that workers from the informal sector would join the formal sector if no entry barriers existed (Günther and Launov 2012). To increase women's labour force participation (LFP) in the formal sector, the enhancement of women's work motivation is critical. Work motivation can be described as 'a set of energetic forces that originate both within as well as beyond an individual's being, to initiate work-related behaviour, and to determine its form, direction, intensity, and duration' (Pinder 1998: 11).

There are four broad categories of theories exploring work motivation (Bezzina, Azzopardi and Vella 2013). The needs-based theories assume that individuals' work participation is driven by needs like self-actualisation, relatedness and authority. Behavioural theories focus on strengthening individuals' observable behaviour to prompt their better work performance. Cognitive process theories suggest that individuals' career goals are shaped by their needs, values and the situational context. Finally, job-based theories identify the satisfaction from the job itself as the major motivation of individual's work participation (Bezzina, Azzopardi and Vella 2013). Other empirical studies indicate that female work motivation could be classified into two internally coherent components: personal and professional development and social and economic well-being (Bezzina, Azzopardi and Vella 2013).

Based on the needs-based theories, Astin (1984) postulated three basic needs as the motivational factors in work behaviour, which include survival, pleasure and contribution. Survival needs refer primarily to physiological survival. Pleasure needs refer to the inherent pleasure of the work involvement and the intellectual and emotional pleasure that stems from work and goal achievement. Contribution needs refer to the need to feel their involvement to the good and well-being of others. These others include family, the close friends, the organisation, the community, the nation or some larger social entity (Astin 1984).

Based on Astin's (1984) three basic needs, the first component of the model is proposed here to illustrate the influence of work motivation on women's participation LFP rates (Figure 3.1). This suggests that women would be motivated by their needs for survival, pleasure and contribution to participate in the labour force. They have intentions to engage in formal work to pursue higher personal and professional development and social and economic well-being.

The influence of social norms

Various factors contribute to female LFP such as education, fertility rates, urbanisation, unemployment and economic growth, and the role of social norms and cultural traditions (Kottis, 1990, Mishra and Smyth 2010). In particular, the relationship between female LFP rates and economic development has been widely discussed (Çağatay and Özler 1995; Goldin 1995; Pampel and Tanaka 1986; Tam 2011).

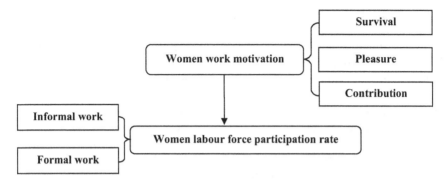

Figure 3.1 Model component one: work motivation and women's LFP rates

Lindbeck, Nyberg and Weibull (1999) examined how social norms influence work choices in the welfare state. They assume that living through working is the social norm and that individual experience a utility loss when they disobey this norm. While economists focused on economic incentives, sociologists emphasised social norms to explain individual's choices (Lindbeck, Nyberg and Weibull 1999). Hazan and Maoz (2002) used the role of tradition and differences in social norms to supplement the explanation based on wage differences between the genders and changes in female LFP rates.

Social norms have been discussed as a critical barrier for women in accepting blue-collar jobs, resulting in the decline of female LFP during the industrialisation period (Mammen and Paxson 2000). For example, according to traditional Korean social norms, working in office jobs or 'blue-collar' jobs is suitable for married women, whereas manual types of work are not (Lee, Jang and Sarkar 2008). Descriptions of tedious assembly line work carried out by young women in Taiwan (Kung 1993) or long work hours and poor health standards in Mexican maquiladoras motivate women to choose marriage over employment (Cravey 1998).

Morrisson and Jütting's (2005) analytical framework proposes that the economic role of women in developing countries is greatly shaped and constrained by a set of laws, norms, codes of conduct and cultural traditions. Social institutions may place direct or indirect restrictions on women's activities through limiting their access to resources that are indispensable for them to join the labour market (Morrisson and Jütting 2005).

In addition to social norms and cultural traditions, studies in South Mediterranean countries revealed the importance of religion and cultural traditions and their manifestations on influencing women's rights and opportunities (Clark, Ramsbey and Adler 1991; Moghadam 2004, 2005). Other empirical research also reveals that culture is essential in interpreting female LFP, economic development, family ties and arrangements (Alesina and Giuliano 2010; Fernandez 2007; Giuliano 2007; Tabellini 2010).

Culture has had a substantial influence on women's participation in the labour force (Ramsbey and Adler 1991). For instance, because of emphasis on the strict separation for men and women in Islamic nations and the traditional prohibition of women from paid agricultural labour and ideological preference for male authority in Latin America, women in Islamic and Latin American nations were significantly less able to participate in the labour force of their countries in 1980 than in other places in the world (Clark et al. 1991).

Different religions have diverse perspectives on gender roles and the classification of labour within a family and society (Lehrer 1995), which influences women's decisions in labour supply. Religions can influence women's fertility rates and desire for children, which might also have an effect on women's LFP (Morgan et al. 2002). In developing countries, religion is one of the primary barriers to the improvement of women's economic and social status (Beit-Hallahmi 1997).

Amin and Alam (2008) compared the labour market behaviour of Muslim women with women of Buddhist, Hindu and other religions. The results suggest that religion has more powerful impacts in areas outside cities and towns; nevertheless, it significantly affects unmarried women's decision to participate in paid work in all areas.

The second component of the model reveals the crucial role of social norms and cultural traditions on influencing women's work motivation and therefore their labour participation intentions (Figure 3.2).

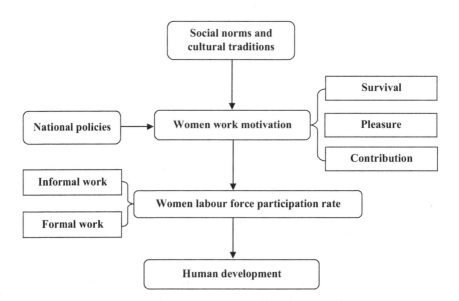

Figure 3.2 Work motivation, social norms and human development

The influence of policies

National policies

National policies influence the relationship between economic growth, social policies and the increase or decrease in informal work (van Klaveren and Tijdens 2012). Research suggests that properly and comprehensively designed policies are helpful in effectively enhancing women's economic opportunities and involvement (Aguirre et al. 2012; Duflo 2012; Revenga and Shetty 2012).

Labour evolution allows women to fully participate in the labour market. For instance, the removal of a ban on part-time work in Argentina triggered a shift from informal work to formal sector, part-time work among mothers (World Bank 2012b). The integration of gender issues in Bangladesh's national budget, activated in 2005, with the aim of promoting a more equal society resulted in improved female LFP rates. The LFP rate of young women almost increased two-fold in the late 1990s (World Bank 2012a). Sufficient health care is also crucial to alleviating women from the obligations of tedious informal health care (World Bank 2012b). In Nepal, the authorities recently amended the Country Code that advances women's access to property other than land (World Bank 2012b). In many LDCs, the accessibility of microfinance has decreased the productivity gap between women and men, and women have higher credit repayment rates than men (Kabeer 2005).

The International Monetary Fund (2012) also examined low female LFP rates, particularly in the Middle East and North Africa, Latin America, Asia and Southern Europe. The proposed policy measures include applying individual taxation instead of family taxation, adopting gender targeted tax exemptions, and alleviating taxes for single parents. Furthermore, the report promotes policies such as improved government-subsidised parental leave schemes, which would provide motivation for mothers to re-enter the labour force and child care subsidies for working mothers.

It is evident that national policies have a significant influence on women's work motivation and female LFP rates. The addition of national policies is depicted in Figure 3.2.

Policy development in Bhutan

Bhutan is a small inland country geographically surrounded by India, Nepal and China (O'Flynn and Blackman 2009). It is predominantly an agrarian society with strong Buddhist roots. Traditional educational and monastic institutions have been influential on the state, its ethical practices and national legislation (Mathou 2000; O'Flynn and Blackman 2009; Thinley 1998). A diarchy of lay and religious leaders governed Bhutan until the establishment of a monarchy in 1907 (Bray 1993; Royal Government of Bhutan 2003). Reforms to the State's legal framework began in 1972, and March 2008 saw the country's first democratic election with constitutional powers being shifted to the Prime Minister.

In 1961, the country commenced modern development and implemented the first five-year plan, which prioritised investment in people (Royal Government of Bhutan 2003). Since the implementation of modern reforms, significant improvements have been noted (O'Flynn and Blackman 2009). Life expectancy at birth in Bhutan increased significantly from 36.9 years old in 1970 to 67.9 in 2012 (United Nations Children's Fund UNICEF [UNICEF] 2013), the adult literacy rate rose from 52.8 per cent in 2005 to 63 per cent in 2012 (National Statistic Bureau n.d.; UNESCO Institute for Statistics 2013) and the GDP per capita average annual growth rate from 1990 to 2012 was 5.4 per cent (UNICEF 2013).

In 1984, 95 per cent of women aged between 15 and 64 worked in agriculture. From 2000 to 2002, a quarter of the total employment in private organisations in Bhutan comprised of women; in 2012, this figure increased to 40.7 per cent (Royal Government of Bhutan [RGB] 2003, 2012). Bhutan's government embarked on progressive strategies to promote and advance women's status in society. These strategies include creating gender awareness and understanding women's rights; promoting child day-care facilities in cities; implementing national policies of flexible breast-feeding schedules, maternity and paternity leave for employees; and encouraging the retention of females in higher education (RGB 2003).

Rapid developments place Bhutan into the medium development category and have primarily been attributed to its leadership, natural resources, administrative system, the commitment of foreign donors such as Denmark and India and the preservation of Bhutanese culture (Ura and Galay 2004). There are criticisms that Bhutan's potential to further accelerate its development is hampered by its commitment to protecting both the environment and culture (Thinley 1998). Yet from Bhutan's persistence of cultural preservation, a distinctive framework of governance and institution-building emerged, named the Four Pillars of Happiness: equitable and sustainable socio-economic development, preservation and promotion of its national culture, conservation of the environment and the promotion of good governance (Mathou 2000).

The Bhutanese reject Gross Domestic Product (GDP) as the criterion of development and prefer the index of Gross National Happiness (GNH), a philosophy of economic and social development activated by the Fourth King of Bhutan in the 1980s (Thinley 2005). GNH represents a set of social and economic approaches that assess societal change with respect to the collective happiness of people, which also promotes the implementation of policies with the objective of improving GNH (Meenawat and Sovacool 2011). Based on the belief of human's destiny in seeking happiness, the concept of GNH focuses on fostering collective happiness and well-being: 'the overarching goal of every aspect of life, including economics, is not seen as the multiplication of material wants but in the purification of the human character' (Priesner 1999: 36). This is in contrast to the rapid development of other Asian economies (China, Japan and Singapore) (UN n.d.) that has resulted in negative outcomes on employee well-being and work–life balance (Galovan et al. 2010; Shimazu et al. 2011; Xiao and Cooke 2012).

The concept of GNH presumes that public policies established in achieving happiness would bring greater harmony than the policies designed with the aim of advancing economic growth. Whilst the concept does not prevent the emergence of conflict among individuals or groups, it acknowledges the necessity for mechanisms to reconcile such conflicts. Women are entitled to employment and fair payment. One of the UN's Millennium Development Goals includes gender equity, which aims to reduce/eliminate gender disparities in access and employment in work, pay equity, recruitment, training, promotions and benefits (UN n.d.).

Despite the GNH concept being subject to wide-ranging discussions and debates of circumventing industrialisation in achieving a post-modern, sustainable state (Ura and Galay 2004), it puts forward key concepts of the way the Bhutanese are pursuing, 'a genuinely non-western development approach' (Priesner 1999: 37), which considers the importance of non-economic goals and provides alternate approaches to work and human development.

In addition to discovering alternative approaches to empowering women, examining workplace performances and national policies from a cultural perspective can provide important learning points for policy makers and organisations to moderate the adverse effects of high levels of gender bias and advance human development (Figure 3.2).

Methodology

This study attempts to gain an understanding into macro-level perspectives on LFP and the roles of social norms and cultural traditions affecting women's employment by utilising a micro-level analysis of the perspectives of women as they describe the ways that they experienced these issues. Anderson et al. (2008) argue that it should not be assumed that findings of women's work experiences and perceptions in the Western context can be generalised to countries and regions where the culture is dissimilar.

To obtain insights into women's work motivations, a number of exploratory interviews were conducted in late 2008, using the focus group technique of interviewing. Effectively, interviews provide an effective approach for capturing personal experiences and associated meanings to people (Denzin and Lincoln 2003). The interviews were in depth and semi-structured and conducted in English, since all the participants had fluent English conversational skills. The interview questionnaire was developed using theory and subsequently contextualised to the Bhutanese experience. The questions included the Bhutanese culture, norms, various traditions and how women perceived these to impact on their work life, how Bhutanese women translate and respond to work policies; what support they received and their interpretation of how likely it is that such measures improve the capacity building of women in Bhutan. Participation was confined to women working in formal work sectors and excluded the agricultural sector.

Since traditionally women were employed informally in the agricultural sector, it was excluded to determine the transition of women into other sectors of employment. Initially professional women working for the Departments of

Table 3.1 Profile of 39 full-time women workers in the focus groups (%)

Age (years)	Education level	Marital status	Number of children
20–29 (75%)	High school or equivalent diploma (23%)	Unmarried (59%)	No child (64%)
30–39 (17%)	Bachelor degree (60%)	Married (33%)	One child (23%)
40–49 (8%)	Master degree (17%)	Divorced (8%)	Two or more children (13%)

Health and Education were recruited, followed by employing a snowball technique to recruit women from other formal workplace sectors. The women worked in the capital region of Thimphu, where the interviews were conducted. There were 6 focus groups comprising of 6–8 participants in each group, with a total of 38 women being interviewed. The focus groups were organised according to seniority and leadership levels; for instance, women in senior leadership roles were in one focus group, those in level two and three positions were in a different groups. Women not occupying leadership positions but employed in a professional capacity were in a separate group. The segmentation of focus groups was to allow the participants to share their varied experiences within similar roles and in different organisational settings. The profiles of participants are shown in Table 3.1 (Dayaram and Pick 2012).

All participants were professional full-time workers with the age range of 20 to 49. The largest share of respondents was between the ages of 20–29 (75 per cent). Over 77 per cent of the women who participated in this study held Bachelor's degrees (60 per cent) and Master's-level degrees (17 per cent). Unmarried women with no children made up 56 per cent of the sample (Dayaram and Pick 2012). The purposeful selection of participants provided an opportunity to examine a relatively unexplored area of understanding work motivation and the influence of social norms, cultural traditions and national policies.

The participants were employed in a wide range of sectors including finance, health, education, pension funds, research and information technology sectors (Dayaram and Pick 2012). Occupational levels varied from administrative assistants in the private sector to senior directors in the public sector. A large percentage of participants worked between 40–45 hours per week, with only one participant indicating that she worked for more than 45 hours due to meeting strict deadlines associated with providing on-time statistical data.

The interviews were audio-recorded and then transcribed verbatim. The researchers read and read the transcriptions to gain a better under of the qualitative data. NVivo 8 software was used to analyse the data according to according themes, by first using a coding process.

The responses were examined to reveal the work motivations of Bhutan female professionals. To scrutinise the impact of social norms and cultural traditions, comments were extracted where the women spoke of culture, notion, and family relationship etc. Note was also made of the significance of the support to the women (Lirio 2007). These were then compared and contrasted to ensure accuracy of data analyses and recurring themes.

Results and analysis

All interviews were transcribed for theme identification and analyses. The main themes that emerged were motivation to work, which comprised of financial survival, achieving key performance indicators, pleasure and job satisfaction, motivation, social norms and culture that influence women's activities in the labour market. It also included national policies in Bhutan that inspired women's work participation.

Work motivation

Work has been considered as one of the great scopes of human activity essential to connecting individuals more closely to the human community (Freud and Strachey 2005). Work behaviour is primarily motivated by three basic needs: survival, pleasure, and contribution (Astin 1984). Some studies indicate that working women are largely motivated by economic independence, career progression, social status, feelings of self-esteem, and developing competencies relating to performance indicators (Bezzina, Azzopardi and Vella 2013; Borg 2007).

The respondents' feedbacks suggest that their work motivation is primarily centred on financial considerations that reflect the basic necessity of survival.

> Actually working does help in our society because here we don't have much land, also and we have studied. I'm a graduate. I don't want to go and work in the fields actually so I have to work and working *brings income* to our family so there's a good cause actually. So we don't have a problem working.
>
> (group 1)

Other interviewees' responses indicate that their involvement in work is associated with helping others in the community and contributing to the country's development. This mirrors the work motivation of gaining a sense of achievement and being recognised for their work contribution (Bezzina, Azzopardi and Vella 2013). This type of response is illustrated here:

> We do contribute because we're doing something through the corporation. We're helping the farmers. Actually we're rural based. So I go myself I'm a huge part of that I go to the field. They [farmers] didn't have to spend extra

money and come here. So farmers as a whole I think income of the country is from the farmers. So when I help the farmers, farmers *help the government* so naturally in that case me in a small way I'm *helping the country*.

(group 2)

Survival, pleasure and contribution, as three basic motivational factors in work behaviour, are interactive. Pleasure can be derived from the satisfaction from survival or contribution at work; it also can be the intrinsic feeling of the work activities themselves. It can be the intellectual and emotional pleasure that originates from the completion of tasks and the accomplishment of goals (Astin 1984; Graham and Weiner 1996). The work motivation of pleasure is closely related to job satisfaction, which stems from enhancing their self-esteem, work responsibility and social contribution.

Most of my friends say why do you work? All the time they're saying my children are grown up and my husband is running a resort in Bhutan you're well off. I said my *job satisfaction*. I wanted to be a nurse. I became a nurse. I want to work until I can *contribute* something that's what I say. Maybe there will be some time where I cannot work and have free time.

(group 3)

Social norms and cultural traditions

In developing countries, the economic identity of women is significantly affected by the combination of laws, norms, codes of conduct and cultural traditions (Morrisson and Jütting 2005). Social norms and cultures may enforce direct restraints on women's activities. They might also indirectly restrict women's access to essential resources for participating in the labour market, such as health, education and social capital (Morrisson and Jütting 2005).

The respondents' views show that in the Bhutanese culture, there is a strong sense of equal gender rights in parental responsibilities and a strong cultural tradition of direct and extended-family support for coping with work–family affairs and tensions, which greatly assist women to participate in economic activity and help to provide women with better access to human capital.

Because this notion has never been in Bhutan you know. Mother and father are always equal. Daughters, we always tell them their upbringing depends on the mother and sons their fathers' responsibility this notion that mother is the key figure is not only part of this *culture*.

(group 3)

Our society is like that. We even support our relatives not only immediate family. Extended or cousins and first cousins, second cousins. We support financially, emotionally.

(group 3)

Yeah our *culture* is I think closely knit and there's all the time full support from our family. If they want to go for studies they will support because they know that it will ultimately help our career building so they support it.

(group 6)

Organisational support and policies

Organisational policies that provide women with child care support benefit women in balancing their work and family responsibilities. Taking time off work hours to feed their babies was deemed to be critical to their family responsibility and mothering duties. As this was paid time off, some women stated that utilizing this benefit was at the discretion of the employer.

> The mothers get one hour off working hours for a year until the baby's one year. I think we had lack of support from *the employers* because we're not given time to breast feed our babies so sometimes it makes us very difficult to work. So most of the people they resign and look for jobs where such kind of facilities are given when *working mothers* are given time to go home and feed their child or spend time with their *child*.

(group 1)

Whilst most women with children valued the time allowance for taking care of their babies, some expressed feelings of guilt when they did exceed the time allowance and trust of their managers.

> It depends on the manager but during the early days of my baby like right after three months we have to leave them and come to office and then we still have to feed them very frequently so sometimes like at 11 o'clock we will leave the office but we'll inform our manager that we are going to feed the baby and sometimes I used to come only after lunch right at 2 o'clock so it is sometimes acceptable but I used to feel guilty and it was not a usual thing.

(group 2)

The work support the employed women could receive from their employers and supervisors is meaningful and has connotations of job satisfaction and self-achievement.

> I did not want to leave is basically it's the environment that we have where I'm working just now is very *positive environment* and we have very close relationship with all staff there and also I get like job satisfaction personally working in that area, these are some of the factors which have kept me there for so many years.

(group 3)

We have very *supportive supervisors*. They will be easily listening to what we want to say very accommodating and that is one reason why I want to be in this department.

(group 4)

The responses also highlight that women in Bhutan receive different forms of organisational gender support that provide women with opportunities to seek financial assistance and work support.

In my case like we have do loan verification and compared to other *organisations* like there are not much women doing these jobs so they want more women and ladies to come up so they encourage us and train us.

(group 2)

If I want to further study or something like that like they *[work organisation]* will be giving like more preference to women.

(group3)

I think they *[work organisation]* do a lot because they always support a woman, if she is educated her whole family is educated so they mostly encourage women to work so that they can work side by side with the men.

(group 4)

Although these types of social support have distinctive definitions, the respondents' feedback indicates that they work together to form a dynamic, Bhutanese social-support family structure.

We can leave our children to my sister in law and other family I can be very, very comfortable. I know they will look after like I would.

(group 4)

Actually when I went for my masters [degree] overseas also when I went only for two years my son was in grade 12 and which was very important for him. So I was a little bit actually worried just to give them moral support when they're studying. So I really didn't want to take that. . . . I had to and then my whole family they encouraged me. I had their full support that's why I could do go.

(group 3)

National policies

The Gross National Happiness (GNH) concept is an approach that considers non-economic goals as a core focus of human development. The Bhutanese have their development priorities embedded within a cultural framework. The overall goal of well-being and environmental conservation were derived from Buddhist normative values; the principles of independence and paternalism were the integral structural attributes of traditional society (Priesner 1999).

Guided by the GNH concept, the Bhutanese government plays an essential role in the improvement of the economic and social well-being of its people. The national policies align towards building a welfare state.

> Other countries they consider gross domestic product and all that stuff but in our country its balance I mean like gross happiness. Like in other countries they have war. People are not happy. When people are not happy they can't contribute to the country but in our country we *take gross national happiness* as development because if people are happy we tend to do things like working here, we give loans to farmers in the rural areas. You know we're happy ok I'll do this that you know in a way it's contributing and helping.
>
> (group 2)

> I think we are trying to push up the *gross national happiness* by providing assistance to the rural people.
>
> (group 2)

Studies have indicated that culture differs in terms of which types of work are independent from family life and which kinds of work prioritise family commitments (Joplin, Nelson and Quick 1999). Anderson et al. (2008) noted that, in Chinese society, work may be considered mainly as a way of improving the family's well-being, whereas in the United States people work for many reasons independent of family well-being (Aryee, Fields and Luk 1999). Women in Bhutan stated they worked to earn a living; some stated that they worked for their families and that work provides inner desire and fulfilment, and others viewed work as giving back to the country.

The welfare state is a notion of government playing an essential role in the protection and advancement of the economic and social well-being of its citizens. It is founded on the principles of equal opportunity, fair distribution of wealth and public responsibility for the disadvantaged who are unable to meet the minimum standards for a good life (Abrantes 2013).

As a country operates based on the principles of a welfare state, its citizens tend to equate the country to a parent and caretaker; therefore, a need for reciprocity appears to be obligatory (Fong, Bowles and Gintis 2006). This metaphor conforms to Stewart-Weeks and Richardson's (1998) argument that the key to democratic and economic efficiency is for institutions to draw on high levels of trust and shared values.

> It's like being good to your parents. If your parents have supported you for your education, your health everything you feel obliged to pay back. In the same way government is not so different from your parenthood. They support you as a child, they give you free education, we're given free health, primary health care is free in Bhutan so it's like government is looking after us.
>
> (group 6)

The Bhutanese are proud of its country's unique GNH approach and are willing to contribute to the country and to the monarch.

> Basically I work as a statistician. . . . So I'm basically working for my country because I'm working for my government. Our king does so many things for us. He's so selfless.
>
> (group 6)

Discussion

Bhutanese organisations tend to reflect the four pillars of GNH, which align with its cultural and economic goals.

The framework proposed here is a needs-based, socio-psychological one that is grounded in three interactive constructs: the psychological construct, the social norms construct and the policy construct. The psychological construct is represented by work motivation wherein work activity is associated with the aim of meeting three basic needs: survival, pleasure and contribution. Work choices depend on expectations relating to the availability of substitutive forms of work with the capacity to fulfil these three basic needs. The social norms construct comprises of a set of social norms and cultural traditions. The social norms may place direct and indirect restrictions (Morrisson and Jütting 2005). The policy construct constitutes labour laws, national policies and workplace policies that promote the access of women to resources and support to improve their LFP.

The proposed framework assumes that, through the interventions of social norms and policy constructs, women's work motivation could be enhanced to promote their LFP and increase women's work contribution in the formal sector. The increase of women's engagement in the labour market would lead to the improvement of a country's human development. Human development is a process of increasing and broadening people's choices, of which the most basic and crucial are a long and healthy life, education and resources needed for a decent life (United Nations Development Programme 1990).

Women's participation in the labour force directly contributes to economic growth. Women's motivation and decision to participate in paid labour is crucial to economic progress. Women's empowerment through work influences human development.

The findings of the focus groups interviews illustrate that Bhutanese professional working women were strongly driven by the motivations of income for living, contributing to family sustainability and societal development, and seeking for pleasure from work itself. These motivations encouraged them to actively participate in formal employment. However, our findings also suggest that women's work participation has been influenced by Bhutan's social norms on gender equity.

The well-established family and community social support system and the national policies aimed at improving women's economic status also contribute to supporting and sustaining professional working women.

The female LFP rate in Bhutan has largely increased over the past decade. Since 1995, it has continued to increase from 47.4 per cent to approximately 68.5 per cent in 2011 (International Labour Office [ILO] 2013). Even though Bhutan has made tremendous progress in female LFP, more Bhutanese women are employed in lower quality jobs and earn less income than men (ILO 2013; World Bank 2013).

The findings on Bhutanese professional women workers verified the proposed framework of women labour force participation based on the interactions of work motivation, social norms construct and the policy construct. Further application of this framework can reveal effective strategies to narrow the job quality gap between women and men and improve women's employment rate in the formal sector in similar LDCs. Further research could also include the social capital construct. This would not only increase job quality and enhance gender equality, but it also could contribute to the economic growth of a country.

Conclusion

Much of the evidence suggests a very strong focus towards social capital, cultural harmony and a fit with the recent policy reforms. Findings emphasise the transformational reform agenda in progress in Bhutan appears to have great potential for achieving multi-level goals. Bhutan's development strategies have created a society that is harmonious and tolerant. The focus of broader policies built around GNH appears to provide a dynamic framework to manage the challenges related to work–life issues and social norms; and cultural traditions appear to be at the centre of that challenge.

The framework of women's LFP proposed in this chapter emphasises increasing women's labour force participation through enhancing their work motivation and initiatives through the intervention of factors such as social norms, cultural traditions and national policies. Based on the proposed framework, some strategies could be derived and used to increase women's LFP rate and enhance the human development especially for other developing countries.

From the social norm and culture perspective, it is important to promote social norms that lead to gender equality for example to encourage men as fathers and caregivers and promote men's participation in housework; promote equality in women's property ownership, inheritance, and land holding and increase women's right in marriage choice.

From the national policy perspective, it is important to improve women's access to finance and entrepreneurship, improve women's job quality and career advancement through vocational and life-skills training, and provide access to health services. In addition to these, improving women's education endowment is crucial to assist women transferring from working in casual and informal employment to formal employment with greater job stability (World Bank 2012b). Government policies aimed at improving flexible working arrangements, establishing family taxation system, and providing childcare support may also significantly influence female LFP rates.

The study has its limitations in that it was confined to the experiences of professional working women, in a single country and at a single point in time. Further studies could explore the experiences of women in other regions where women have transitioned have the informal work sector into formal work roles. There is also potential for further study in Bhutan, particularly after the country has transitioned from a monarchical rule to a democracy.

References

Abrantes, J.J. 2013, 'Welfare state and globalisation of the economic area', *Tribuna Juridică*, vol. 3, no. 1, pp. 194–202.

Aguirre, D., Hoteit, L., Rupp, C. and Sabbagh, K. 2012, *Empowering the third billion: women and the world of work in 2012*, Booz & Company, New York, NY.

Alesina, A. and Giuliano, P. 2010, 'The power of the family', *Journal of Economic Growth*, vol. 15, no. 2, pp. 93–125.

Amin, S. and Alam, I. 2008, 'Women's employment decisions in Malaysia: does religion matter?', *The Journal of Socio-Economics*, vol. 37, no. 6, pp. 2368–2379.

Anderson, S.E., Coffey, B.S., Liu, Y. and Zhao, S. 2008, 'Employees in Chinese enterprises: antecedents and outcomes of work–family balance', *Chinese Economy*, vol. 41, no. 5, pp. 22–50.

Aryee, S., Fields, D. and Luk. V. 1999, 'A cross-cultural test of a model of the work–family interface', *Journal of Management*, vol. 25, no. 4, pp. 491–511.

Astin, H.S. 1984, The meaning of work in women's lives: 'a sociopsychological model of career choice and work behavior', *The Counseling Psychologist*, vol. 12, no. 4, pp. 117–153.

Beit-Hallahmi, B. 1997, 'Biology, destiny and change: women's religiosity and economic development', *Journal of Institutional and Theoretical Economics no. JITE)/ Zeitschrift für die gesamte Staatswissenschaft*, vol. 153, no. 1, pp. 166–178.

Beneria, L. and Roldan, M. 1987, *The cross-road of class and gender*, University of Chicago, Chicago, IL.

Bezzina, F., Azzopardi, R.M. and Vella, G. 2013, 'Understanding and assessing the work motivations of employed women insights into increasing female participation rates in the maltese labor market', *Sage Open*, vol. 3, no. 3, pp. 1–14.

Borg, A. 2007, *Women and work: findings from a study on the work aspirations of Maltese women*, Employment and Training Corporation, Hal Far, Malta.

Bray, J. 1993, 'Bhutan: the dilemmas of a small state', *World Today*, vol. 49, no. 11, pp. 213–216.

Çağatay, N. and Özler, Ş. 1995, 'Feminization of the labor force: the effects of long-term development and structural adjustment', *World Development*, vol. 23, no. 11, pp. 1883–1894.

Castells, M. and Portes, A. 1989, 'World underneath: the origins, dynamics, and effects of the informal economy', in A. Portes, M. Castells and L.A. Benton (eds.), *The informal economy: studies in advanced and less developed countries*, John Hopkins University Press, Baltimore, MD, pp. 11–37.

Charmes, J. 2012, 'The informal economy worldwide: trends and characteristics', *Margin: The Journal of Applied Economic Research*, vol. 6, no. 2, pp. 103–132.

Chaudhuri, S. and Mukhopadhyay, U. 2009, 'Chapter 1: introduction', in S. Chaudhuri and U. Mukhopadhyay (eds.), *Revisiting the informal sector: a general equilibrium approach*, Springer, New York, NY, pp. 1–15.

Clark, R., Ramsbey, T. W. and Adler, E. S. 1991, 'Culture, gender, and labor force participation: a cross-national study', *Gender and Society*, vol. 5, no. 1, pp. 47–66.

Cravey, A. J. 1998, *Women and work in Mexico's maquiladoras*, Rowman and Littlefield, Lanham, MD.

Crompton, R. 2006, *Employment and the family: the reconfiguration of work and family life in contemporary societies*, Cambridge University Press, Cambridge, UK.

Dayaram, K. and Pick, D. 2012, 'Entangled between tradition and modernity: the experiences of Bhutanese working women', *Society and Business Review*, vol. 7, no. 2, pp. 134–148.

Denzin, N. K. and Lincoln, Y. S. 2003, *Strategies of qualitative inquiry: volume 2 of Handbook of qualitative research*, Sage Publications, Thousand Oaks, CA.

Duflo, E. 2012, 'Women empowerment and economic development', *Journal of Economic Literature*, vol. 50, no. 4, pp. 1051–1079.

Emslie, C. and Hunt, K. 2009, '"Live to work" or 'work to live'? a qualitative study of gender and work–life balance among men and women in mid-life', *Gender, Work and Organization*, vol. 16, no. 1, pp. 151–172.

Fernandez, R. 2007, 'Women, work, and culture', *Journal of the European Economic Association*, vol. 5, no. 2–3, pp. 305–332.

Fields, G. S. 1990, 'Labour market modelling and the urban informal sector: theory and evidence', in D. Turnham, B. Salomé and A. Schwarz (eds.), *The informal sector revisited*, Organisation for Economic Co-operation and Development, Paris, France, pp. 49–69.

Fong, C. M., Bowles, S. and Gintis, H. 2006, 'Strong reciprocity and the welfare state', in K. Serge-Christophe and Y. Jean Mercier (eds.), *Handbook of the economics of giving, altruism and reciprocity: fundations*, Elsevier, Amsterdam, Netherlands, pp. 1439–1464.

Freud, S. and Strachey, J. 2005, *Civilization and its discontents*, WW Norton, New York, NY.

Galovan, A. M., Fackrell, T., Buswell, L., Jones, B. L., Hill, E. J. and Carroll, S. J. 2010, 'The work–family interface in the United States and Singapore: conflict across cultures', *Journal of Family Psychology*, vol. 24, no. 5, pp. 646–656.

Giuliano, P. 2007, 'Living arrangements in western europe: does cultural origin matter?', *Journal of the European Economic Association*, vol. 5, no. 5, pp. 927–952.

Goldin, C. 1995, 'The U-shaped female labour force function in economic development and economic history', in T. P. Schultz (ed.), *Investment in women's human capital and economic development*, University of Chicago Press, Chicago, IL, pp. 61–90.

Graham, S. and Weiner, B. 1996, 'Theories and principles of motivation', in D. C. Berliner and R. C. Calfee (eds.), *Handbook of educational psychology*, Routledge, New York, NY, pp. 63–84.

Greenhaus, J. H. and Powell, G. N. 2006, 'When work and family are allies: a theory of work–family enrichment', *Academy of Management Review*, vol. 31, no. 1, pp. 72–92.

Gregory, A. and Milner, S. 2009, 'Editorial: work–life balance: a matter of choice?', *Gender, Work and Organization*, vol. 16, no. 1, pp. 1–13.

Günther, I. and Launov, A. 2006, '*Competitive and segmented informal labor markets*', *Discussion Paper, no. 2349*, Institute for the Study of Labour, Bonn, Germany.

Günther, I. and Launov, A. 2012, 'Informal employment in developing countries: opportunity or last resort?', *Journal of Development Economics*, vol. 97, no. 1, pp. 88–98.

Harris, J. R. and Todaro, M. P. 1970, 'Migration, unemployment and development: a two-sector analysis', *The American Economic Review*, vol. 60, no. 1, pp. 126–142.

Hazan, M. and Maoz, Y. D. 2002, 'Women's labor force participation and the dynamics of tradition', *Economics Letters*, vol. 75, no. 2, pp. 193–198.

Heintz, J. and Posel, D. 2008, 'Revisiting informal employment and segmentation in the South African labour market', *South African Journal of Economics*, vol. 76, no. 1, pp. 26–44.

Henley, A., Arabsheibani, G. R. and Carneiro, F. G. 2009, 'On defining and measuring the informal sector: evidence from Brazil', *World Development*, vol. 37, no. 5, pp. 992–1003.

Hussmanns, R. 2004, *Statistical definition of informal employment: guidelines endorsed by the seventeenth international conference of labour statisticians (2003)*, International Labour Office, Geneva, Switzerland.

International Labour Office 2013, *Key indicators of the labour market*, International Labour Office, Geneva, Switzerland.

International Monetary Fund 2012, *Fiscal policy and employment in advanced and emerging economies*, International Monetary Fund, Washington, DC.

Joplin, J. R., Nelson, D. L. and Quick, J. C. 1999, 'Attachment behavior and health: relationships at work and home', *Journal of Organizational Behavior*, vol. 20, no. 6, pp. 783–796.

Kabeer, N. 2005, 'Is microfinance a 'magic bullet' for women's empowerment? analysis of findings from South Asia', *Economic and Political Weekly*, vol. 40, no. 44/45, pp. 4709–4718.

Kottis, A. P. 1990, 'Shifts over time and regional variation in women's labour force participation rates in a developing economy: The case of Greece', *Journal of Development Economics*, vol. 33, no. 1, pp. 117–132.

Kung, L. 1993, *Factory women in Taiwan*, Columbia University Press, New York, NY.

Lee, B. S., Jang, S. and Sarkar, J. 2008, 'Women's labor force participation and marriage: the case of Korea', *Journal of Asian Economics*, vol. 19, no. 2, pp. 138–154.

Lehrer, E. L. 1995, 'The effects of religion on the labor supply of married women', *Social Science Research*, vol. 24, no. 3, pp. 281–301.

Lewis, W. A. 1954, 'Economic development with unlimited supplies of labour', *The Manchester School*, vol. 22, no. 2, pp. 139–191.

Lindbeck, A., Nyberg, S. and Weibull, J. W. 1999, 'Social norms and economic incentives in the welfare state', *The Quarterly Journal of Economics*, vol. 114, no. 1, pp. 1–35.

Lirio, P., Lituchy, T. R., Monserrat, S. I., Olivas-Lujan, M. R., Duffy, J. A., Fox, S., Gregory, A., Punnett, B. J. and Santos, N. 2007, 'Exploring career-life success and family social support of successful women in Canada, Argentina and Mexico', *Career Development International*, vol. 12, no. 1, pp. 28–50.

Mammen, K. and Paxson, C. 2000, 'Women's work and economic development', *The Journal of Economic Perspectives*, vol. 14, no. 4, pp. 141–164.

Marcinkus, W. C., Whelan-Berry, K. S. and Gordon, J. R. 2007, 'The relationship of social support to the work–family balance and work outcomes of midlife women', *Women in Management Review*, vol. 22, no. 2, pp. 86–111.

Mat Zin, R. B. 2006, 'The relationships between family and career-related factors and organizational commitment: a Malaysian case', *The Business Review*, vol. 5, no. 2, pp. 117–121.

Mathou, T. 2000, 'The politics of Bhutan: change in continuity', *Journal of Bhutan Studies*, vol. 2, no. 2, pp. 250–262.

Meenawat, H. and Sovacool, B. K. 2011, 'Improving adaptive capacity and resilience in Bhutan', *Mitigation and Adaptation Strategies for Global Change*, vol. 16, no. 5, pp. 515–533.

Mishra, V., and Smyth, R. 2010. 'Female labor force participation and total fertility rates in the OECD: New evidence from panel cointegration and Granger causality testing', *Journal of Economics and Business*, vol. 62, no. 1, pp. 48–64.

Moghadam, V. M. 2004, 'Patriarchy in transition: women and the changing family in the Middle East', *Journal of Comparative Family Studies*, vol. 35, no. 2, pp. 137–162.

Moghadam, V. M. 2005, 'Women's economic participation in the Middle East: what difference has the neoliberal policy turn made?', *Journal of Middle East Women's Studies*, vol. 1, no. 1, pp. 110–146.

Morgan, S. P., Sharon, S., Smith, H. L. and Mason, K. O. 2002, 'Muslim and non-Muslim differences in female autonomy and fertility: evidence from four Asian countries', *Population and Development Review*, vol. 28, no. 3, pp. 515–537.

Morrisson, C. and Jütting, J. P. 2005, 'Women's discrimination in developing countries: a new data set for better policies', *World Development*, vol. 33, no. 7, pp. 1065–1081.

National Statistic Bureau n.d., *Key Indicators*, National Statistic Bureau, Thimphu, Bhutan, viewed 6 March 2014, <www.nsb.gov.bt/main/main.php#&slider1=4>.

O'Flynn, J. and Blackman, D. 2009, 'Experimenting with organisational development in Bhutan: a tool for reform and the achievement of multi-level goals?', *Public Administration and Development*, vol. 29, no. 2, pp. 133–144.

Pampel, F. C. and Tanaka, K. 1986, 'Economic development and female labor force participation: a reconsideration', *Social Forces*, vol. 64, no. 3, pp. 599–619.

Pinder, C. C. 1998, *Work motivation in organizational behavior*, 1st ed., Prentice Hall, Upper Saddle River, NJ.

Pocock, B. 2003, *The work/life collision: what work is doing to Australians and what to do about it*, The Federation Press, Sydney, Australia.

Priesner, S. 1999, 'Gross National Happiness–Bhutan's vision of development and its challenges', in P. N. Mukherji and C. Sengupta (eds.), *Indigeneity and universality in social science: a South Asian response*, Sage Publications India, New Delhi, India, pp. 24–52.

Revenga, A. and Shetty, S. 2012, 'Empowering women is smart economics', *Finance & Development*, vol. 49, no. 1, pp. 40–43.

Royal Government of Bhutan 2003, *Convention on the elimination of all forms of discrimination against women – an updated summary of the report of the Kingdom of Bhutan*, Royal Government of Bhutan, Thimphu, Bhutan.

Royal Government of Bhutan 2012, *Labour force survey 2012*, MOLHR Department of Employment, Royal Government of Bhutan, Thimphu, Bhutan.

Saget, C. 2006, *Wage fixing in the informal economy: evidence from Brazil, India, Indonesia and South Africa*, International Labour Office, Geneva, Switzerland.

Samad, S. 2006, 'Assessing the effects of work and family related factors on women well-being', *Journal of American Academy of Business*, vol. 9, no. 1, pp. 52–57.

Shimazu, A., Demerouti, E., Bakker, A. B., Shimada, K. and Kawakami, N. 2011, 'Workaholism and well-being among Japanese dual-earner couples: a spillover-crossover perspective', *Social Science and Medicine*, vol. 73, no. 3, pp. 399–409.

Stewart-Weeks, M. and Richardson, C. (eds.) 1998, *Social capital stories: how 12 Australian households live their lives*, The Centre for Independent Studies Limited, St Leonards, Australia.

Stiglitz, J. E. 1976, 'The efficiency wage hypothesis, surplus labour, and the distribution of income in LDCs', *Oxford Economic Papers*, vol. 28, no. 2, pp. 185–207.

Tabellini, G. 2010, 'Culture and institutions: economic development in the regions of Europe', *Journal of the European Economic Association*, vol. 8, no. 4, pp. 677–716.

Tam, H. 2011, 'U-shaped female labor participation with economic development: some panel data evidence', *Economics Letters*, vol. 110, no. 2, pp. 140–142.

Thinley, J. Y. 2005, 'What does gross national happiness (GNH) mean?', paper presented at The Second International Conference on Gross National Happiness, at Antigonish, Canada, 20 June 2005.

Thinley, L. J. 1998, 'Values and development: gross national happiness', paper presented at the Millennium Meeting for Asia and the Pacific, Seoul, Korea, 30 October 1998.

Tsui, A. H. 2008, 'Asian wellness in decline: a cost of rising prosperity', *International Journal of Workplace Health Management*, vol. 1, no. 2, pp. 123–135.

UNESCO Institute for Statistics 2013, *Adult and youth literacy: national, regional and global trends, 1985–2015*, UNESCO Institute for Statistics, Paris, France, viewed 6 March 2014, <www.uis.unesco.org/Education/Documents/literacy-statistics-trends-1985–2015.pdf>.

United Nations 2010, *The world's women 2010: trends and statistics*, Department of Economic and Social Affairs, United Nations, New York, NY, viewed 16 March 2014, <http://unstats.un.org/unsd/demographic/products/Worlds-women/WW_fullper cent20report_color.pdf>.

United Nations n.d., *Goal 3: promote gender equality and empower women*, United Nations, New York, NY, viewed 10 March 2014, <www.un.org/millenniumgoals/gender.shtml>.

United Nations Conference on Trade and Development 2013, *The least developed countries report 2013*, United Nations Conference on Trade and Development, Geneva, Switzerland, viewed 15 March 2014, <http://unctad.org/en/PublicationsLibrary/ldc2013_en.pdf>.

United Nations Development Programme 1990, *Human development report*, United Nations Development Programme, New York, NY.

UNDP Bhutan Country Office 2007, *Gender mainstreaming strategy 2007–2008*, United Nations Development Programme, Thimphu, Bhutan, viewed 10 March 2014, <www.bhutancensus.gov.bt>.

United Nations Children's Fund UNICEF 2013, *Bhutan statistics*, The United Nations Children's Fund, New York, NY, viewed 12 March 2014, <www.unicef.org/infobycountry/bhutan_statistics.html>.

Ura, K. and Galay K. (eds.) 2004, 'Gross national happiness and development', proceedings of the First International Conference on Operationalization of Gross National Happiness Thimphu, 18–20 February 2004, viewed 20 March 2014, <www.bhutanstudies.org.bt/gross-national-happiness-and-development/>.

Van Daalen, G., Willemsen, T. M. and Sanders, K. 2006, 'Reducing work–family conflict through different sources of social support', *Journal of Vocational Behavior*, vol. 69, no. 3, pp. 462–476.

van Klaveren, M. and Tijdens, K. 2012, *Empowering women in work in developing countries*, Palgrave Macmillan, New York, NY.

World Bank 2012a, *Accelerating progress on gender mainstreaming and gender related MDGs: progress report*, World Bank, Washington, DC.

World Bank 2012b, *World development report 2012: gender equality and development*, World Bank, Washington, DC.

World Bank 2013, *Bhutan gender policy note*, World Bank, Washington, DC.

Xiao, Y. and Cooke, F. L. 2012, 'Work–life balance in China? social policy, employer strategy and individual coping mechanisms', *Asia Pacific Journal of Human Resources*, vol. 50, no. 1, pp. 6–22.

4 'Scarcity in plenty'

Skills shortages and HRM competencies in Vietnam

Alan Nankervis, Prikshat Verma and Alan Montague

Introduction

Vietnam is a development success story. Political and economic reforms (*doi moi*) launched in 1986 have transformed Vietnam from one of the poorest countries in the world, with a per capita annual income below US$100, to a lower-/middle-income country within a quarter of a century with per capita income of US$1,130 per annum by the end of 2010. The percentage of the population in poverty has fallen from 58 per cent in 1993 to 14.5 per cent in 2008 (Benuyenah and Phoon 2014), and most indicators of welfare have improved. Vietnam has already attained five of its ten original Millennium Development Goal targets and is well on the way to attaining two more by the end of 2015. Following the implementation of the *doi moi* policy, the Vietnamese economy has demonstrated consistent growth, considerable industrial expansion and a significant transition from low- to high-tech manufacturing (Benuyenah and Phoon 2014; Truong 2013; Warner 2013; Zhu et al. 2008).

It is estimated that Vietnam's past quarter century has witnessed a healthy annual per capita growth of approximately 5.3 per cent 'with annual growth rates averaging as high as 7.6 per cent from 1991 to 2000' (Benuyenah and Phoon 2014: 96). The *doi moi* system represented 'a new economic system which would move to a multi-sector economic system, streamline the development of the non-state sector, and allow the economic system freedom to respond to market forces' (Collins, Sitalaksmi and Lansbury 2013: 135). It worked: 'Vietnam has been one of the fastest growing economies over the last 25 years' (Benuyenah and Phoon 2014: 96).

The rationalisation of the state-owned enterprises (SOEs) sector over the last 20 years has also led to significant management challenges for the remaining government-owned entities, including the rise of 'a new cadre of managers . . . with a dynamic business spirit characterized by the ability . . . to minimize threats and take advantage of opportunities as a consequence of the open-door policy' (Pham 2011: 81). This transformation of former SOEs, together with the associated broadening of the economy to encompass significant numbers of new privately owned enterprises, collective enterprises, household companies, joint ventures and wholly foreign-owned enterprises (Hoe 2013; Thang and Quang 2005; Truong 2013), has also inevitably resulted in 'changes for enterprises, making human resource management (HRM) a vital matter' (Pham 2011: 79). The new breed of managers, including those in HRM positions, have significantly increased opportunities to develop and 'exercise their own leadership and management competencies' (Pham 2011: 81). They have greater choices with respect to HRM strategies, policies and processes, and more accountability for their decisions in relation to organisational productivity, competitiveness and profitability (Collins, Sitalaksmi and Lansbury 2013; Pham 2011; Thang et al. 2007; Warner 2013).

Concomitant with economic growth, there has been a series of legislative developments designed both to facilitate industrial development and to protect workers from the ravages of unbridled capitalism. These include new labour codes in 1994 and 2013 and revisions of prior vocational training laws (2006, 2013) (Ministry of Labour, Invalids and Social Affairs 2014). The former introduced modest temporary and foreign labour contracts and new employee disciplinary provisions together with wage increases, working hour regulations and maternity leave entitlements (Collins et al. 2013; Warner 2013); the latter aims 'to enhance the quality of Vocational Education Training (VET) and to strengthen articulation between vocational education institutions, employers and higher education' (Nankervis et al. 2014). To date, it has yet to achieve these aims, although the Ministry of Labour, Invalids and Social Affairs (MoLISA) is currently implementing revisions to the legislation (Ketels et al. 2010).

As a consequence of its success in terms of rapid economic growth and emerging industry transformation, Vietnam, like China and India, is also facing substantial challenges in addressing an immense talent shortage (Gross 2013; Hoe 2013; Montague 2013; Montague et al. 2014; Quang and Thang 2009; Thang and Quang 2005). The extent of the problem has been highlighted by recent research. The Manpower Group (Manpower 2011: 2) concluded that 'while low cost labour has helped fund Vietnam's growth, it is likely to be an impediment if the country does not improve its workers' skills quickly', whilst others have suggested that 'Vietnam has an over-supply of available labour but an under-supply of quality skilled employees' (Montague 2013: 209). Pham and Tran (2013: 8) similarly observed that there is 'a paradox regarding the employment market in Vietnam . . . [whilst it is] facing severe skills shortages in various sectors . . . up to 60 per cent of Vietnam graduates are unable to secure employment . . . and many do not work in areas of their major, or need to be retrained' (Pham and Tran 2013: 8). More specifically, Nguyen (2013) found that 83.5 per cent of the labour market was 'non-qualified and qualified without certificate', with less than 4.5 per cent holding vocational qualifications. The majority of jobs available reside in vocational fields as opposed to the professions (Nguyen 2013).

In response to these challenges, the Vietnamese government has developed a Socio-Economic Development Strategy (SEDS) for 2011–2020 (World Bank 2014). This strategy directs policy development in terms of 'structural reforms, environmental sustainability, social equity, and emerging issues of macroeconomic stability' (World Bank 2014: para 4) and focuses on three 'breakthrough areas: (i) promoting human resources/skills development (particularly skills for modern industry and innovation), (ii) improving market institutions, and (iii) infrastructure development. The overall goal is for Vietnam to lay the foundations for a modern industrialised society by 2020 (World Bank 2014).

SEDS defines the development of Vietnam's human resources, particularly 'high-quality' resources, as a national strategic priority (Baur 2012). The strategy is underpinned by reformation of the VET system as a whole to address the needs of local and national labour markets (United Nations Educational, Scientific and Cultural Organization [UNESCO] 2014). A five-level National Vocational Qualifications (NQV) framework is being implemented with MoLISA leading social and professional organisational participation to support the key strategies of SEDS (UNESCO 2014). The expectation is that the Vietnam NQV VET qualifications will achieve international recognition, paving the way to educational and vocational mobility (UNESCO 2014).

Like other rapidly developing economies within the Association of Southeast Asian Nations (ASEAN), Vietnam has experienced a continuous and serious shortage of skilled workers since the advent of *doi moi* (UNESCO 2014). The under-supply of skilled workers has been aggravated by a technical and vocational education and training (TVET) system in need of reform (UNESCO 2014):

> [The TVET] system has been unable to produce sufficient numbers of qualified workers for the labour market. One reason for this is that TVET offered in formal educational settings often lacks a workplace orientation. It is divorced from real-life practice and does not integrate placements in the world of work. Moreover, curricula are built around knowledge and skills that do not correspond to labour market and employer demands for skills.
>
> (UNESCO 2014: 1)

The Vietnamese NVQ (see Figure 4.1) aims to promote and foster improved articulation pathways between TVET and academic and pathways 'at each of the

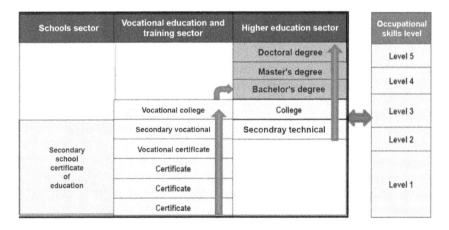

Figure 4.1 Vietnam qualifications framework
Source: UNESCO (2014).

five levels, national occupational skills standards will form the foundation of the qualifications offered' (UNESCO, 2014: 2).

In response to these challenges, neither the central and provincial governments nor most Vietnamese organisations, whether SOEs, locally owned private firms or multinational corporations, have yet demonstrated that they are well-equipped with the managerial acumen, HRM expertise or necessary resources to adequately address its challenges (Asian Development Bank 2011; Baughn et al. 2011; Benuyenah and Phoon 2014; Hoe 2013; Montague 2013; Nankervis et al. 2014). Baughn et al. (2011: 1017), for example explored HRM staff competencies in Vietnamese companies involved in international joint ventures and concluded that HRM professionals 'must address control, trust and conflict issues, establishing mechanisms to enhance trust and performance' in the workplace if they are to attract and retain qualified and experienced staff. Warner (2013) suggested that many Vietnamese organisations have 'simply changed their personnel function to 'HR' without any change in its administrative focus or the adoption of a strategic role' (p. 219), with associated consequences for HR planning, talent attraction and retention. He also proposed three developmental stages for HRM in Vietnamese organisations, namely, nascent, interim and mature stages (Warner 2013: 220).

This chapter explores the nature of Vietnam's 'scarcity in plenty' labour market phenomenon together with the roles, capacities and competencies of its HRM professionals to face the associated challenges by examining the findings of a recent empirical study through the prism of HRM competency theory. The latter findings are compared with HRM roles and competencies contained in the HRM Competency Framework (see Figure 4.2) designed by the Australian Human Resources Institute (AHRI), in association with Ulrich et al. (2007).

Previous skills shortage research studies and the HRM competency theory are reviewed prior to an analysis of the research findings, a discussion of the links between skills shortages and Vietnamese HR professionals' competencies and recommendations for future research and HRM practice.

Literature review

Labour markets and skills shortages in Vietnam

With an estimated population of 88 million, almost 58 per cent of whom are in the labour market (Central Intelligence Agency [CIA] 2013; Gross 2013; Hoe 2013), there is a significant imbalance in sectoral participation in Vietnam, with nearly half in agriculture, approximately 30 per cent in services and only 22 per cent in the growing industrial sector (Economist Intelligence Unit [EIU] 2012). With a median age of 28.7 (CIA 2013), Vietnam has the considerable human capital advantage of a 'demographic dividend' (Montague et al. 2014). However, this potential productivity benefit may be offset by the 'scarcity in plenty' paradox, namely, 'an over-supply of available labour but an under-supply of qualified and skilled employees' (Montague 2013: 209). It is estimated that

AHRI MODEL OF EXCELLENCE

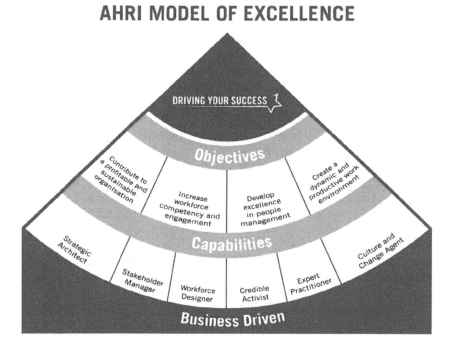

Figure 4.2 AHRI Model of Excellence

Source: HR Competency Model (Ulrich et al. 2013) and AHRI HR Management Model 2013.

nearly 85 per cent of the Vietnamese workforce has no formal post-secondary qualifications, with only 6 per cent being university graduates (EIU 2012: 9; Nguyen 2013). The Human Development Index (HDI) ranking also suggested that Vietnam had a lower percentage age of its population with 'high educational attainment compared to countries with almost similar (or even lower) HDI rankings, such as Mongolia and South Africa' (United Nations Population Fund [UNFPA] 2011: 1).

Table 4.1 (Nguyen 2013) illustrates that the qualifications spectrum in Vietnam is improving. But, like the UNFPA (2011) data, it also shows that the labour supply available to employers in Vietnam has a noticeably low formal qualifications rate. The 'non-qualified and qualified without certificate' group in 2012 shows a disturbingly high proportion (83.54 per cent) of the Vietnamese labour force lacking credentials, with only 16.46 per cent holding some form of qualification, with a mere 4.53 per cent possessing formal vocational qualifications.

The breadth and depth of these vocational and capability shortages has been explored by many researchers, including Hoe (2013: 54) who estimated that two-thirds of potential Vietnamese employees lack work-ready training and that three-quarters are currently in 'uncertain jobs with low income' (Hoe 2013: 54). Two-thirds of foreign-owned enterprises reported lower productivity due to an

Table 4.1 Vietnam's labour market – qualifications (%)

	2009	2010	2011	2012
Non-qualified and qualified without certificate	82.63	85.37	84.5	83.54
Primary vocational training	3.83	1.92	2.08	2.56
Secondary vocational training	2.11	1.64	1.60	1.61
Secondary professional school	4.28	3.43	3.66	3.61
Vocational college	0.30	0.27	0.29	0.36
College	1.67	1.68	1.72	1.92
University	5.17	5.69	6.15	6.4

Source: Nguyen (2013).

absence of skilled workers (Gross 2013; McKinsey Global Institute 2012; World Bank 2012, 2014). The latest labour and social trends report issued by MoLISA (2010) discovered significant shortages in trades and professions – automobile technicians, electricians, hospitality workers, Information and Communication Technology (ICT) and accounting, financial planning and construction surveyors (Montague 2013: 215). Others have noted significant shortages in burgeoning industry sectors such as textiles, plastics, oil and gas, chemicals and mining (EIU 2012), together with specialist professional skills in healthcare, aviation, manufacturing, natural science, agriculture and waste treatment. Overall, there are particular demand–supply gaps in both professional and technical occupations – labourers, skilled trades, managers and engineers (EIU 2012). As an example, a study commissioned by the Vietnam Chamber of Commerce and Industry (VCCI) and the International Labour Organisation (ILO) found that 70 per cent of employers anticipated shortfalls in managerial positions, with a further 77 per cent expecting gaps in their technical workforce (Centre for Labour Market Studies [CLMS] 2011).

The key question for Vietnam is how to overcome the lack of qualifications amongst its workforce – with the vast majority no longer in education and who may have no desire to return to classroom environments. One solution may lie in the formal recognition of prior learning (RPL) (Montague 2013; UNESCO 2014). Improving the overall education system is another objective (World Bank 2014), together with a higher priority for organisational human resource development (Nankervis et al. 2014).

Part of a potential solution is for human resource professionals to work with educators and locate the student in the workplace (Bosch and Charest 2010; Organisation for Economic Co-operation and Development 2012). Many talented people are employed in numerous industries without qualifications. Creating a higher qualification level through the ethical use of RPL by means of an improved partnership between education and industry has merit, but working to boost the numbers of persons gaining qualifications in both formal educational and industry settings is the fastest way to boost skills and qualifications cost effectively (Montague et al. 2014).

UNESCO (2014) for example called for a move to recognise learners' prior skills in Vietnam gained through informal study and experience. The aim is 'to encourage enhancement of skill levels, improving workforce quality and boosting the international competitiveness of Vietnamese industry' (UNESCO 2014: 1). Vietnam's MoLISA has adopted a policy of assessment and granting of national qualifications and occupational skill standards through recognising prior skills developed through education and experience.

RPL is considered an aspect of education that can be undertaken in workplaces that may enhance individual and organisational effectiveness, wellbeing and productivity (Wheelahan et al. 2003). The RPL is defined in the Australian Qualifications Framework (AQF):

> Recognition of prior learning is an assessment process that involves assessment of an individual's relevant prior learning (including formal, informal and non-formal learning) to determine the credit outcomes of an individual application for credit.

This is underpinned by the AQF's definition of credit:

> Credit is the value assigned for the recognition of equivalence in content and learning outcomes between different types of learning and/or qualifications. Credit reduces the amount of learning required to achieve a qualification and may be through credit transfer, articulation, recognition of prior learning or advanced standing.
> (Australian Qualifications Framework Council [AQFC] 2013, 94)

UNESCO (2012: 5) refers to RPL as the recognition, validation and accreditation (RVA) of all forms of learning with a focus on non-formal and informal learning to 'translate learning outcomes from working and life experiences into credits and/or qualifications'. It also recommended that an awareness and acceptance of RVA be adopted in industry and education and training bodies among its country members including Vietnam (UNESCO 2012); that learning outcomes and skills development be formally recognised within an assessment and validation framework, regardless of its origin, and where possible and ethical, that qualifications be issued and recognised. Finally, UNESCO (2014: 6) called for 'all stakeholders to develop clearly defined roles and responsibilities in developing a coherent and coordinated national structure to oversee the design, implementation and quality assurance of the RVA system'. Figure 4.2 later in this chapter illustrates that a major outcome of the HRM role is to develop key competencies in the workplace.

Associated skills shortages may be divided into 'vocational and capability' (Montague 2013) or 'industry- and enterprise-specific' (Manpower 2011) skills. Vocational skills include specific professional and technical qualifications and experience, whilst capability skills incorporate 'soft' competencies such as interpersonal communication, teamwork, critical thinking, decision-making, data collection and analysis, cross-cultural understanding and managerial capabilities (Montague et al. 2014). Many of these skills have been perceived to be lacking in potential and current Vietnamese employees. From a slightly different perspective, the Manpower Group (Manpower 2011: 6) suggested that many applicants lacked 'industry-specific' knowledge (about materials, production, products and services; new technology; occupational health and safety; business planning) and/or 'enterprise-specific' capabilities (about customer knowledge, work procedures, group interactions; operation of machines, equipment and work tools) (Montague et al. 2013).

Causal factors for these skill shortages are associated with both labour demand and supply. Demand has been a direct outcome of rapid economic growth, increasing technological change and the more recent shift from low- to high-tech manufacturing, together with the more demanding expectations of local, private and foreign-owned companies (Montague et al. 2014). Supply issues have arisen from problems with Vietnam's vocational and higher education systems and the reluctance of many employers to provide supplementary workplace training programmes or even to collaborate with vocational or higher education service providers for such purposes (UNESCO (2014). The current educational infrastructure at both vocational and university levels suffers from an over-emphasis on theory rather than practice – 'a failure to combine theoretical learning with practical or behavioural skills' (Economist Intelligence Unit 2012: 9) – as well as a societal preference for university rather than technical education and outdated curricula (Truong 2013: 17) – 'a curriculum that is isolated from the employment market and employers' needs in association with low-level commitment to skills development in tertiary education' (Pham and Tran 2013: 16). Many vocational and higher education professionals themselves lack either the training or experience needed to pass on such practical skills (Montague et al. 2014). Whilst the Vietnamese government is cognisant of these deficiencies, and is revising the previous Vocational Training Law to address them, the demand–supply gap is widening with no indication that it will be resolved in the immediate future (Montague et al. 2014). As a consequence of the skills shortages, wages in Vietnamese organisations are constantly rising, reportedly as much as 15 per cent annually (McKinsey Global Institute 2012), thus threatening the low labour costs which have provided Vietnam's competitive global advantage, especially in the manufacturing sector.

HRM competency theory

One of the pervasive themes of recent management literature has been consideration of the meaning and importance of 'competencies' in job design, learning and development and rewards systems amongst leaders and their subordinates (Montague et al. 2014; Nankervis et al. 2014). Competencies have replaced descriptors such as knowledge and skills (Gilbert 1978; Raven and

Stephenson 2001; Robinson et al. 2007) in job design, learning and development, rewards and remuneration, promotions and career development systems (Raven and Stephenson 2001; Robinson et al. 2007). Despite imprecise terminology, ambiguity associated with different levels of competence and the blurring of 'broad' (leadership/managerial functions) and 'narrow' (mechanistic skills) capabilities (Colin 1989), competency theory has been widely accepted in both theory and professional HRM practice (Nankervis et al. 2014; Raven and Stephenson 2001).

Birenbaum (1996) provided a four-factor taxonomy of professional competencies, namely:

- cognitive competencies, such as problem solving, critical thinking, making informed judgements, inventing and creating new things, analysing data, presenting data communicatively, oral and written expression;
- meta-cognitive competencies, such as self-reflection or self-evaluation;
- social competencies, such as leading discussions and conversations, persuading, cooperating, working in groups; and
- affective dispositions, such as perseverance, internal motivation, initiative, responsibility, self-efficacy, independence, flexibility (Tait and Godfrey 1999: 246).

Whilst these competencies obviously apply to professionals, including managers and HR specialists, they may also be relevant in skilled technical positions. HRM theorists have been modelling the key competencies which underlie their strategic and operational functions for more than 20 years (Boudreau and Ramstad 2003; Brockbank and Ulrich 2003; Brockbank, Ulrich and James 1997; Carroll 1990; Nankervis et al. 2014; Ulrich 1997; 1998; Wright, Dunford and Snell 2001). These efforts have been driven by strategic human resource management (SHRM) concepts (Nankervis et al. 2014; Wright, Dunford and Snell 2001). They represent a search for professional legitimacy on the one hand – 'the HR profession can evolve into a true decision science . . . and aspire to the level of influence of disciplines such as finance and marketing' (Boudreau and Ramstad 2003: 86) – and prescriptive frameworks for professional practice on the other – 'a competency model can serve as an integrative framework for an organisation's entire human resources system' (Ramlall 2006: 29). HRM roles and competencies provide practitioners with legitimacy, confidence, measurable and accountable performance criteria and the capability to align HR strategies with business goals and objectives (Nankervis et al. 2014). Towards these objectives, Schuler (1990) proposed six key HRM roles – business person, shaper of change, consultant to the organisation, strategic formulator and implementer, talent manager, asset manager and cost controller (Boselie and Paauwe 2005: 5), which to some degree reflect the initial consideration by Ulrich et al. (2013) of broad HRM responsibilities – financial management, cultural change, strategic decision-making and market-focus (Long and Khairuzzaman 2008; Nankervis et al. 2014).

These early taxonomies derived from two crucial concepts associated with SHRM theory, namely, 'internal-external fit' (Lepak and Snell 2002; Wright and Snell 1998) and 'horizontal-vertical integration' (Becker, Huselid and Ulrich 2001; Losey 1999; Ulrich and Lake 1990).These concepts suggest, on the one hand, that HRM strategies and processes should clearly address both the challenges of the external business environment and internal company priorities and that all HRM functions should be integrated with each other (horizontal) and with HRM strategies (vertical), on the other (Nankervis et al. 2014). As Crouse, Doyle and Young (2011: 379) concluded, 'the former functional HRM role has been supplanted by a more strategic role which requires new competencies'. The common features of these early taxonomies lie in their emphasis on business knowledge (marketing and financial acumen), change management, data collection and analysis, consulting skills, HRM functional competence, programme evaluation and accountability.

Whilst later models of HRM roles and competencies reflect similar emphases, they are more clearly focused as they are derived from national and global research studies. As examples, the 1997 University of Michigan survey concluded that there were four broad HRM competencies, namely, strategic partner, change agent, employee champion and administrative expert (Barney and Wright 1998; Boselie and Paauwe 2005: 6). Later versions of this study (2002, 2007 and 2012) have attracted large global research samples, leading to successive revisions of these competencies (Nankervis et al. 2014). The most recent study (2012) surveyed 20,000 respondents (HR and non-HR managers) in ten countries and developed an HR competency model – *strategic positioner, capability builder, change champion, technology proponent, HR innovator and integrator* and *credible activist* (Ulrich et al. 2013: 24).

Professional associations in many countries have tried to convert HRM competency theory into measurable practitioner competencies and capabilities. As examples, the US Society of HRM has distilled nine key professional competencies (technical expertise, relationship management, consultation, organisational leadership, communication, diversity and inclusion, ethical practice, critical evaluation and business acumen), together with one technical competency and eight behavioural competencies/professional standards (Dolan 2013: 4).The UK Chartered Institute of Personnel Development (Chartered Institute of Personnel and Development 2010) uses an 'HR Profession Map', which includes ten professional areas, eight professional behaviours, and four 'bands' (levels) of competency (Dolan 2013: 7–8). The Australian Public Service Commission promotes six 'capabilities' for its HR professionals, namely, knowledge, credibility, alignment, innovation, relationships and 'performance achieving high quality business results', whilst the Western Australian Public Service Commission's 'capability framework' includes strategic alignment, workforce capability, results-driven, relationship management, credible influence, professional expertise, culture and change management (Dolan 2013: 9–10; Nankervis et al. 2014).

Finally, the AHRI developed a 'Model of Excellence' as a framework for both the recognition of its members' proficiency and the formal accreditation of all

Australian vocational and higher education HRM qualifications (see Figure 4.2, Nankervis et al. 2014). Its 'capabilities' (rather than 'competencies') derive from a business-driven focus towards its component HRM capabilities: strategic architect, stakeholder manager, workforce designer, credible activist, expert practitioner and culture and change agent. The model was used as the analytical framework for the study of skills shortages and HRM competencies in Vietnam reported later in this chapter.

Methodology

The study combined an exploration of the skills shortages experienced by a range of Vietnamese organisations (large, medium and small; public, local private and multinational) as well as of insights into the current competencies of their HRM professionals, with a view to analysing their capacities to address the crucial labour market challenges in Vietnam. It was hoped that some overall observations might be made about the links between Vietnamese HRM professionals' competencies and their likely contribution to the skills shortages faced by their organisations, as an impetus for more rigorous future research studies. However, the limitations of a modest research sample and the difficulty of such extrapolations are acknowledged. The specific research questions were:

1) What are the main skills shortages in a range of Vietnamese organisations?
2) What are the key roles, competencies and functions of HRM professionals in these organisations?
3) How might the identified HRM competencies equip such professionals to address these skills shortages?

The research methodology included a comprehensive literature review; a National Skills Summit (NSS) convened in Ho Chi Minh City in April 2013; and an associated e-survey supported and administered by the research partners, the AHRI and the VCCI. The survey was presented in both English and Vietnamese, using only closed questions and Likert scales to encourage responses and to facilitate data analysis.

The survey comprised five sections, including information on the organisation; respondents; HRM department; HRM competencies and functions; professional and technical skills shortages, and their causes. It was conducted during 2013, using the networks of the VCCI and the MoLISA. The target sample of the survey was managers working in companies operating in Vietnam. A total of 82 responses were received with 3 incomplete questionnaires, which were thus eliminated from the analysis (Montague et al. 2014, Nankervis et al. 2014). The remaining 79 responses were analysed using Statistical Package for Social Sciences (SPSS). The data sample and findings on skills shortages are reported first, followed by those on HRM competencies, and the possible links between them are discussed in a later section of this chapter.

Research findings

Sample profile

While a small majority of the respondents are from government departments or agencies (42.7 per cent), there is also a significant representation from local private organisations (34.7 per cent) and a smaller number of respondents from multinational enterprises (MNCs, 12 per cent) – (see Table 4.2). These proportions are more or less parallel to those in the broader Vietnamese economy (Nankervis et al. 2014). A large majority of the respondents work in small (63.5 per cent) or small-medium (83.7 per cent) organisations, whether in government or the private sector, with fewer in large organisations (20.3 per cent). Many of the latter are likely to be employed by MNCs. Again, these proportions largely reflect the size distributions in the overall economy.

The spread of industry sectors generally reflects the expanse of industry, noting that the administrative/support (19 per cent), education/training (20 per cent), and manufacturing (16 per cent) sectors are predominant.

Professional and technical skills shortages – vocational and capability

As Table 4.3 indicates, *professional* (vocational) skills shortages are most evident in large organisations (73 per cent) and medium-sized organisations, mostly multinationals (62.5 per cent) and local private enterprises (56 per cent), with less concern in smaller organisations or government agencies. The key skills shortages reported in this category included HR specialists, managers (29.1 per cent), marketing specialists (20.3 per cent), engineers (17.7), accountants (13.9 per cent), IT specialists (10.1 per cent); doctors and nurses (8.9 per cent). Causes were ranked in ascending order as inability to provide adequate salary (39.2 per cent), inability to provide employee benefits/industry competition (22.8 per cent); lack of career opportunity (15.2 per cent), unattractive location (11.4 per cent), lack of sufficient university graduates (10.1 per cent), and organisation's reputation (7.6 per cent).

Technical (vocational) skills shortages (Table 4.4) were of less concern, with only larger (87 per cent) and mainly foreign-owned organisations having significant shortfalls. This finding is at odds with those from earlier studies. Electricians (13.7 per cent), mechanics (8.9 per cent), welders (5.1 per cent), chefs (2.5 per cent), plumbers (1.3 per cent) and carpenters (1.3 per cent) appear difficult to find. Causes of these lesser shortages include inability to provide adequate salary (24.1 per cent) and inability to provide employee benefits (15.2 per cent). Other causes included industry competition and lack of career opportunity (13.9 per cent each), lack of sufficient university graduates (6.3 per cent) and unattractive location (1.3 per cent).

In both categories, 'inability to provide adequate salary' is the main causal factor identified for skills shortages, together with an 'inability to provide employee

Table 4.2 Profile of respondents

Status	Profile	Numbers	Percentage
Ownership (n = 75)	Government	32	42.7
	Private	26	34.7
	International	9	12.0
	Other	8	10.7
Number of employees (n = 74)	Less than 20	4	5.4
	20–100	43	58.1
	101–500	12	16.2
	More than 500	15	20.3
Number of HRM staff (n = 76)	1–3	15	19.7
	4–7	36	47.3
	8–12	16	21.1
	More than 12	9	11.8
Industry type (n = 74)	Accommodation and food service	3	4.1
	Administrative and support services	14	18.9
	Agriculture forestry and fishing	3	4.1
	Arts and recreation services	3	4.1
	Construction	5	6.8
	Education and training	15	20.3
	Electricity, gas, water and waste services	3	4.1
	Financial insurance services	2	2.7
	Health care and social assistance	2	2.7
	Information media and telecommunication	5	6.8
	Manufacturing	12	16.2
	Professional scientific and technical services	1	1.4
	Retail trade	1	1.4
	Transport postal and warehousing/logistics	3	4.1
	Wholesale trade	1	1.4
	Others	1	1.4

Table 4.3 Professional skills shortages by size and ownership

| | | Number (%) | | Total |
		Yes	No	
Number of employees	< 20	1 (25.00)	3 (75.00)	4 (100.00)
	21–100	19 (46.34)	22 (53.66)	41 (100.00)
	101–500	7 (58.34)	5 (41.66)	12 (100.00)
	> 501	11 (73.33)	4 (26.67)	15 (100.00)
Ownership	Government department or agency	12 (37.50)	20 (62.50)	32 (100.00)
	Private business	14 (56.00)	11 (44.00)	25 (100.00)
	International company	5 (62.50)	3 (37.50)	8 (100.00)

Table 4.4 Technical skills shortages by size and ownership

| | | Number (%) | | Total |
		Yes	No	
Number of employees	< 20	0 (0%)	4 (100.00)	4 (100.00)
	21–100	9 (25.00)	27 (75.00)	36 (100.00)
	101–500	4 (33.33)	8 (66.67)	12 (100.00)
	> 501	13 (86.67)	2 (13.33)	15 (100.00)
Ownership	Government department or agency	8 (26.67)	22 (73.33)	30 (100.00)
	Private business	7 (30.43)	16 (69.57)	23 (100.00)
	International company	4 (57.14)	3 (42.86)	7 (100.00)
	Other	6 (85.71)	1 (14.29)	7 (100.00)

benefits'. 'Industry competition' and 'lack of career opportunity' also contribute to the recruitment difficulties for both professional and technical staff. However, the reported levels of professional and technical skills shortages are more modest than those suggested in some earlier studies (Montague et al. 2014).

Skills enhancement requirements

Figure 4.3 demonstrates the main capability skills requiring improvement for both professional and technical employees. With respect to 'capability' skills, it is clear that both occupations are deficient in some areas. Thus, whilst 'leading teams' is a priority for professionals, it is of lesser importance for technical

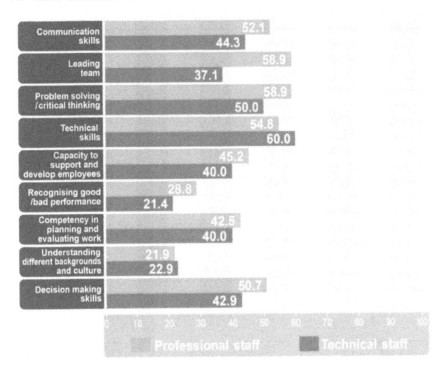

Figure 4.3 Skills enhancement requirements for professional and technical staff

staff. However, 'problem solving/critical thinking' skills are equally important for both professionals and technical staff. 'Recognising good/bad performance' and 'understanding how to work with people from different backgrounds and culture' are apparently of little importance for either occupational group (Montague et al. 2014).

HRM departments: key roles, competencies and functions

Most HRM departments (67.1 per cent) include less than seven employees (with most between four and seven), which is appropriate for small and medium-sized organisations. However, larger organisations may employ more than eight HRM professionals. Almost all respondents (97.4 per cent) suggested that either a relevant diploma (14.3 per cent) or a bachelor's degree (83.1 per cent) is a mandatory minimum qualification for HRM staff, a very high expectation in comparison with the situation in other countries (Nankervis et al. 2014).

With respect to the *three key HRM roles* – namely, strategic business partners, functional HRM specialists, administrative experts – clearly most respondents (see Figure 4.4 and Table 4.5) believe that their HRM professionals adopt a 'functional HRM specialist' (73.7 per cent) rather than either 'strategic business

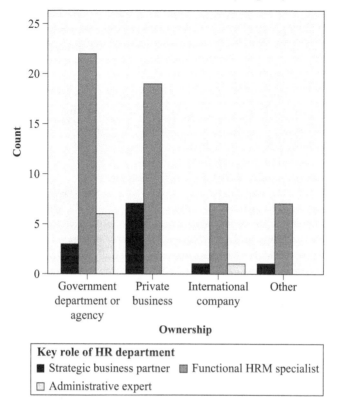

Figure 4.4 Key HRM role by ownership type

Table 4.5 Key role of HR department

		Frequency	Per cent	Valid (%)	Cumulative (%)
Valid	Strategic business partner	13	16.5	17.1	17.1
	Functional HRM specialist	56	70.9	73.7	90.8
	Administrative expert	7	8.9	9.2	100.0
	Total	76	96.2	100.0	
Missing	System	3	3.8		
Total		79	100.0		

partner' (17.1 per cent) or 'administrative expert' (9.2 per cent) roles. This is not an unexpected finding, and in fact, it reinforces Warner's (2013) observation that HRM in Vietnam is in an 'interim' (or 'transitional') rather than a 'nascent' or 'mature' stage (p. 220). Figure 4.4 indicates that this predominant HRM role is more common in government agencies and local private businesses but that the strategic business partner role is more evident in private businesses than in government agencies. This finding, to some extent, strengthens the authenticity of the responses in view of the risk of exaggerated role perceptions with a self-reporting research methodology.

With respect to the *HRM competencies* included in the AHRI Model of Excellence (see Figure 4.2 earlier in the chapter), it is clear that most respondents perceive that their levels of expertise are relatively high on all the measured competencies (see Table 4.6). In descending order, the greatest support was given to 'culture and change agent' (mean = 3.67), followed by 'expert practitioner' (3.60), 'credible activist' (3.56), 'stakeholder manager (3.47), 'strategic architect' (3.45) and 'business driven' (3.42). There was no evidence of significant differences between the measured competencies. Whilst the culture and change agent competency might reflect a strategic business partner role; expert practitioner, credible activist, and stakeholder manager competencies are more supportive of a functional HRM specialist role, especially one performed within a transitional industry context such as Vietnam, moving as it is from socialism to a market-driven economy (Nankervis et al. 2014).

Cross-correlation analyses were also undertaken with respect to the associations between organisational type/company size and the specific HRM competencies. With regard to the correlations between company size and the key role of HR department, most HR professionals in Vietnam are performing their tasks as functional specialists (< 20 = 100 per cent; 21–100 = 78.6 per cent; 101–500 = 50 per cent and > 501 = 66.7 per cent). However, there is a tendency for the role to change according to the size of the organisation. Thus, in larger organisations, more HR professionals are involved in strategic planning (< 20 = 0 per cent; 21–100 = 14.3 per cent; 101–500 = 25 per cent and > 501 = 26.7 per cent, respectively) (Nankervis et al. 2014).

Table 4.7 reports the level of expertise that the HR professionals perceive in themselves against the seven HR competencies and skills across the three types of organisations. According to the table, HR professionals who are working for government agencies see themselves as having a high level of expertise on four key competencies (strategic architect, stakeholder manager, workforce designer and expert practitioner). HR professionals in local private businesses assess themselves as experts on six out of the seven competencies and skills (business driven, strategic architect, stakeholder manager, workforce designer and expert practitioner). However, HR professionals working for MNCs perceive their key competencies as strategic architect, culture and change agent and workforce designer (Nankervis et al. 2014).

The findings also illustrate that HR professionals in medium-sized and larger organisations feel that they have higher levels of the seven competencies and skills than their counterparts in smaller organisations. For example the HR professionals in small organisations reported a high level of expertise in only one competency (strategic architect), while their colleagues in large companies regarded their expertise as encompassing five of the seven competencies and skills (stakeholder

Table 4.6 HRM competencies

		Business driven	Strategic architect	Stake-holder manager	Work-force designer	Credible activist	Expert practitioner	Culture and change agent
N	Valid	73	73	72	72	73	73	73
	Missing	6	6	7	7	6	6	6
Mean		3.4247	3.4521	3.4722	3.4583	3.5616	3.6027	3.6712
Std. deviation		.89625	1.10606	.90339	1.06066	.92776	.92406	.89837
Range		4.00	5.00	4.00	5.00	4.00	4.00	5.00

Table 4.7 Organisational types and HR competencies and skills

HR competencies and skills	Government	Private	International
Business driven	Medium	High	Medium
Strategic architect	High	High-very high	High
Stakeholder manager	High	High	Medium
Workforce designer	High	High	High
Credible activist	Medium	Very high	Medium
Expert practitioner	High	High	Medium
Culture and change agent	Medium-high	Medium-high	High

manager, workforce designer, credible activist, expert practitioner and culture and change agent). There is a mixed finding for HR professionals who work for medium-sized companies (21–100 and 101–500).

Drilling down to *the top five HRM* functions from the 16 provided (see Table 4. 8), 'HR policy development' is reported as the most important function (34.2 per cent) of their HR department, followed by 'HR planning' (25.3 per cent), with less support given to 'work and job design/analysis/evaluation' (22.8 per cent), 'recruitment and selection' (16.5 per cent) and 'employee training and development' (13.9 per cent). We would argue that 'employee training and development' need to be seen as a higher priority by HRM professionals through enhanced relationships with the education and training sectors to facilitate RPL/RVA as outlined earlier.

An inconsistency that is apparent in the survey findings is that, while 'employee training and development' is only ranked in the fifth place as the most important HR function, it has the highest percentage age (75.9 per cent) when the top five HR functions are considered at the same time. This indicates that, although 'employee training and development' is not perceived as the key HR function, it is apparently one of the most important and popular HR functions perceived by the respondents when multiple HR functions are considered (Nankervis et al. 2014). Given the skill shortages and low levels of qualifications discussed earlier in this chapter, this is an important HRM priority in addressing such issues. Another HR function central to resolving the skills shortage dilemma, whilst 'recruitment and selection' is only ranked fourth as the most important HR function, it ranks second (69.7 per cent) when all five functions are considered. These findings are generally consistent with functional HRM specialist roles, and expert practitioner, credible activist, workforce designer, stakeholder manager and culture and change agent professional competencies, and not surprisingly, HR policy and planning capabilities and skills are consistent with the management of staff within a dynamic economic context. There is considerably less support for HR information management, knowledge management, career development, employee

Table 4.8 Top five HRM functions

HR function	Ranked 1st important	Ranked 2nd important	Ranked 3rd important	Ranked 4th important	Ranked 5th important	Total
HR policy development	34.2	6.3	1.3	0.0	5.1	46.9
HR planning	25.3	21.5	7.6	3.8	2.5	60.7
HR information system design and management	7.6	13.9	7.6	6.3	3.8	39.2
Knowledge management	6.3	5.1	11.4	7.6	2.5	32.9
Ethics, governance and/or CSR	11.4	7.6	12.7	6.3	3.8	41.8
Work job design/ analysis/ evaluation	22.8	8.9	13.9	5.1	3.8	54.5
Recruitment and selection	16.5	20.3	16.5	10.1	6.3	69.7
Talent management	13.9	5.1	8.9	5.1	1.3	34.3
Career development	8.9	5.1	7.6	5.1	0.0	26.7
Employee training and development	13.9	11.4	15.2	25.3	10.1	75.9
Employee counselling and discipline	2.5	7.6	7.6	3.8	3.8	25.3
Performance management	11.4	7.6	2.5	11.4	13.9	46.8
Employee rewards and benefits	6.3	12.7	3.8	3.8	11.4	38.0
Industrial relations	12.7	6.3	8.9	3.8	5.1	36.8
Occupational health and safety	10.1	8.9	6.3	2.5	6.3	34.1
HR evaluation and accountability	10.1	7.6	3.8	1.3	7.6	30.4

rewards and benefits systems or talent management competencies, which might be more reflective of strategic business partner roles (Nankervis et al. 2014).

Cross-correlations between organisation type and HR functions show that the HR professionals in government and local private organisations regard 7 of the 16 choices as the most important function (HR policy development, HR planning, ethics, governance and/or corporate social responsibility, work/job design/ analysis/evaluation, industrial relations, occupational health and safety and HR evaluation and accountability). Similar analyses between organisational size and HR functions demonstrate that larger organisations appear to regard most of the HR functions as top priorities as compared with their smaller counterparts. In particular, the emphases on HR policy development and HR planning may reflect concerns with addressing the identified present and future implications of the skills shortages in their organisations.

Discussion

The findings from this study of skills shortages and HRM roles, competencies and functions in Vietnamese organisations are generally consistent with those from similar local studies (Collins, Sitalaksmi and Lansbury 2013; Hoe 2013; Ketels et al. 2010; Warner 2013) and reflect transitional phases in the economy and development of the HRM profession in Vietnam (Barney and Wright 1998; Benuyenah and Phoon 2014; Boselie and Paauwe 2005; Boudreau and Ramstad 2003; Brockbank, Ulrich and James 1997; Warner 2013).

With respect to skills shortfalls, whilst some of our findings accord with prior research in Vietnam, there are differences concerning the particular vocational and capability shortages in different organisational types and sizes. The paradox of 'scarcity in plenty' reflects the quandary of the Vietnamese workforce – the shortfalls in workforce quantity and quality are likely to impede the future economic growth of the economy (Hoe 2013; Thang and Quang 2005). With respect to the *first research question:* What are the main skills shortages in Vietnamese industry? The study suggests that, for vocational shortages, there may be less of a problem with technical specialists than professionals, although both areas are of concern. These shortages have resulted from rapid economic development (demand), on the one hand; inadequate secondary, higher and vocational education systems; and the inability of employers to attract qualified and experienced employees from a static local labour market, to establish appropriate linkages with these education systems, or to provide complementary on-the-job learning and development systems (supply), on the other hand.

Key capability skills are deficient amongst both technical specialists and professionals. These include strategic and human resource management capabilities such as planning and evaluation, employee support and development and the identification and management of talent, which further exacerbate supply challenges. It can be argued that these capability skills shortages are of more concern than the vocational shortages, as they encompass the supervisory, managerial and team competencies required to attract and retain competitive talent into the future (Montague et al. 2014). Providing potential and current employees with both vocational and capability skills is perhaps the key strategic priority for Vietnam's future economic growth and will need to integrate the efforts of the central and provincial governments, and education providers in concert with employers of all types and sizes. As a recent ILO (2010) report suggests, 'good-quality primary and secondary education, complemented by relevant vocational training and skills development opportunities, prepare future generations for their productive lives, endowing them with the core skills that enable them to continue learning' (p.1).

Implementing a robust policy framework to implement RPL/RVA is arguably crucial to boosting qualification levels in Vietnam. UNESCO (2012; 2014) rightly concluded that it was essential for the industry, education and training bodies to develop a clear understanding and facilitate ethical assessment and learning practices to alleviate skill gaps resulting in formal qualifications being issued regardless of where employees obtained their skills.

The *second research question:* what are the key HRM roles, competencies and functions designed to elicit respondents' views on the stage of development of HRM professionals, their priorities and capacities to address the human capital issues facing their organisations due to these skills shortages? As indicated earlier in this chapter, the major HRM role in most types of organisations is that of a functional HRM specialist, including key functions such as HR policy development, HR planning, job design, recruitment and selection, learning and development, performance management and rewards systems. In Warner's (2013) categorisation, these roles and functions suggest an 'interim' HRM stage of development, with considerably smaller proportions of 'nascent' and 'mature' HRM functions (p. 220).

As might be expected, larger (and possibly local private) organisations are marginally more likely to adopt a strategic business partner role (Ulrich 1997, 1998; Ulrich et al. 2013; Wright and Snell 1998) than their smaller and government counterparts. This finding suggests that HRM in Vietnam has transitioned away from 'personnel management' traditions of an 'administrative expert' (Brockbank, Ulrich and James 1997; Carroll 1990; Warner 2013) towards a more contemporary professional status but has yet to truly embrace its more strategic potential including a heightened role in talent management and human resource development (Nankervis et al. 2014). There are also some related findings concerning the key competencies and functions of HR professionals, which largely support a functional HRM specialist role (expert practitioner, credible activist, stakeholder manager) with a complementary focus on 'culture and change agent' (Collins, Sitalaksmi and Lansbury 2013; Hoe 2013; Ketels et al. 2010). Crosscorrelation analysis revealed that government, local private organisations and MNCs place importance on strategic architect and workforce designer capabilities, but government and local private HRM professionals emphasise stakeholder management and expert practitioner competencies as well. Local private business respondents also stressed the importance of business-driven skills, while MNCs reiterated culture and change agent capacities(Nankervis et al. 2014). Larger organisations appear to show greater expertise in higher level HRM competencies than their medium-sized and smaller counterparts (Quang and Thang 2009). With respect to the associated HRM functions, learning and development, and recruitment and selection functions are high priorities, with job design, analysis and programme evaluation also mentioned. These represent functional HRM specialist roles and expert practitioner competencies rather than strategic business partner roles and 'strategic architect' or 'culture and change management' capabilities/competencies (see Figure 4.2).

Importantly, there was considerable support for HR planning and policy development functions in all organisation types, which may suggest that they are attempting to respond proactively to Vietnam's dynamic economy and labour market conundrum (research question 3) (Collins, Sitalaksmi and Lansbury 2013; Montague 2013; Nguyen 2013; CLMS 2008). In contrast, however, crucial support functions for addressing the identified vocational and capability skills shortages, such as HR information management, knowledge management, career development, talent management and rewards systems, are not as common. This may merely reflect the transitional nature of the HRM profession in Vietnam, the limited nature of the research sample or both. In any case, all of these functions will need to be utilised if government, local private and multinational organisations are to respond effectively to the present and future skills deficits of the Vietnamese economy (Collins, Sitalaksmi and Lansbury 2013; Nguyen 2013; Thang et al. 2007). Given the dynamic nature of this economy, movements towards more business-driven, integrated HRM strategies, supported by appropriate practitioner competencies and key HRM functions would seem the essential ingredients for growth and competitiveness; 'strategic decision-making, culture management, fast change and market-driven connectivity' (Brockbank and Ulrich 2003; Long and Khairuzzaman 2008).

Conclusion

This chapter reports on the perceptions of a sample of managers in a variety of Vietnamese organisations about their skills shortages and associated HRM professionals' roles, competencies and functions. It suggests that, despite some diversity in their implementation in different ownership types and sizes, very few claim to have adopted strategic business partner roles or possess the competencies (Warner's [2013] 'mature' stage of HRM) required to proactively and effectively address the immense vocational and capability skills facing the Vietnamese economy into the future. Whilst an HRM functional expert role is appropriate for the overall management of an organisation's human capital, it may not be sufficient for the strategic attraction, development and retention of large numbers of skilled and qualified employees in order to ensure the competitiveness of their organisations. RVA/RPL may also need to be embedded in strategic HRM roles. There are, however some encouraging signs of environmental changes that might strengthen Vietnamese HRM professionals' capacities to embrace these challenges, including the relatively high proportion of graduates in HR departments, recent government initiatives focused on modernising vocational and higher education systems and the learning and development programmes provided by many multinational corporations, which may encourage replication in local private and government organisations.

For HRM professionals, the study suggests that they might assess their present competency levels in relation to the ongoing skills development challenges facing their organisations, with a view to developing those competencies that have not yet been acquired. Thus, government HRM specialists might focus on business-driven and credible activist competencies; local private company practitioners could consider culture and change agent roles; and those in MNCs might embrace business-driven, stakeholder manager, credible activist and/or expert practitioner competencies.

Acknowledgements

We acknowledge the assistance of Lyn Goodear, CEO of the Australian Human Resources Institute (AHRI) and Ms Ha Nguyen, former Deputy Director of the Vietnam Chamber of Commerce and Industry (VCCI) in supporting this research study. We also acknowledge the contributions of our colleagues – Dr Nuttawuth Muenjohn and Dr Jiang Zhang (RMIT), and Dr Poonsri Vate-U-Lan (Assumption University, Bangkok).

References

Asian Development Bank 2011, *Vocational education and training in Vietnam*, Asian Development Bank, Geneva, Switzerland.

Barney, J.B. and Wright, P.M. 1998, 'On becoming a strategic partner: the role of HR in gaining competitive advantage', Human *Resource Management*, vol. 37, no. 1, pp. 31–46.

Baughn, C., Neupert, K.E., Anh, P. and Hang, N. 2011, 'Social capital and human resource management in international joint ventures in Vietnam: a perspective from a transitional economy', *International Journal of Human Resource Management*, vol. 22, no. 5, pp. 1017–1035.

Baur, M. 2012, 'International experience in occupational standard development and implementation', keynote inputs at the *Regional TVET-Conference*, Vietnam, 10–11 October 2012.

Becker, B., Huselid, M. and Ulrich, D. 2001, *The HR scorecard: linking people, strategy and performance*, Harvard Business School Press, Boston, MA.

Benuyenah, V. and Phoon, M. 2014, 'Population, property and productivity: a theoretical prediction of economic growth in Vietnam', *Journal of Global Business & Economics*, vol. 8, no. 1, pp. 1–13.

Birenbaum, M. 1996, 'Assessment 2000: towards a pluralistic approach to assessment', in M. Birenbaum and F.J.R.C. Dochy (eds.), *Alternatives in assessment of achievements, learning processes and prior knowledge*, Kluwer Academic Press, Boston, MA, pp. 3–29.Bosch, G. and Charest, J. (eds.) 2010, *Vocational training: international perspectives*, Routledge, New York, NY.

Boselie, J.P. and Paauwe, J. 2005, 'Human resource functional competencies in European companies', *Visiting Fellow Working Papers*, no.11, School of Industrial and Labour Relations, Cornell University, Ithaca, NY.

Boudreau, J.W. and Ramstad, P.M. 2003, 'Strategic HRM measurement in the 21st century: from justifying HR to strategic talent leadership', in M. Goldsmith, R.P. Gandossy and M.S. Efron (eds.), *MM in the 21st Century*, Wiley, New York, NY, pp. 79–90.

Brockbank, W. and Ulrich, D. 2003, *The new HR agenda: 2002 HRCS executive summary*, University of Michigan Business School, Ann Arbor, MI.

Brockbank, W., Ulrich, D. and James, C. 1997, *Trends in HR competencies*, University of Michigan School of Business, Ann Arbor, MI.

Carroll, S.J. 1990, 'The new HRM roles, responsibilities and structures', in R.S. Schuler (eds.), *Managing Human Resources in the Information Age*, Bureau of National Affairs, Washington, DC, pp. 204–226.

Centre for Labour Market Studies 2008, *Youth employment in Vietnam: report of survey findings for VCCI and* ILO, The Centre for Labour Market Studies, University of Leicester, UK.

Centre for Labour Market Studies 2011, *Youth employment in Vietnam: report of survey findings*, Report for Vietnam Chamber of Commerce and Industry (VCCI)/ International Labour Organisation (ILO), The Centre for Labour Marker Studies (CLMS), University of Leicester, UK.

Central Intelligence Agency 2013, *The world factbook*, Central Intelligence Agency, Washington, DC, viewed 7 August 2013, <www.cia.gov/library/publications/the-world-factbook/geos/vn html>.

Chartered Institute of Personnel and Development 2010, *CIPD HR Profession Map (HRPM) 2010–2012*, Chartered Institute of Personnel and Development (CIPD), London, UK.

Colin, A. 1989, 'Managers' competence; rhetoric, reality and research', *Personnel Review*, vol. 18, no. 6, pp. 20–25.

Collins, N., Sitalaksmi, S. and Lansbury, R. 2013, 'Transforming employment relations in Vietnam and Indonesia: case studies of state-owned enterprises', *Asia Pacific Journal of Human Resources Special Issue: 'HRM in Vietnam'*, vol. 51, no. 2, pp. 131–151.

Crouse, P., Doyle, W. and Young, J.D. 2011, 'Trends, roles and competencies in human resource management practice: a perspective from practitioners in Halifax, Canada', proceedings of the American Society of Business and Behavioral Sciences (ASBBS) Annual Conference, Las Vegas, NV, 22–27 February 2011, pp. 377–390.

Dolan, A.-M. 2013, *AHRI Model of Excellence redevelopment project: literature review*, The Australian Human Resource Institute, Melbourne, Australia.

Economist Intelligence Unit 2012, *Skilled labour shortfalls in Indonesia, the Philippines, Thailand and Vietnam: a custom research report for the British Council*, The Economist, London, UK.

Gilbert, T.F. 1978, *Human competencies: engineering worthy performance*, Routledge, London, UK.

Gross, A. 2013, *Vietnam: HR update 2013*, Pacific Bridge Medical, Bethesda, MD.

Hoe, P.T. 2013, 'Human resource management in the transitional economy in Vietnam', unpublished Master's thesis, Vaasan Ammattikorkeakoulu, University of Applied Sciences, Helsinki, Finland.

International Labour Office 2010, *A skilled workforce for strong, sustainable and balanced growth: a G20 training strategy*, International Labour Office, Geneva, Switzerland.

Ketels, C., Nguyen, D.C., Nguyen, T.T.A. and Do, H.H. 2010, *Vietnam competitiveness report*, Central Institute for Economic Management, Ha Noi, Vietnam, viewed 10 June 2011, <www.isc.hbs.edu/pdf/Vietnam_CompetitivenessReport_2010_Eng.pdf>.

Lepak, D.P. and Snell, S.A. 2002, 'Examining the human resources architecture: the relationships between human capital, employment and human resource configurations', *Journal of Management*, vol. 28, no. 4, pp. 517–543.

Long, C.S. and Khairuzzaman, W. 2008, 'Understanding the relationship of HR competencies & roles of Malaysian human resource professionals', *European Journal of Social Science*, vol.7, no. 1, pp. 88–103.

Losey, M. 1999, 'Mastering the competencies of human resources management', *Human Resource Management*, vol. 38, no. 2, pp. 99–103.

Manpower 2011, *Building a high-skilled economy: the new Vietnam*, Manpower Group, Ha Noi, Vietnam.

McKinsey Global Institute 2012, *Sustaining Vietnam's growth: the productivity challenge*, McKinsey Global Institute, Ha Noi, Vietnam.

Ministry of Labour, Invalids and Social Affairs 2014, *Circular: providing guidance on implementation of some articles of decree No.102/2013/Nd-Cp Dated September 05, 2013 of the Government detailing the implementation of some articles of labour code on foreign employees in Vietnam*, Ministry of Labour, Invalids and Social Affairs (MoLISA), Ha Noi, Vietnam, viewed 1 June 2015, <http://thuvienphapluat.vn/archive/Circular-No-03–2014-TT-BLDTBXH-guiding-Decree-No-102–2013-ND-CP-labor-code-on-foreign-vb223036.aspx>.

Montague, A. 2013, 'Vocational and skill shortages in Vietnamese manufacturing and service sectors, and some plausible solutions', *Asia Pacific Journal of Human Resources Special Issue: 'HRM in Vietnam'*, vol. 51, no. 2, pp. 208–227.

Montague, A., Zhang, J., Muenjohn, N., Nankervis, A. and Vate-U-Lan, P. 2014, 'Exploring vocational and capability skills in Vietnam by organisational type and size', unpublished manuscript.

Nankervis, A., Montague, A., Zhang, J., Muenjohn, N. and Vate-U-Lan, P. 2014, 'HRM roles, competencies and functions in Vietnamese organisations: a preliminary study', unpublished manuscript.

Nguyen, T. l. H. 2013, 'Labour market trends and vocational strategy', paper presented at Meeting Today's and Tomorrow's Skills Needs Conference, Ho Chi Minh City, Vietnam, 25 April 2013.

Organisation for Economic Co-operation and Development 2012, *Better skills, better jobs, better lives: a strategic approach to skills policies*, Organisation for Economic Co-operation and Development (OECD) Publishing, Geneva, Switzerland, viewed 4 November 2014, <http://dx.doi.org/10.1787/9789264177338-en>.

Pham, L. 2011, 'Impact of applying human resource management practices on equitized state-owned enterprises' financial performance in Vietnam', *Journal of International Business Research*, vol.10, no. 2, pp. 79–90.

Pham, H. and Tran, L. 2013, 'Develop graduate skills and knowledge for the world of work: the case of the translation curriculum in Vietnam', *Journal of Language, Culture and Society*, vol. 36, pp. 7–17.

Quang, T. and Thang, L. C. 2009, 'HRM in Vietnam', in P. Budhwar (eds.), *Managing human resources in Asia-Pacific*, Routledge, London, UK, pp. 173–199.

Ramlall, S. J. 2006, 'Identifying and understanding HR competencies and their relationships to organisational practices', *Applied HRM Research*, vol. 11, no. 1, pp. 27–38.

Raven, J. and Stephenson, J. (eds.) 2001, *Competencies in the learning society*, Peter Lang, New York, NY.

Robinson, M. A., Sparrow, P. R., Clegg, C. and Bird, K. 2007, 'Forecasting future competency requirements: a three-phase methodology', *Personnel Review*, vol. 36, no.1, pp. 65–90.

Schuler, R. S. 1990, 'Repositioning the human resources function: transformation or demise?', *Academy of Management Executive*, vol. 4, no. 3, pp. 49–59.

Tait, H. and Godfrey, H. 1999, 'Defining and assessing competence in generic skills', *Quality in Higher Education*, vol. 5, no. 3, pp. 245–253.

Thang, L. C. and Quang, T. 2005, 'Human resource management practices in a transitional economy: a comparative study of enterprise ownership forms in Vietnam', *Asia Pacific Business Review*, vol. 11, no. 1, pp. 25–47.

Thang, L. C., Rowley, C., Quang, T. and Warner, M. 2007, 'To what extent can management practices be transferred between countries? the case of HRM in Vietnam', *Journal of World Business*, vol. 42, no. 1, pp. 113–127.

Truong, Q. 2013, 'Vietnam: an emerging economy at a crossroads', *Working Paper*, no. 2013/09, Maastricht School of Management, Maastricht, Netherlands.

Ulrich, D. 1997, *Human resource champions: the next agenda for adding value and delivering results*, Harvard Business School Press, Boston, MA.

Ulrich, D. 1998, 'A new mandate for human resources', *Harvard Business Review*, vol. 76, no. 1, pp. 124–135.

Ulrich, D., Brockbank, W., Johnsonand, D. and Younger, J. 2007, 'Human resource competencies: responding to increased expectations', *Employment Relations Today*, vol. 34, no. 3, pp. 1–12.

Ulrich, D., Brockbank, W., Ulrich, M. and Younger, J. 2013, *Global HR competencies: mastering competitive value from the outside in*, McGraw-Hill, New York, NY.

Ulrich, D. and Lake, D. 1990, *Organizational capability: competing from the inside out*, Wiley, New York, NY.

United Nations Educational, Scientific and Cultural Organization 2012, *UNESCO guidelines for the recognition, validation and accreditation of the outcomes of non-formal and informal learning*, UNESCO Institute for Lifelong Learning, Hamburg, Germany, viewed 4 July 2014, <http://unesdoc.unesco.org/images/0021/002163/216360e.pdf>.

United Nations Educational, Scientific and Cultural Organization 2014, *UIL's Contribution to the Global Inventory of National Qualifications Frameworks (NQFs)/ Asia and the Pacific/Vietnam*, United Nations Educational, Scientific and Cultural Organization, New York, NY, viewed 7 July 2014, <http://uil.unesco.org/home/programme-areas/lifelong-learning-policies-and-strategies/recognition-validation-and-accreditation-of-non-formal-and-informal-learning-rva/news-target/uils-contribution-to-the-global-inventory-of-national-qualifications-frameworks-nqfs/d2bc960671bdee>.

United Nations Population Fund 2011, *Fact sheet on education in Viet Nam: evidence from the 2009 census*, United Nations Population Fund, Ha Noi, Vietnam, viewed 10 July 2014, <http://vietnam.unfpa.org/public/pid/12209>.

Warner, M. 2013, 'Comparing HRM in China and Vietnam: an overview', *Human Systems Management*, vol. 32, no. 4, pp. 217–229.

Wheelahan, L., Miller, P., Newton, D., Dennis, N., Firth, J., Pascoe, S. and Veenker, P. 2003, *Recognition of prior learning: policy and practice in Australia,* Report to Australian Qualifications Framework Advisory Board, Southern Cross University, East Lismore, Australia, viewed 7 July 2014, <http://epubs.scu.edu.au/gcm_pubs/34/>.

World Bank 2014, *Vietnam overview*, World Bank, Washington, DC, viewed 4 July 2014, <www.worldbank.org/en/country/vietnam/overview>.

World Bank 2012, *Vietnam development report: pillars of development.* Report no. 20018-VN, World Bank, Washington, DC.

Wright, P.M., Dunford, B.B. and Snell, S.A. 2001, 'Human resources and the resource-based view of the firm', *Journal of Management*, vol. 27, no. 6, pp. 701–721.

Wright, P.M. and Snell, S.A. 1998, 'Toward a unifying framework for exploring fit and flexibility in strategic human resource management', *Academy of Management Review*, vol. 23, no. 4, pp. 756–772.

Zhu, Y., Collins, N., Webber, M. and Benson, J. 2008, 'New forms of ownership and HR traditions in Vietnam', *Human Resource Management*, vol. 47, no. 1, pp. 157–175.

5 Gender development in Myanmar

An exploration of women's leadership trajectory

Kantha Dayaram, Maria Fay Rola-Rubzen and John Burgess

Introduction

Historically, in developing economies, the status and role of women were limited to and defined as that of 'farmer's wife', positioning women's work as unimportant and rendering women with very little decision-making powers. Over the last two decades, the status of women has changed in many ways; for instance women are now recognised as farmers in their own right. Women have also increasingly participated in paid labour. This shift in economic status has facilitated women's empowerment and encouraged labour mobility allowing women to move from the agricultural sector to the manufacturing and services sector. Women are moving out of unpaid and informal employment into paid and formal employment.

Myanmar as one of these developing economies is unique in its history and policy development, as noted in the report of Chhor et al. (2013: 4):

> Myanmar is a very unusual case: a large country with a rich history that remains an underdeveloped agrarian economy in the heart of the world's fastest-growing regional economy – perhaps one of the few remaining, largely untapped markets in the world.

The Organisation for Economic Co-operation and Development (OECD 2013) report states that, whilst the overall labour participation in Myanmar is high at 78 per cent, approximately 70 per cent of the population are considered under-employed in the agricultural sector. Within this sector, whilst women's labour participation in the workforce is high, they still face disadvantages compared to males. Despite its military rule and economic sanctions, women in Myanmar have endeavoured to forge career pathways into sectors outside of agriculture.

In this chapter, we examine the strategies and practices that women deliberately seek to develop and empower themselves to assume leadership roles in the formal sector. Employing a qualitative analysis of interviews undertaken with women in leadership roles, the study explores the factors that contribute and influence gender development in Myanmar. It examines the challenges and perceived barriers, how these were overcome and the current practices that support women in leadership roles. These findings will be useful for government policymakers, planners and organisations that support the development of women.

Leadership development of women in less developed countries

The United Nations (2013) lists a number of countries within Asia, such as Bangladesh, Nepal, Bhutan, Myanmar and Afghanistan, as less developed countries (LDCs). In this section, we highlight the challenges and progress in women's participation in the market economy and engagement with leadership opportunities, in some of these LDCs.

Bangladesh is one of the least developed South Asian nations. Although Bangladeshi women's labour force participation rate has increased since 1971, the ratio of female-to-male labour force participation (68 per cent at 2012) remains considerably low (World Bank (2013). Moreover, Bangladeshi women's work tends to be concentrated within the informal sector of the economy and predominantly as unpaid labour. Lucy, Ghosh and Kujawa (2010) note that a lack of Bangladeshi females' access to education is a critical factor that limits the female labour force to the informal job market. Other factors that hinder Bangladeshi women's empowerment include male-dominated social structures (Lucy, Ghosh and Kujawa 2010); poor access to health facilities for women, a high burden of domestic responsibilities, low awareness of women rights and lower political representation (Narayan et al. 2000); and mobility constraints imposed by the culture (Sperandio 2011). Conversely, initiatives such as training programmes (aimed at providing supporting Bangladeshi women in managing and operating small businesses), have contributed to women's empowerment, enhanced decision-making abilities and helped women build their confidence levels (Lucy, Ghosh and Kujawa 2010). Importantly, non-governmental organisations have achieved considerable success in empowering Bangladeshi women through various support programmes aimed at facilitating money lending for small business development (Rabbani 2009), women's skills development (Lucy et al. 2010), women's rights awareness and women's education (Sperandio 2011).

Nepalese women experience social, cultural and structural barriers in their leadership development, with a key challenge being women's inability to obtain financial assistance and provide collateral because of their limited access to family inheritance, especially land (Bushell 2008). Other important challenges highlighted by Bushell's (2008) study include the lack of support via subsidies and policies for women entrepreneurs; non-recognition of women's abilities as businesspersons; husbands' dominance; high levels of family obligation; lower access to education and training facilities; poor representation of women-owned businesses in the various business associations; and a lack of awareness of opportunities for women. Bushell's (2008) research suggests that increased access to credit, implementation of property rights law, equitable treatment of women clients by the financial institutions, literacy education, skills development and access to a variety of entrepreneurial networks can potentially build Nepalese women's business skills and leadership competencies.

Whilst Bhutanese women have traditionally been employed in the informal agrarian sector, there have been concerted efforts to include women in the country's strategic development plans (Royal Government of Bhutan 2003). Policies are designed to foster women's rights, build child day-care facilities, implement parental leave and undertake measures targeting the promotion of women in higher levels of education (OECD 2010; Royal Government of Bhutan 2003). Although these measures are in place, few women have access, and progress tends to be concentrated in the urban region. Recent findings by Dayaram and Pick (2012: 145), in their study of Bhutanese women in formal employment, indicate that the Bhutanese women are 'entangled between tradition and modernity' and an influencing 'Western-style' culture. For these women, it has been especially challenging as they attempt to juggle their resources between formal work, competing family demands and conforming to cultural norms and traditions. Whilst the women expressed confidence about their contribution to society and the economy, they were despondent about the changes that were occurring in their lives and the lack of support towards societal and family expectations of them being both the traditional woman (wife, homemaker, mother, etc.) and the modern woman (a Western-style, career-oriented image) (Dayaram and Pick 2012: 145).

In Afghanistan, the status of women lags far behind men in social, political as well as the economic spheres of life. Despite the unfavourable local environment for Afghan women, notable achievements have also been made, including the introduction of a national constitution that ensures equal rights for women, the introduction of the National Plan of Advancement of Women of Afghanistan 2007–2017, and the establishment of various civil society organisations to empower Afghan women (Islamic Republic of Afghanistan 2007). Ahmed-Ghosh (2006) emphasises the need to prioritise economic and social empowerment of Afghan women through education, jobs, mobility and public visibility.

Other countries that are no longer in the United Nations' 2014 LCD listing (United Nations 2013) include Pakistan, India, Jordan and Vietnam. An outline of development in these countries indicates that, in Pakistan, despite several women's empowerment initiatives, women continue to struggle with breaking cultural and religious barriers, which act as obstacles to their progress (Repila 2013). The study further notes that non-governmental organisations such as the Aurat Foundation (AF) and Raising Her Voice (RHV, the global programme led by Oxfam) have actively been working in Pakistan to motivate civil society, the judiciary, government officials, private sector, financial institutions and media agencies to develop strategies for women's empowerment. A case study conducted by RHV in 2014 (Green 2015) concludes that building women's confidence, knowledge, expertise and networking skills can potentially contribute to strengthening Pakistani women's leadership capabilities. Other findings (Khan 2010) note that Pakistani women are falling far behind their male counterparts when it comes to control over resources, labour force participation rates, schooling, decision making abilities, mobility, social networking and access to information. Khan's (2010) study suggests the active involvement of governmental and non-governmental agencies in bridging the inter-sexual divide on all these fronts by enhancing female labour force participation rates, knowledge, skills, awareness and their political involvement.

Studies on Indian women advocate female entrepreneurship as a potential opportunity in building the social and economic status of Indian women and helping develop their leadership competencies (Kaushik 2013). It is suggested that women aged 36 years and above are more likely to be entrepreneurs than women under 36 years of age, whilst married women with fewer children show more interest in becoming entrepreneurs. Key barriers to female entrepreneurs and leadership development include lower access to finances, difficulties in marketing the product, health related issues and high levels of family responsibilities, and their disadvantaged physical locations inhibit women in starting and managing a new business (Sinha 2003).

Vietnam tends to have a relatively smaller proportion of women occupying senior leadership positions, with patriarchal attitudes being a key obstacle to women's leadership development (Le 2011; Truong 2008). Cultural obligations include expectations of women placing family as priority in their lives. This leaves working women with little choice except to work extraordinarily hard so as to meet the social expectations of a 'good woman' and a 'good leader'. Le's (2011) study notes that prevailing patriarchal Vietnamese culture has shaped women's leadership perspectives to the extent that women consider their male counterparts more suitable for leadership roles. It is suggested that a speedier cultural shift is needed in Vietnam to match the requirements of women's human capital development as well as a more responsive global economy.

R. Al Maaitah et al.'s (2012) study of Jordanian women notes that social and organisational constraints pose significant challenges to women's leadership. In particular, the study suggests that the lack of family and tribal support, negative social norms regarding working women, unequal sharing of domestic responsibilities between men and women and the existence of a wide gap between the career promotional opportunities available to men as compared to women potentially discourage women seeking leadership positions. The study further suggests that various training and development schemes, awareness raising, empowerment programmes for women, financial support schemes and professional training programmes could be the real impetus to women's leadership.

The literature illustrates the segregation of women in LDCs into the informal economy, into low paid or unpaid work, and their exclusion from participation in civil governance and leadership roles. The barriers to leadership and governance roles are a mix of tradition, culture, experience, resources, support and opportunities. The enablers and barriers for women to pursue leadership roles can be illustrated in Figure 5.1. Supporting mechanisms can be grouped into their sources: NGOs, community and government. Barriers are grouped into cultural, socio-economic and political factors.

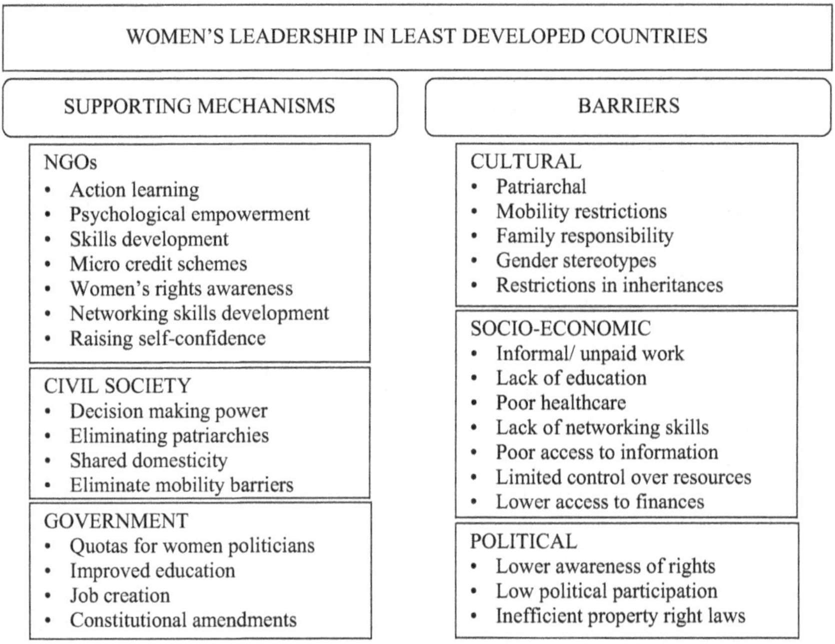

WOMEN'S LEADERSHIP IN LEAST DEVELOPED COUNTRIES	
SUPPORTING MECHANISMS	**BARRIERS**
NGOs • Action learning • Psychological empowerment • Skills development • Micro credit schemes • Women's rights awareness • Networking skills development • Raising self-confidence	CULTURAL • Patriarchal • Mobility restrictions • Family responsibility • Gender stereotypes • Restrictions in inheritances
CIVIL SOCIETY • Decision making power • Eliminating patriarchies • Shared domesticity • Eliminate mobility barriers	SOCIO-ECONOMIC • Informal/ unpaid work • Lack of education • Poor healthcare • Lack of networking skills • Poor access to information • Limited control over resources • Lower access to finances
GOVERNMENT • Quotas for women politicians • Improved education • Job creation • Constitutional amendments	POLITICAL • Lower awareness of rights • Low political participation • Inefficient property right laws

Figure 5.1 Women's leadership in LDCs (current study)

Using these studies of women's formal work and leadership experiences in LDCs, as well as the progress to date, Figure 5.1 illustrates that the factors supporting and inhibiting the leadership capacity of women in such countries are multifaceted. Some of the socio-economic barriers include the lack of education and skills required to seek paid employment; poor health care facilities affecting child birth and mortality rates; lack of networking opportunities; access to finances in the form of loans; obstacles to land ownership, etc. The political barriers include women's lack of knowledge and awareness of their rights, the ability to have their voices heard and contribution to the country's policy making and current ineffective property right laws. Notwithstanding the structural barriers, women in these countries also experience a mix of cultural barriers, which includes living in a predominantly patriarchal environment with gender stereotyping such as being a 'good', 'traditional' wife, mother and house keeper. Simultaneously, women are also limited in terms of what they may seek as family inheritance and experience restrictions on job mobility.

Support for women's development has largely come through the efforts of non-governmental organisations (NGOs) and civil society. For instance, Oxfam has worked with women's groups in Pakistan to develop business skills; other NGOs have been actively working to enhance women's psychological empowerment and financial acumen and to build awareness of women's rights (Green 2015). Despite these efforts, several avenues for further improvements remain especially in the areas of building women's networking skills and in increasing their representation at community and business forums. Turning to the role of government, quotas for women politicians and workers have been introduced in some LDCs such as Pakistan to facilitate the active involvement of women in these fields (Green 2015; Repila 2013). Moreover, governments in India, Pakistan and Afghanistan have made several constitutional amendments to empower women. However, there is a need to fully implement female protection laws. Additionally, women need better access to education, civic participation and a wider range of occupations and industries (Sperandio 2011; Sinha 2003).

Given the widespread popularity of equal opportunity principles in the developed world, the huge gender leadership divide prevailing in LDCs demands special attention from policy makers, NGOs and the broader civil society. Although LDCs have made considerable progress in empowering women, a significant avenue for further improvement remains. For example civil society needs to facilitate women's participation in the decision-making process. Additionally, family responsibilities could be equitably (or to some extent) shared between men and women. There is a dire need to reduce the cultural inhibitors and barriers to women's mobility and participation (Dayaram and Pick 2012).

Gendered leadership development

The debate on whether culture or gender tends to have a greater influence, either as opportunities or obstacles to women's leadership development, continues. Some argue (Stoeberl et al. 1998) that culture has a greater impact on differences in leadership styles than gender and that gender differences are observable only within specific cultures. Kandola (2004) explores why women and ethnic minorities failed to progress from middle management to senior management levels in greater numbers in the United Kingdom. They identified individual barriers (stereotyping, interpersonal dynamics and informal networks) and organisational barriers (organisational culture, organisational systems and procedures and token status) as impediments to women's leadership development. The meaning assigned to managerial success is often associated with the male gender (Anthony and Dayaram 2013); hence, a shift in thinking from focussing only on recruitment and selection to placing emphasis on the promotion and retention of women and ethnic minorities might help advance such marginalised groups into more senior leadership positions. Kandola (2004) proposed training and development initiatives that aim to further develop the skills of women and ethnic minorities and to encourage managers to reflect on their own behaviours.

Studies (Chandler 2008; Lucy, Ghosh and Kujawa 2010; Sperandio 2011) reinforce the importance of social modelling, cultural values and support systems on leadership development and support for women. Emerging women leaders from countries such as Croatia, India, Japan, Jordan, Ukraine and Zambia note the critical function that role models and support systems play in the development of self-confidence, value formation, self-efficacy and leadership aspirations

(Chandler 2008). Prominent female politicians in the United States argue that key skills for women's leadership are the competent self, creative aggression, and women power (Cantor, Bernay and Stoess 1992). The competent self indicates strong self-sense and the ability to perceive possibilities instead of obstructions; creative aggression comprises of initiative, leading ability and speaking out; women's power means strength and force with nurturance and the ability to contribute to a better society (Cantor, Bernay and Stoess 1992; Denmark 1993). Furthermore, effective female leaders must be able to empower those women who are least empowered themselves (Denmark 1993). A key criticism in organisations is the 'non gender-neutral' environment that continues to exist where women leaders' performances are examined and evaluated differently from their male counterparts (Hopkins et. al. 2008). Their study further notes that women tend to more frequently encounter unique challenges in leadership; however, they receive little or no recognition from peers. Lucy, Ghosh and Kujawa (2010: 23) advocate that leadership development with women in group settings can lead to the 'empowerment of women in their local communities' and within society as a whole.

Mattis (2001) believes that both senior and middle managers have shared individual responsibilities in retaining and advancing women in their careers through feedback and coaching, which are often more readily provided to male employees than females. The development of women's leadership requires specific and effective developmental and support mechanisms. Hopkins et al. (2008) propose a framework comprising of seven categories for women's leadership development: assessment, training and education, coaching, mentoring, networking, experiential learning and career planning, through which women's individual and organisational leadership contributions can be maximised. Ely, Ibarra and Kolb (2011) discuss effective ways of using standard leadership development tools of '360-degree feedback, networking, negotiations, leading change, and managing career transitions' to facilitate women's transition to more senior leadership positions.

Figure 5.2 summarises the factors relevant to understanding women's leadership development presented in the broader international literature, especially that of developed nations. Based on the literature, the factors affecting the leadership capacity of women can be grouped into two categories – individual factors and organisational factors – as illustrated in Figure 5.2.

In LDCs such as Myanmar, whilst the overall labour participation is high at 78 per cent, approximately 70 per cent of the population are considered underemployed in the agricultural sector (OECD 2013). Within this sector, whilst women's labour participation in the workforce is high, they still experience drawbacks as compared to their male counterparts. Despite its military rule and economic sanctions, women in Myanmar have endeavoured to forge career pathways into sectors outside of agriculture (OECD 2013), with a high reliance on the individual self and societal supporting structures (as illustrated in Figure 5.1 for LDCs). Moving beyond the LDCs, two-dimensional supporting structures, as illustrated in Figure 5.2, can retrospectively act as impediments to women's leadership advancement. This study therefore employs empirical data to further

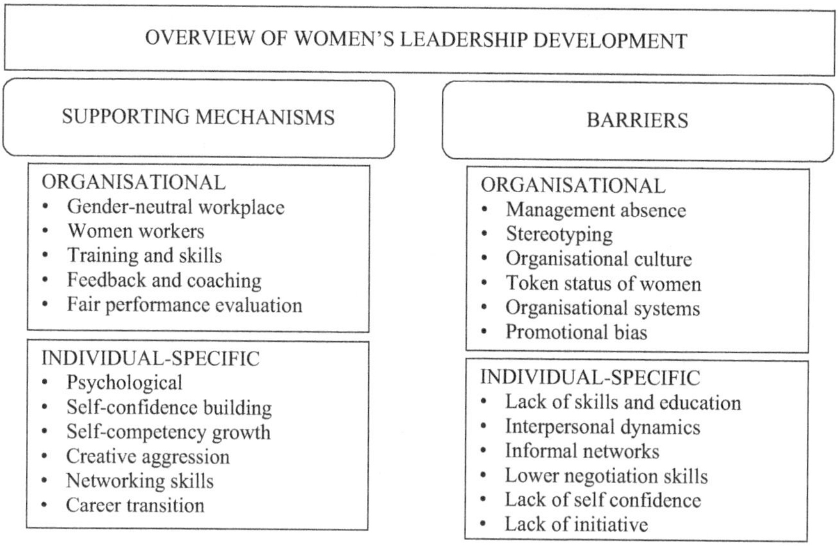

OVERVIEW OF WOMEN'S LEADERSHIP DEVELOPMENT

SUPPORTING MECHANISMS	BARRIERS

ORGANISATIONAL
- Gender-neutral workplace
- Women workers
- Training and skills
- Feedback and coaching
- Fair performance evaluation

ORGANISATIONAL
- Management absence
- Stereotyping
- Organisational culture
- Token status of women
- Organisational systems
- Promotional bias

INDIVIDUAL-SPECIFIC
- Psychological
- Self-confidence building
- Self-competency growth
- Creative aggression
- Networking skills
- Career transition

INDIVIDUAL-SPECIFIC
- Lack of skills and education
- Interpersonal dynamics
- Informal networks
- Lower negotiation skills
- Lack of self confidence
- Lack of initiative

Figure 5.2 Factors affecting women's leadership capacity: a general perspective

explore structures that support and/or impede women's leadership growth particularly LDCs such as Myanmar.

Myanmar: background

Myanmar has a history of foreign occupation, followed by independence, then one-party rule and political isolation, with an easing of political controls and international engagement only taking place within the last five years. In the nineteenth century, Myanmar was occupied by the British and became part of the empire. In World War II, Myanmar was occupied by the Japanese and, following it, achieved independence in 1948. A succession of coups, assassinations and army rule heralded a turbulent 50 years for the country. The country has suffered from political instability, internal regional uprisings, religious and ethnic conflict and difficult relations with its neighbours (especially Thailand). Myanmar and a new flag came into being in 2010, and since then, there has been greater economic and political engagement with the international community, though the military still occupies the direct and indirect position of control in government (British Broadcasting Corporation 2014).

The country has extensive natural resources, minerals and gas deposits, and these are currently attracting foreign investment and being developed. The United Nations Development Programme (2014) provides the following information and data for Myanmar: Traditional industries of employment include garments, timber and rice and pulse production. The economy has been growing around 6 per cent of GDP for the past five years. The largest trading partners and investors are

Thailand, China and India. Despite the recent growth surge, Myanmar remains a poor and rural-based economy. Despite its oil and gas reserves, around 85 per cent of the population do not have access to electricity. The per capita GDP is US$1100, and one-third of the population lives below the poverty line. Females are underrepresented in political and economic spheres. There is only one female Member of Parliament. The female labour force participation rate is 20 per cent as opposed to 74 per cent for males, while only 8 per cent of females over 25 years of age have secondary education as opposed to 24 per cent of their male counterparts (United Nations Development Programme 2014). Not surprisingly, the United Nation's 2014 Human Development Index ranks Myanmar 150 out of 185. In terms of the gender equality index, Myanmar ranks 83 out of 185, largely reflecting very low maternal mortality rates in births. On other indicators such as schooling, the labour force and parliamentary representation, women are well behind (United Nations Development Programme 2014).

A recent report on Myanmar was very upbeat about its integration into the global economy and into the region and saw a long period of future growth and expansion. However, it cautioned that 'Growth should be pro-poor, inclusive and balanced, and environmentally and socially sustainable. In a nutshell, human-centred growth is required' (Kudo, Kumagai and Umezaki 2013: 1).

The government has developed a modernisation plan (the Framework for Economic and Social Reform), which includes the following strategic priorities (Kudo, Kumagai and Umezaki 2013: 1.i):

1) Fiscal and tax reform
2) Monetary and finance sector reform
3) Trade and investment liberalisation
4) Private sector development
5) Improvements in health and education
6) Food security and agricultural growth
7) Governance and transparency
8) Mobile telephony and Internet
9) Infrastructure investment
10) Efficient and effective government

These priority areas for reform are not surprising, and clearly behind many of these priorities is the purpose of capacity building. However, there is also an opportunity to develop capability through investing in opportunities and human capital for women, a vast under-utilised resource for a developing economy given the very low labour force and leadership participation for women.

Research on women's business leadership in Myanmar is scant. A study conducted in 1999 about female entrepreneurs in Myanmar found that most of the female entrepreneurs were relatively young and married to supportive husbands who were not necessarily leaders. They felt the pressure of having dual responsibilities at home and in business, but they managed their responsibilities well with confidence. They were likely to be actively involved in social and religious affairs.

These female entrepreneurs were attracted to their current work by the expected higher incomes and independence. They appraised themselves as having very good or excellent skills in management, especially in leadership. Most of them had university-level education, and most of these educated women were from families in the private sector benefiting from existing resources and networks (Friedrich Ebert Stiftung [FES] 2009).

Another source (FES 2009) of Myanmar graduate women's participation in private enterprises in 1996 showed that marketable skills such as proficiency in English, computer literacy and accounting were essential, in addition to university degrees for women, to qualify for jobs in the private sector. Additionally it has been found that young women in these lines of business were mostly unmarried. Women in this study also considered their jobs lacking in personal relations, job satisfaction and security. Many expressed a wish to venture into business on their own despite the benefits provided by their employment (FES 2009).

Currently, there is a dearth of material on female businesses and women and leadership in Myanmar. Little is known about the mechanisms needed to support women in leadership. Hence, this study was designed to examine the factors supporting leadership development and capacity building of women employed in local and international organisations operating in Myanmar. The research questions the study sought to address are:

1) What support mechanisms did women in Myanmar employ in developing their leadership?
2) What leadership skills and or competencies did they find to be most needed?
3) What national policies were in place to help support women in leadership?
4) What were the barriers and challenges to their leadership development?

Methods

This study examines the strategies and practices that Myanmar women implement or seek to acquire in developing their leadership roles in the formal work sector. The focus is on women who occupy business leadership roles. To obtain an understanding into women's leadership roles and developmental practices in Myanmar, the semi-structured interview approach has been adopted for this study. Semi-structured interviews are an effective approach for investigating the perceptions of respondents in association to complex topics and exploring more detailed information and clarification of answers. It enables the exploration and comparison of the sample groups with diversified professional, educational and personal backgrounds (Louise Barriball and While 1994).

The study explores the factors that influence gender development and identifies the barriers and challenges for women's leadership development in Myanmar. Twenty women participated in the interviews. All participants held leadership positions in domestic or international organisations based in Myanmar. Table 5.1 provides a demographic overview of the participants. The participants were employed in a wide range of sectors including finance, education, family business,

Table 5.1 Participants' details

	Age group	Education	Field	Sector	Position
1	40–49	Master's degree	Auditing	Private	Owner
2	40–49	Bachelor degree	Marketing	Private	Co-founder and Managing Director
3	40–49	Secondary schooling	Training/ education	NGO	Director
4	Above 50	Master's degree	Training/ education	NGO	Social Welfare Worker and Writer
5	–	Secondary schooling	Social development	NGO	Media Advocacy Advisor
6	30–39	Master's degree	Media	Private	General Manager
7	–	Secondary schooling	Social development	NGO	Director
8	–	Secondary schooling	Legal	Private	Advisor Corporate Affairs
9	40–49	Doctorate degree	Furniture	Private	Owner
10	–	Secondary schooling	n/a	Private	Programme Manager
11	40–49	Doctorate degree	Production	Private	General Manager/ Owner
12	-	Secondary schooling	Community development	NGO	Programme Coordinator
13	40–49	Secondary schooling	Arts	NGO	Executive
14	–	Secondary schooling	–	–	Community development supervisor
15	–	Secondary schooling	Community development	NGO	Executive Director
16	Above 50	Master's degree	Community development	n/a	Livelihood advisor
17	40–49	Master's degree	Jewellery	Private	Owner and CEO
18	30–39	Master's degree	Development	NGO	Manager
19	–	Secondary schooling	Community development	NGO	Freelance trainer
20	30–39	Master's degree	Retail	Private	Owner and CEO

international NGOs, retail and media sectors and with occupations ranging from business owners, managers and executives to community leaders. A large percentage of participants worked up to 45 hours per week, largely due to their responsibilities as leaders in their organisations.

The semi-structured interview comprised of 3 themes and a total of 15 questions. The theme of the first group was leadership roles and comprised of seven questions. In order to explore labour policies and practices, as well as barriers women in Myanmar experienced in advancing their employment and leadership roles, questions included 'What are the labour policies and practices in Myanmar?', 'Are there policies in Myanmar that specifically target women's employment?' and 'In general, what do you see as the main barriers to women accessing leadership roles in Myanmar?' In addition to these seven questions, the question of 'How did social norms and traditions shape or influence your preferences in your choice of work?' and 'How did these influence your career aspirations and your choice to take on leadership positions/roles?' were also asked to examine the influence of social norms and traditions on women's choice of work.

The second theme of the interview was leadership support with the aim of finding the available organisational and other types of support for women leaders. There were five questions in this group, such as 'Can you describe any specific organisational programmes (training and development) that facilitate women into management and leadership roles in your organisation?' The last group of interview questions focused on exploring the capacity building including three questions, such as 'How has this leadership role influenced your standard of living?'

The interviews with 20 participants were transcribed in Burmese and then translated to English. The data were imported to the software NVivo 10 for organising and analysing transcripts to all questions (QSR 2014). Based on the categories of the three major themes, the researchers employed NVivo to identify common key words and sub-themes of each question, as well as the frequencies of these sub-themes and specific factors in relation to major themes. The responses were examined to reveal and determine the contributors in influencing Myanmar women's leadership development, the challenges, the perceived barriers in their workplace and how these were overcome. The study also made efforts to uncover the current practices that support women in leadership roles, with an emphasis on identifying best practice programmes.

Of the 20 participants, all were above 30 years of age; they were all educated, lived in urban areas and held senior management positions (see Table 5.1). They are not representative of the age, educational, occupational or spatial profile in Myanmar. This is a purposeful sample of women who have been successful in leadership roles and in career development; we wished to gauge from them what were the important factors that contributed to their successes.

Findings

The participants' responses were analysed by the key themes and research questions as discussed here. Majority of the respondents worked in small businesses where family and community networks were important. Organisational and formal policies were not considered to be major factors contributing to the success of these female leaders.

What support mechanisms did women in Myanmar employ in developing their leadership?

The support mechanisms were found in the family, in the community and in the organisations in which the women worked. These are largely informal, personal networks that offer support, encouragement and advice. Whilst influential teachers and role models were acknowledged, the education system and policy support were rarely mentioned. Moreover, family (parents, husband and children) was the major source of support for 15 out of 20 professional women. The forms of family supports included mentorship, emotional support, moral support, financial support and child-care and family caring support.

> I got most of the support from my family, especially my mum. She has encouraged me in many ways.

Respondents also received mentorship from female friends, female leaders in the organisations and women community members. In some cases, they were role models for the respondents.

> The first woman general manager for XX group gave me a lot of expectation. Her ways of working (sometimes it is very hard as she is very strong person), her dedication on her work and her communication skills to different types of people make me see the world better.

In addition to the family and female role models, the supervisors and colleagues from the workplace were also often mentioned as mentors.

> My program director. Not that much mentoring, you know if I have a problem I can call him directly. So he gives for you know, good suggestion. Sometimes blame, but it's okay. But you know at least good.

Community and teacher support were also mentioned by some respondents as, the considerable support mechanisms.

> Social norms, choice of work, how started. What drive you to sacrifice for the good of community. I planned to do something for the community since I was the law student.

Some respondents highlighted the significant role of the employing organisation in developing women's careers and leadership capabilities.

The [organisation's] motto is push females right at the heart of what we do. The profile starts with being educated, self-skills and traits and male regard female as the same.

What leadership skills and or competencies did they find to be most needed?

The respondents identified several important skills required for their roles, including expertise (theoretical and technical knowledge related to their work fields and positions), work experience, leadership and management skills, communication skills, interpersonal skills, trust-building skills and marketing skills. The characteristics like self-confidence, passion, sympathy and dedication were also mentioned as merits for their leadership roles.

> Dedication, expert knowledge on the subject, strong commitment and self-confidence plays pivotal role for me. Empathy also plays an important role.

Respondents identified continuous learning as their primary way to develop these skills. Learning can transpire from practice, academic courses, professional training and also through families, others and experience.

> Before I open as a company, I have learned this knowledge from my parents, aunties and friends. Later, I attended the related courses in the country and as well as overseas to upgrade my knowledge and capacity of this sector. Continuous learning is necessary for me to keep in the position as a leader of the jewellery business in Myanmar.

What national policies were in place to help support women in leadership?

The discussion of national policies centred on fundamental employment rights around equal pay, non-discrimination and violence against women. The absence of an extensive discussion on policy is not surprising since there is an absence of formal policy or basic employment rights, let alone leadership programmes. Fifty per cent of respondents acknowledged the presence of labour policies and practices (social security, minimum wages) in Myanmar; however, they expressed concerns on the absence of any specific labour policies related to female workers.

> So far I know, there are no specific policies which target women's employment.

What were the barriers and challenges to their leadership development?

The majority of respondents identified culture, traditions and social norms as the main barriers for women to access leadership roles in Myanmar. Traditionally, men are considered more powerful and suitable for assuming leadership roles in Myanmar. Often, and compared with males, female workers in the same positions were harder to get accepted, earn trust and respect compared to their male counterparts. Additionally, family care, patriarchal views and non-acceptance of women leaders were seen as major barriers.

Discussion

Comparing the supporting mechanisms, as illustrated in Figure 5.1 (LDC experiences) and Figure 5.2 (general leadership development), with Myanmar women's experiences, it is noted that the most commonly reported support mechanisms have been the access, skills and the ability to network. The women reported that their family and friends provided the most support and access to networks, whilst generally it has been noted in the literature that NGOs work towards creating network opportunities that women can access (Green 2015). Literature on leadership development also stresses the importance of networks in helping to provide leadership opportunities and further development (Bushell 2008). Figure 5.2 illustrates the role of the individual and the organisation in seeking and providing mentorship opportunities. This has been reinforced with the Myanmar women's experience. Mentorship was accessed informally through family, friends, work colleagues and the work organisation; however, there was a lack of formalised mentoring.

The leadership skills and competencies that respondents indicated as being highly valuable included work experience, management skills such as decision making and negotiation, communication and interpersonal skills and developing the ability to market products. The values that were highly rated included trust, passion, sympathy and commitment. They also ranked psychological empowerment favourably, which includes building self-confidence, as critical to women's enablement.

With regard to national policies centred on women's inclusion and recognition in formal work structures as well as policies supporting employee rights, some participants were not aware of either supporting policies or rights in the workplace. Some participants expressed their dissatisfaction with the lack of policies to support women in the workplace, and others noted the need for improved government support. Less than half of the participants were aware of the presence of family-friendly policies supporting women's participation such as paid maternity leave. The lack of awareness of employee and women's rights are also highlighted in Figure 5.1 as being prevalent amongst the LDCs. However, those women who worked in NGOs (44 per cent of whom held directorate positions) indicated the support and encouragement they received to build their leadership capabilities and work in an organisation that was gender neutral.

Women in Myanmar held similar experiences to women in the LDCS as illustrated in Figure 5.1, which included barriers relating to cultural norms and traditions. They voiced their discontent with the level of patriarchy that discouraged their leadership development. There were also cultural stereotypes of women's roles that the participants had to conform to. Notwithstanding these barriers, these women viewed themselves as 'fortunate' for having access to education and noted that the lack of education as a critical barrier to women's formal employment and their leadership trajectory.

Conclusion

Women in Myanmar noted similar barriers to participation and leadership development as those faced by their counterparts in developed and LDC countries. This aligns with the general view of gendered leadership development in the broader international literature, especially that of developing nations. However, their reports did not include organisational and systemic barriers such as fair performance evaluation systems, action learning programmes, female worker retention approaches and gender quotas associated with the token status of women. These may be perceived to be associated with sophisticated and extensive human resource management systems in developed country contexts or workplaces that aim towards gender-neutral policies and female-friendly policies. From an individual development perspective, these women did not refer to policies or mechanisms that supported development such as career transition management and building creative aggression. Interestingly, none of the women alluded to a lack of initiative, yet they noted their personal courage and ambitions to seize opportunities such as international education scholarships and developing personal networks. The common themes throughout the literature on women's experiences in LDCs, developing countries and this study on Myanmar women highlight the need for education, training and development; national policies supporting women's leadership and support mechanisms in the formal workplace. Education and training on labour policies and supporting structures are much needed. In developing and less-developed countries in particular, patriarchy and cultural stereotyping act as high inhibitors to women's leadership development.

The study is limited by the small number of participants, by their success in achieving leadership positions, by their location in urban areas and by their participation in the formal economy. In remote and rural regions, dominated by informal arrangements, the leadership challenges faced by women are extensive with few support mechanisms and extensive barriers across all the criteria identified in Figure 5.1. Given the large rural sector in Myanmar and its importance to the country's development, future studies should look into expanding research on the leadership trajectory of women in rural areas and the barriers and enablers in obtaining leadership roles. Women face different sets of challenges in rural areas, and understanding these constraints can help in setting strategic directions to increase women's chances in participating in the development of Myanmar.

Acknowledgments

We would like to acknowledge the assistance of Kathy Shein in interviewing the women respondents for this project. We would also like to acknowledge Hasnat Ahmad for research assistance particularly with the literature review. Funding for this project was provided by Curtin University's School of Management

References

Al Maaitah, R., Oweis, A., Olimat, H., Altarawneh, I. and Al Maaitah, H. 2012, 'Barriers hindering Jordanian women's advancement to higher political and leadership positions', *Journal of International Women's Studies*, vol. 13, no. 5, pp. 101–122.

Ahmed-Ghosh, H. 2006, 'Voices of Afghan women: human rights and economic development', *International Feminist Journal of Politics*, vol. 8, no. 1, pp. 110–128.

Anthony, M. and Dayaram, K. 2013, 'Gendered leadership strategies: where are the women police?', in G. Ogunmokun and R. Gabbay (eds.), *Marketing, management and international business: contemporary issues and research in selected countries*, Global Publishing House, Perth, Australia, pp. 175–192.

British Broadcasting Corporation 2014, 'Myanmar profile, a chronology of key events', British Broadcasting Corporation (BBC) News: Asia, London, UK, viewed 4 December 2014, <www.bbc.com/news/world-asia-pacific-12992883>.

Bushell, B. 2008, 'Women entrepreneurs in Nepal: what prevents them from leading the sector?', *Gender & Development*, vol. 16, no. 3, pp. 549–564.

Cantor, D. W., Bernay, T. and Stoess, J. 1992, *Women in power: the secrets of leadership*, Houghton Mifflin, Boston, MA.

Chandler, D. J. 2008, 'The impact of social modelling, cultural values, and support systems on the leadership development of emerging global women leaders', *Advancing Women in Leadership*, vol. 28, p. 7.

Chhor, H., Dobbs, R., Nguyen Hansen, D., Thompson, F., Shah, N. and Streiff, L. 2013, *Myanmar's moment: unique opportunities, major challenges*, The McKinsey Global Institute, Singapore.

Dayaram, K. and Pick, D. 2012, 'Entangled between tradition and modernity: the experiences of Bhutanese working women', *Society and Business Review*, vol. 7, no. 2, pp. 134–148.

Denmark, F. L. 1993, 'Women, leadership, and empowerment', *Psychology of Women Quarterly*, vol. 17, no. 3, pp. 343–356.

Ely, R. J., Ibarra, H. and Kolb, D. M. 2011, 'Taking gender into account: theory and design for women's leadership development programs', *Academy of Management Learning & Education*, vol. 10, no. 3, pp. 474–493.

Friedrich Ebert Stiftung 2009, *Country gender profile: Myanmar*, Friedrich Ebert Stiftung, Singapore.

Green, D. 2015, *The raising her voice Pakistan programme: active citizenship case studies*, Oxfam, Oxford, UK.

Hopkins, M. M., O'Neil, D. A., Passarelli, A. and Bilimoria, D. 2008, 'Women's leadership development strategic practices for women and organizations', *Consulting Psychology Journal: Practice and Research*, vol. 60, no. 4, pp. 348.

Islamic Republic of Afghanistan 2007, *National action plan for the women of Afghanistan 2007–2017*, Kabul, Islamic Republic of Afghanistan.

Kandola, B. 2004. 'Skills development: the missing link in increasing diversity in leadership', *Industrial and Commercial Training*, vol. 36, no. 4, pp. 143–147.

Kaushik, S. 2013, 'Challenges faced by women entrepreneurs in India', *International Journal of Management and Social Sciences Research*, vol. 2, no. 2, pp. 6–8.

Khan, T. M. 2010, 'Socio-cultural determinants of women's empowerment in Punjab, Pakistan', PhD thesis, University of Agriculture, Faisalabad, India.

Kudo T., Kumagai S. and Umezaki S. 2013, 'Five growth strategies for Myanmar: re-engagement with global economy', *IDE Discussion Paper*, no. 427, The Institute of Developing Economies, Chiba Prefecture, Japan.

Le, N.T.T. 2011, 'How does culture impact on women's leadership in higher education? a case study in Vietnam', PhD thesis, University of Waikato, New Zealand.

Louise Barriball, K. and While, A. 1994, 'Collecting data using a semi-structured interview: a discussion paper', *Journal of Advanced Nursing*, vol. 19, no. 2, pp. 328–335.

Lucy, D.M., Ghosh, J. and Kujawa, E. 2010, 'Advancing individual and societal development at the community level: the role of NGO microcredit and leadership training', *SAM Advanced Management Journal*, vol. 75, no. 1, pp. 23.

Mattis, M.C. 2001, 'Advancing women in business organizations: key leadership roles and behaviors of senior leaders and middle managers', *Journal of Management Development*, vol. 20, no. 4, pp. 371–388.

Narayan, D., Patel, R., Schafft, K., Rademacher, A. and Koch-Schulte, S. 2000, *Voices of the poor: can anyone hear us*, World Bank, Washington, DC.

Organisation for Economic Co-operation and Development 2010, *Atlas of gender and development: how social norms affect gender quality in Non-OECD countries*, Organisation for Economic Co-operation and Development (OECD) Publishing, Paris, France.

Organisation for Economic Co-operation and Development 2013, *Multi-dimensional review of Myanmar: volume 1, initial assessment*, OECD Development Pathways, Organisation for Economic Co-operation and Development (OECD) Publishing, Paris, France.

QSR International 2014, *An overview of NVIVO*, QSR International, Doncaster, UK, viewed 4 December 2014, <http://download.qsrinternational.com/Resource/NVivo10/NVivo-10-Overview.pdf>.

Rabbani, G. 2009. 'Gender and NGO governance: evidence from local NGOs of Bangladesh', Social Science Research Network (SSRN), no. 1440097, viewed 5 December 2014, <http://ssrn.com/abstract=1440097>.

Repila, J. 2013, The politics of our lives: the raising her voice in Pakistan experience, Oxfam, Oxford, UK.Royal Government of Bhutan 2003, *Convention on the elimination of all forms of discrimination against women: an updated summary of the report of the Kingdom of Bhutan*, United Nations, New York, NY.

Sinha, P. 2003, 'Women entrepreneurship in the north east India: motivation, social support and constraints', *Indian Journal of Industrial Relations*, vol. 38, no. 4, pp. 425–443.

Sperandio, J. 2011, 'Context and the gendered status of teachers: women's empowerment through leadership of non formal schooling in rural Bangladesh', *Gender and Education*, vol. 23, no. 2, pp. 121–135.

Stoeberl, P.A., Kwon, I.W.G., Han, D. and Bae, M. 1998. 'Leadership and power relationships based on culture and gender', *Women in Management Review*, vol. 13, no. 6, pp. 208–216.

Truong, T.T.H. 2008, 'Women's leadership in Vietnam: opportunities and challenges', *Signs*, vol. 34, no. 1, pp. 16–21.

United Nations 2013, *General Assembly resolution draft 68/L.20*, United Nations, New York, NY, viewed 4 December 2013, <www.un.org/en/development/desa/policy/cdp/ldc/ldc_list.pdf >.

United Nations Development Programme 2014, *Human development report 2014*, United Nations, New York, NY.

World Bank 2013, *World development indicators 2013*, World Bank, Washington, DC.

6 The political economy of capacity building in the French Pacific territories

Stéphane Le Queux and Stéphanie Graff

Introduction

Polynesia and New Caledonia are the main French colonial territories in the South Pacific. While Polynesia is celebrating their 30-year anniversary of 'autonomy' (1984–2014), New Caledonia is engaged in a far-reaching process of decolonisation dating from the 1980s Kanak people insurrection – euphemistically referred to as the 'Events' and which resulted in the *Accords de Matignon* in 1988. Both territories have their own distinctive institutions for self-governance, yet are considered as 'overseas *collectivities*' within the framework of the French Constitution: Polynesia is ruled under article 74 (as per a few other French overseas colonies), and New Caledonia has become a '*sui generis collectivity*' since the 1998 *Accord de Nouméa* (Bill no. 99–209, 19 March 1999, Title XIII of the French Constitution). This chapter sets out to provide an examination of capacity building in the specific context of emancipation from the colonial order looking at factors of *independence* (here to be understood analytically as capacity for self-determination) and of *dependencies* in the management of geo-political, economic and ethnic *inter-dependencies*.

Following some background information, we will first expose the socio-economic divides between and within both territories as well as the challenges lying ahead. Next, we will turn to the world of work as employment and institutions of labour relations represent key determinants for capacity building in addressing inequalities and enhancing citizenship, with a particular attention to indigenous activism within the labour movement and beyond.[1] Prospects for capacity building will be discussed by way of conclusion.

Socio-economic background

For being French 'overseas collectivities', New Caledonia and Polynesia[2] are granted some degree of political sovereignty and autonomous powers of jurisdiction, especially the so-called '*loi du pays*', which is a legal disposition allowing them to legislate territorial affairs. Polynesian institutions for self-governance include an Assembly and a Presidency in charge of the legislative functions and external affairs, and the government is responsible for the executive and the territorial administration. New Caledonia institutions include a government in charge of the executive and a Congress dealing with the legislative, further subdivided into three Provincial Assemblies (North/South/Loyalty Islands) with internal competencies, hence reflecting the socio-demographic and regional disparity of the territory. In both territories, France has a *Haut Commissariat* in place to administer national affairs. Both territories have representation in the French National Assembly, and both are, to significant degrees, subject to French laws.

It is important to note that New Caledonia, and more recently Polynesia (in 2013), have been registered on the UN list of countries to be decolonised, which in legal terms means that they are technically recognised as 'non-self-governing territories' by the international community. New Caledonia is leading the way towards independence and is planning to organise an additional electoral consultation on further or full sovereignty in 2018, as concluded in the *Accord de Nouméa*. This particular issue is highly contentious in Polynesia due to Polynesia's heavy dependence on French financial support and the multi-cultural character of its social fabric. Both territories benefit from a considerable level of assistance from France in relation to social (health care, education, police, justice, etc.) and broader infrastructure, which differentiates them significantly from other self-reliant Pacific nations and which may also explain why they usually disappear from the radar in Pacific studies, for often, they are assimilated to France.

Socio-economic divides between and within territories

New Caledonia is by far the most developed Pacific economy, thanks principally to its large mining sector – an estimated 25 per cent of the world reserves of nickel are found on the main island, which recently attracted almost US$7 billion of foreign direct investments (FDI). As a result, New Caledonia's GDP per capita is higher than that of New Zealand and almost the same as France itself.[3]

In contrast, Polynesia, which has long been maintained on a lifeline by French subsidies, is experiencing economic difficulty. The territory is struggling to overcome a triple crisis: the end of French nuclear experimentations in the mid-1990s and consequently the loss of the large financial transfer that it conveyed; the 2008 global financial crisis that hit tourism hard, which had been estimated to provide around three-quarters of all self-generated revenues; and ten years of political turmoil. The political rise of the *Tavini Huiraatira* (Polynesian Liberation Front) to the Presidency in 2004 and the repudiation of the *Bolliet* report, which was to condition French subsidies to budget stringency in the early 2010, did not help either for a while, convincing the French to maintain fully fledged financial support. The economic downfall and years of recession have had devastating consequences on the Polynesian labour market; unemployment has almost doubled in five years, from 11.7 per cent in 2007 to 21.8 per cent in 2012.

While the New Caledonian and Polynesian economic situations differ sharply, they share a common problem of wealth distribution, which is a major cause of social inequity, coupled with a low participation in the labour market overall and particularly among the indigenous population. Both territories thus display a relatively high Gini coefficient: 0.40 and 0.43 for Polynesia and New Caledonia, respectively;[4] the difference between the richest 10 per cent and the poorest 10 per cent households is six-fold in Polynesia (remote islands excluded) and up to seven-fold in New Caledonia. It is estimated that almost 30 per cent of the population live below the poverty line in Polynesia (based on living conditions); estimates are up to a third in New Caledonia, based on the median revenue of Nouméa regional area (Syndex 2010, p.73). It is commonly acknowledged in both contexts that access to employment is the key factor in explaining and addressing inequalities, although both territories have a welfare system in place. Labour market statistics indicate that, while participation rates are estimated at around 60 per cent and 55 per cent in New Caledonia and Polynesia, respectively, in each context, the number of 'other inactive' people surpasses by far those unemployed. In Polynesia, for instance, for 90,000 people in a job, there are 80,000 people on unemployment benefits and around another 90,000 listed as inactive: over half of the persons of working age indicate that they were not looking for a job.

In both contexts, there is a spatial, racial and politico-administrative segmentation of the labour market. With the exception of tourism hubs like Bora Bora or mining sites across New Caledonia, the vast majority of jobs are concentrated in the main urban centres, Papeete in Tahiti and Nouméa in New Caledonia. The further away from those centres, the more prevalent is the informal economy, usually reliant on traditional community-based modes of self-subsistence and as a rule among the indigenous population. Indeed, in establishing their agenda to address social inequalities, the *Union des Syndicats des Ouvriers et Employés de Nouvelle-Calédonie* (USOENC, the dominant trade union in New Caledonia) stated that 'there were not one, but two or more New Caledonia' in reference to this spatial (*ipso facto* racial) divide in the context of New Caledonia. The situation is similar in Polynesia but based on geo-spatial terms, from Tahiti at the epicentre to remote islands at the periphery. This segmentation of the labour market and the unequal capacity to access a decent job is compounded with lesser investments in infrastructure and uneven access to either social services or education and training in regional areas.

The third source of labour market segmentation stems from the political-administrative apparatus, which further entrenched existing social segregation. This feature is not exclusive to New Caledonia and Polynesia and is commonly found in other French colonies. French expatriates working for the colonial administration benefit from a generous wage package including pay indexation and fiscal exemptions plus other fringe benefits, an indexed revenue that is usually matched to some extent by territorial administrations. For instance in Polynesia, wages in the public sector are 60 per cent higher than in the private sector. Providing more qualified jobs on average, the public sector pays twice as much than the private sector in New Caledonia (Frappier 2013). As a result, the colonial and territorial administrations together constitute a class in itself, a core component of the upper class that drives inflationary pressures on housing and consumer goods, notwithstanding being a potential source for corruption and nepotism.

Those socio-economic divisions and resulting inequalities have led to ongoing social protests and union-based common fronts across French colonies since the mid-2000s: a campaign geared on the 'cost of life' (*campagne contre la vie chère*), based on holistic claims around economic governance and social inequalities and also targeting fiscal reforms in favour of low-revenue households, such as claims for a direct tax on mining extraction in New Caledonia.[5] The 2014 Labour Day joint declaration from USOENC and CSTNC (*Confédération Syndicale des Travailleurs de Nouvelle-Calédonie*) read '[E]ach picket strike on the ground must bring something to the nation'. Labour agency for capacity building is indeed critical in both regions, and even more so in New Caledonia, as we will detail after outlining the major challenges ahead.

Challenges to capacity building: engaging the youth and balancing the economy

In the presence of a political, legal and industrial relations framework that provides a solid institutional background for decent working conditions in both territories, up-skilling and access to employment are seen as the way forward to reduce broader social inequalities. In Polynesia, employment statistics show that low-qualified men and especially the youth have been particularly impacted by the economic downturn; between 2007 and 2012, the youth job rate has dropped by an estimated 32 per cent (ISPF 2012). Young people bear the brunt of the crisis: half of unemployed people are between 15 to 25 years old, and two-thirds of them are 30 years old or less. In New Caledonia, while unemployment levels have remained fairly stable, albeit with a slight increase to 12 per cent, it is estimated that 35 per cent of job seekers are between 20 to 30 years old, and around the same proportion of those are unskilled. This prompted New Caledonia to engage in a series of policy initiatives in 2013 to target youth unemployment and promote access to vocational training. There is already a range of educational resources in place whilst continuous vocational training is a compulsory requirement for employers (as per the French legislation and up to almost 2 per cent of the payroll annually). In Polynesia, the employers' association is monitoring an initiative focusing on youth vocational training in partnership with the Defence Force to enhance youth employability, one of their core commitments to the Polynesian community. The challenge lies in the connectivity of youth to the labour market, especially bridging the gap with the indigenous (urban) youth who often find themselves in a situation of double exclusion: from the formal labour market and decent jobs and from traditional means of subsistence and community support.

If access to employment and up-skilling at the lower end of the labour market represents the main area of concern, union officials in both territories report the existence of a 'glass ceiling' at the other end, with native employees and especially indigenous people being under-represented in the ranks of management, and broadly in professional occupations. There is thus a call for positive action to break this 'glass ceiling', a call for a so-called *Océanisation des Cadres*.

Labour and politics as agency of capacity

Although technically territorially bound, the labour legislation is moulded into or derived from French legislation, thus matching standards expected in advanced socio-democratic economies. Some discrepancies, however, are found in specific fields (for example retirement, tax and social benefits). In particular, both territories have sought to foster positive discrimination of local employment using their jurisdictional prerogative. While there is now a legal obligation for employers to hire territorial labour if available at equal qualification levels in New Caledonia (Act n° 2010–9, July 2010) in the private sector only,[6] the Polynesia's 2009 *Loi du pays* on the protection of local employment was rebuked by the French *Conseil d'État* for being 'too restrictive'.

Progress in gender equity is a showcase illustration of supportive legislation and labour institutions. Although Polynesian and New Caledonian labour law alike prohibit any form of discrimination in employment, there is an identified gender gap in New Caledonia, while according to several union observers, inequality in Polynesia is more likely to be based on ethnicity rather than gender, especially as mentioned earlier when it comes to the higher end of the labour market. The gender gap in New Caledonia is mostly a consequence of the employment structure, with male- and female-dominated jobs, as in many other national contexts. From their sample of the private sector, the *Institut pour le Développement des Compétences en Nouvelle-Calédonie* (IDC-NC 2013) identified that only 28 per cent of managerial positions were filled by women and, moreover, that the gender pay gap was widening correlatively to education levels: the gap being the wider at the higher end of qualification levels. This said, New Caledonian labour experts signal two counter trends: the gradual feminisation of traditionally male dominated industries (mining, constructions), but still generally in low-qualified and technical jobs, and women becoming more educated than men. In Polynesia, female participation in the labour market has actually increased (+1.9 points from 2007 to 2012, reaching 49.1 per cent in 2012), which may be an enduring trend as women are likewise increasingly involved in higher levels of education and vocational training, with unions being proactive in fostering access to the latter.

Employment relations very much resemble those in France, marked by union (conflictual) pluralism, and despite low union density, as in France, sector-based (branch) bargaining provides a fairly high level of union coverage guaranteeing level working conditions across the board, at least in large businesses. Labour organisations are not only instrumental in advancing working conditions through their industrial arm and collective representation but they are also pivotal in the struggle for decent living standards, either directly through political activism or indirectly within the parameters of institutionalised social dialogue – e.g. the political platform for a 'Common Destiny' and a Social Pact in New Caledonia and the *Conseil Économique Social et Culturel* (CESC) and the Tripartite Commissions in Polynesia – including, importantly, their participation in the management of social welfare. In the wake of the campaign against cost-of-living and social inequalities, unions' efforts over the last few years have translated into substantial increases in minimum wages (+8.6 per cent between 2011 to 2013 in New Caledonia; well above the inflation rate) in addition to active social and fiscal dispositions to increase the purchasing power of low-income earners or families on welfare payment.

Indigenous labour and political activism

In both regions, the prevalence of indigenous trade unions in the representative chessboard exacerbates union rivalry. Yet, it is fair to say that indigenous as well as non-indigenous labour organisations alike are altogether contributing to decent work to all, although indigenous-led unions are more likely to be engaged in direct representation of indigenous workers, as in the case of *Otahi* in Tahiti, a newly formed union actively involved in organising workers across sectors at the lower end of the labour market.

The dominant, French-affiliated trade unions – the USOENC (New Caledonia); A TI'A I MUA (*Confédération Française Démocratique du Travail* [CFDT]) and the *Confédération Syndicale des Travailleurs de Polynésie/Force Ouvrière* (CSTP/FO) (Polynesia) – openly condemn the political orientation of indigenous (pro-independence) trade unions, i.e. the *Union Syndicale des Travailleurs Kanak et des Exploités* (USTKE) in New Caledonia and *O Oe To Oe Rima* in Polynesia. While the USOENC and A TI'A I MUA are homegrown trade unions, relatively autonomous and with a long-standing history, they both align themselves to the CFDT's culture of social dialogue and business unionism. In contrast, indigenous trade unions fully embrace a model of political unionism. In both regions, indigenous trade unions are capitalising from having political leverage, although much more so organically in New Caledonia, through the Kanak people liberation movement (*Front de Libération Nationale Kanak et Socialiste* [FLNKS]) and the Labour Party, than in Polynesia.

Indeed, USTKE established in December 1981 was subsequently involved with pro-independence political parties such as the *Union Calédonienne* and *Palika* in the creation of the FLNKS in September 1984. USTKE left the FLNKS in 1989 but continued to provide support for their political action. USTKE later decided to return to politics and present candidates in pro-independence lists in the 2007 legislative elections and then, in November of the same year, went on to create its own political arm, the *Parti Travailliste* (Labour Party). The leader of the New Caledonia Labour Party, Louis Kotra Uregei, is a founding member of USTKE. The Labour Party is now part of UC-FLNKS and Nationalists Group in the Congress of New Caledonia.

O Oe To Oe Rima is a relatively weak under-resourced trade union (in terms of organisation and membership) compared to USTKE, which is the second dominant union in New Caledonia after the USOENC, but for long, the union was led by the charismatic Ronald Terorotua, who was able to reach out to Tahitian working families. In the view of Ronald Terorotua, trade unionism was a way to 'provide traction to the struggle for independence', which otherwise was 'without direction'. Although sympathetic to the cause, *Otahi* has no official position towards Polynesian independence but clearly brands itself as a movement for the working class *de facto* Tahitian in vast majority.

While *Otahi*'s leadership recognises that, perhaps much more than capitalism, the territorial administration (and its politico-bureaucratic class) may be the 'enemy', *O Oe To Oe Rima* and USTKE are fundamentally anti-capitalist. One particular challenge according to *O Oe To Oe Rima*'s new leader, Atonia Teriino-horai, is to mobilise the youth. In his view, the political chaos of the last decade has disengaged young people from politics making it difficult to rebuild a new generation of social militancy.

USTKE's slogan '*Usines, Tribus, Même Combat*' ('Factories, Tribes, Same Struggle') as well as their foundation manifesto (see abstract following) both illustrate the distinctive role of indigenous labour activism as a catalyst in the broader struggle for colonial emancipation in New Caledonia.

> Us as a People are different and the 'cultural', 'social' and 'political' distinctiveness of Kanak workers are improperly represented by existing unions. . . . Before colonisation, our society was a rich civilisation, a culture based on ancestral rules which command respect; a culture that the colonial (brutal) forces wanted to break but that is still alive and standing and which is our distinctive identity. . . . We are numerically superior but economically subordinated (our value systems not being the same) and we are considered as inferior beings. . . . The exploitative violence of capitalism does not suit the Kanak way of life. . . . We are a colonised People, our dignity has been scorned; we seek to regain our freedom and we will carry on the struggle till we see the day of an independent and socialist Kanak country.
>
> (1981 USKTE foundation statement, author's translation; see also Israël 2007: 285–286)

It is unequivocal to USKTE that the anti-capitalist struggle is an underlying component of the broader struggle for independence. The preamble of USTKE thus states:[7]

> In reference to the Universal Declaration of Human Rights and the Charter of the United Nations, USTKE appeals for the right of the Kanak people to self-governance and to the free exercise of their national sovereignty, and to the suppression of capitalist exploitation. . . . We are thus committed to the Kanak people's struggle for independence and socialism.
>
> (authors' translation)

That is the reason why USTKE leaders' public declarations usually combine mixed calls for political and labour activism. On May Day 2012, USTKE leader Marie-Pierre Goyetche, hence, declared that the union was 'committed to the country's emancipation and access to full sovereignty'.[8] History provides insights on why indigenous labour and political activism intersect that way. New Caledonia was taken over by France in the mid-nineteenth century, it was first established as a convict colony but later opened to free settlers. The Kanak people were ruled apart from European settlers under a regime of '*indigénat*' and only accessed French citizenship in 1946; the right to vote was subsequently granted to all Kanak people in 1957 (Mohamed-Gaillard 2010). In 1975, in a context similar to apartheid, a Kanak coalition involving the *Union Calédonienne* and labour activists (among others) self-proclaimed independence (Leblic 1993, p. 61). USTKE emerged six years after. Thus, the colonial context explains how the indigenous union struggle is embedded in the struggle for independence and therefore that the struggle for independence is carried on by indigenous organised labour.

Prospects for capacity building

As outlined, in the contexts of institutional frameworks that in each territory are conductive to decent working conditions and protection of employees' rights, labour market participation is regarded as the key policy challenge to address economic disparity and nurture social inclusion. However, inequalities have to be understood in broader terms and require forward-looking policy making aimed at balancing and diversifying economic activity and cascading down its dividends (and public investments) to community-based (sustainable) development, a viewpoint commonly shared by social partners (unions and employers' associations alike). The 'split' nature of the economy in both contexts is putting social cohesion under strain, a phenomenon exacerbated by youth exclusion and disengagement. The 2014 Labour slogans in New Caledonia were precisely along those lines: 'equity' ('*rééquilibrage*'), '[local] employment' and 'citizenship'.[9]

In both regions, the political economy weighs heavily on capacity building, as a matter of path-dependency shaping corridors and constraints to further autonomy and sovereignty; as such, it appears to be a relevant heuristic device to understand capacity for (colonial) emancipation. To put it bluntly, New Caledonia is so rich in mineral resources that it is unlikely that global capital and multinational mining corporations will leave while there is so much wealth to exploit. SMSP and Xstrata have recently invested US$3.8 billion in what is to become one of the biggest nickel mining operations in the world. This explains why Robert Forest, one of the founding members and a co-leader of USTKE interviewed in 2011, himself quoting the late Kanak political leader Tjibaou, came to explain that the challenge (of independence) was rather to manage '*inter-dependencies*'. Those inter-dependencies are also to be understood in the context of a symbolic struggle over the notion of a 'Caledonian citizenship' brought about by the *Accord de Nouméa*. Caledonian citizenship is part of a political setup for reconciliation, which can be referred to as the 'politics of "Common Destiny"' (Graff 2012). While at the starting point there is recognition of the precedency of the Kanak people, it is encapsulated in a broader conception of a 'Caledonian' identity. In principle, jobs, land and resources belong to this newly constituted 'Caledonian People', which today includes the majority of the non-indigenous population. Down the track, it does explain the underlying importance of and intense scrutiny upon the legislation on local employment: beyond jobs, it is a question of restraining migration and changing demographics, which has been one long-standing colonial strategy to shift the racial balance. Abstracts of a correspondence from the French Prime Minister Pierre Messmer to Xavier Deniau, State Secretary to French overseas colonies, dated 19 July 1972, illustrates this strategy:

> French presence in New Caledonia can only be threatened, albeit a world war, by nationalist claims from indigenous people. . . . In the short and medium term, the massive immigration of metropolitan French citizens or from other overseas colonies should help in preventing this danger by improving the numerical balance between communities. . . . In the long run nationalist claims will be circumvented if communities from non-Pacific background become the majority demographics.
>
> (authors' translation)

The downside of being *exotic*, literally, is to be cast away. 'We're far away, you know, very much afar' was the first thing raised by Angelo Frebault, spokesperson for the CSTP/FO and also President of the CESC, interviewed in 2014. His observation says much: it explains why France decided to set up its nuclear experimentation centre in the territory; it explains too the high cost of living and the insularity of social (and industrial) relations as much as the specific constraints and limitations upon economic development. Whereas New Caledonia is somewhat 'cursed' by (mineral) abundance, Polynesia is not that resource-rich, can hardly cope with welfare demands and has not yet reached capacity for self-development. While the operating budget of the Polynesian government is around US$ 1.28 billion annually, welfare expenses are estimated at around US$ 1.21 billion. It thus represents a considerable burden on the economy that three-quarters of welfare expenditures are waved by the world of work through employers' and employees' contributions. Pressures on the welfare system can be explained by two factors, health and unemployment: while some are pointing at the oncological cost linked to past nuclear experimentations (a total of over 180 A-bombs were tested between1966 to 1996), the stark increase of beneficiaries of unemployment benefits, from 45,000 to 80,000 in a matter of a few years (45 per cent being young people between 20 to 29 years old),[10] explains much of the budgetary problem. Despite kin-based solidarity, a strong component of Polynesian culture, this situation yields serious consequences in terms of social cohesion and indigence. Behind the safety net provided by the welfare system, church associations are helping to reduce resentment. There is a question as to whether the situation has reached a critical point, with many Polynesian families under financial distress. The government has announced a plan to relaunch the economy.[11] Yet, the plan will not go ahead without substantial FDIs, with China being the likely source. Chinese investors are very likely to condition their investments on concessions. They have already signalled that they want special derogations to lower labour costs and relief from constraints in the labour law.

Some express their concern over the potential of having Chinese investors using the Polynesian-born Chinese business community to obtain political leverage. What then will be the effect on the Polynesian inter-ethnic cohesion? Here, the Polynesian-led trade union leaders, as many Polynesians, do make it clear that there is a line drawn in the sand: they do not mind having the Chinese run the economy, but politics must remain in the hands of indigenous Maoris.

Capacity building for what? It so begs the question. Kanak leaders are fully aware of the adversity and of the nature of 'inter-dependencies' at play. Yet, when asked about the struggle, Robert Forest concluded that, for him, 'after all', it was ultimately 'a matter of dignity', a word also echoed by Polynesians, while others in the same register would say 'freedom'. If not contrary, the context of capacity building is indeed contradictory. Polynesian autonomy is leading to greater heteronomy. Development is occurring with a trade-off with sustainability. It is obvious in the case of extensive mining excavation in New Caledonia, but what of the ecological impact of mass Sino-tourism and extensive Chinese-led aquaculture in Polynesia? Prospects for meaningful capacity will depend on how both regions in their own way will manoeuvre between prosperity and de-culturation, wealth and well-being. A Gini coefficient is a measure of wealth disparity, not of well-being, which does not make much anthropological sense in traditional or remote communities that are essentially non-capitalist, where not having the latest smart phone would not matter much to a Marquesan fisherman. As a member of the Polynesian CESC expressed it, away from wage labour and consumerism, 'the (remote) islands fare better after all'.

For these reasons, the Melanesian Spearhead Group (MSG) has made the choice to invest on the development of the 'Alternative Indicators of Well-being for Melanesia'. Those indicators of well-being are for example life satisfaction, life expectancy and the ecological footprint. On those indicators, in 2006, Vanuatu was declared the happiest country in the world by the UK-based New Economics Foundation in a report named *The Happy Planet Index: An Index of Human Well-Being and Environmental Impact*, whereas the United Nations, based on GDP growth, measured Vanuatu as one of the world's most impoverished countries. At the 2008 MSG Leaders' Summit Trade and Economic Officials Meeting (TEOM), held in Port-Vila, Vanuatu delivered a paper called 'Enhancing Our Traditional Systems and Values for a Stronger and More Integrated Melanesia in Addressing Global Challenges'. MSG TEOM further decided to follow Vanuatu's initiative by developing alternatives indicators of well-being within the context of Melanesia.

Conclusion

Contextualised comparisons in political economy can be performed through the identification of 'fault lines' and 'sticking points' (Locke and Thelen 1995). There are significant fault lines between the two territories. The first, not to be neglected, is ethnographic. Melanesians and Polynesians are different people. Race is a dividing factor in New Caledonia but is not an issue in Polynesia.

Anthropologically speaking, the Melanesian social structure is based around clans and tribes and is dominantly patriarchal. The Polynesian one is organised along kinship, and Polynesia is reputably a matriarchal society. Polynesians are by large the majority population on their territory (around 85 per cent of the population), and the Kanak people have been turned into a minority (at the time of the USTKE foundation manifesto, they were 60 per cent; they are now 40 per cent of the population). The second fault line is economic, as we insist, although we find similar patterns of wealth disparity, structural high cost of living and youth disengagement.

Those factors underlie the contrasted political dynamics in each context and by extension the differing colonial strategies in response to them. Whereas social dialogue has been imposed upon social actors in response to the Kanak people's struggle and as part of a wider political strategy to promote a 'Common Destiny' in New Caledonia, social partnership does emanate from the Polynesians themselves in a common effort to get out of the crisis they are bogged into and to build a future that is much more self-reliant. Independence or further sovereignty is high on the agenda in New Caledonia, while Polynesians seem, in their majority, satisfied with the *status quo*. Indeed, recent interviews at the Polynesian Presidency and the CESC indicated that France was fully respecting Polynesian autonomous decision making in relation to their economic plan and even more so committed to financially backing it up with a contribution up to US$250 million, amounting to half of the government stimulus package. Conversely, at the time of writing, dissensions within majority parties against independence has led to a political deadlock and the fall of the government in New Caledonia that, compounded with a declining economic performance and inaction towards the high cost of living and social inequalities, is a situation that is fuelling tensions. Future assessments of the political economy of capacity building in the region will have to consider the contested process of decolonisation on the road to independence in New Caledonia and the consequences of shifting economic dependency in Polynesia.

France, as a colonial ruler, is the major sticking point, notwithstanding that France appears to be keen to reinforce their presence in the Pacific, arguably in response to the rise of Chinese interests in the region. Metropolitan France provides significant assistance in terms of social and physical infrastructure, which makes a sharp difference with self-dependent neighbouring countries. Consequently, capacity building ought not to be understood in those terms but rather in the ground of 'moral economy'. Or say, in classic Maussian terms, that an economy can be ultimately defined as a construct of social relations reflecting a value system that determines what is or has 'value'. And that is, we argue, a determinant sticking point for the analysis. Both regions face exogenous forces through FDIs, more extensively in New Caledonia and yet to come in Polynesia. How to compromise development and sustainability, how to maintain the '*enoughness*' and inclusiveness that used to characterise traditional indigenous value systems and way of living may be the true yardstick of capacity building, at least for the South Pacific indigenous peoples.

Notes

1 A comprehensive account of each context can be found in Le Queux (2015) and Le Queux and Graff (2015).
2 New Caledonia is approximately 1500 km off Australia's east coast, while Tahiti is further afield at 5700 km from Sydney and 3900 km from Auckland. The area of New Caledonia itself is of 19,000 km², and the territory covers an overall Exclusive Economic Zone of around 1.5 million km². French Polynesian territory covers an area of over 5 million km² (mostly oceanic). Tahiti is the economic and administrative centre of French Polynesia. Tahiti and surrounding islands have a population of around 205,000 people out of a total population of 270,000 (around 85 per cent indigenous Polynesians), hence approximately three-quarters of the Polynesian population (www.ispf.pf). New Caledonia is host to around 250,000 people, 2 out 5 of which are native Melanesians. Most of the population is to be found around the urban region of Nouméa.
3 Business Advantage, New Caledonia 2010–2011, www.businessadvantagenew caledonia.com/
4 www.ispf.pf/themes/EmploiRevenus/NiveauVie.aspx
5 $0.5 per pound of nickel extracted to generate funding for future generations and sustainable development. *Propositions de l'USOENC pour lutter contre la vie chère et contre les inégalités*, Finitemps, October 2010.
6 The extension of this provision to the public sector is being discussed.
7 http://ustke.org/statuts/statuts-ustke/Statuts-de-lUSTKE-at_131.html
8 http://ustke.org/communiques/b.c/Discours-de-M.P-Goyetche-lors-du-1er-mai-2012-au-siege-du-syndicat-(VDT)-at_239.html
9 La marche du 1er-Mai de l'USTKE prend des accents politiques: www.lnc.nc/article/pays/defiler-c-est-voter
10 Caisse de Prévoyance sociale, '1956–2013, 57 ans d'avancées sociales. Chiffres clés de la PSG 2013', Polynésie Française, p. 4.
11 Plan de Relance 2014. *50 mesures pour l'avenir*. Présidence de la Polynésie Française. http://web.presidence.pf/files/PlandeRelance-BD.pdf

References

Frappier, J. 2013, *Les Salaires Entre 2007 et 2010*, Synthèse No 26, Institut de la Statistique et des Études Économiques (ISEE), Nouvelle Calédonie.
Graff, S. 2012, 'Quand combat et revendications kanak ou politique de l'État français manient indépendance, décolonisation, autodétermination et autochtonie en Nouvelle Calédonie', *Journal de la Société des Océanistes*, no. 134, pp. 61–83.
IDC-NC 2013, *Focus sur les femmes – Édition 2013*, Observatoire de l'Emploi, des Qualifications, des Salaires et de la Formation, Institut pour le Développement des Compétences en Nouvelle-Calédonie (IDC-NC), Nouvelle Calédonie.
ISPF 2012, 'Points forts de la Polynésie Française, Études, Les actifs peu qualifiés pénalisés par la crise', Institut de la Statistique de la Polynésie Française (ISPF), La Polynésie Française.
Israël, H. 2007, *Une histoire du mouvement syndical en Nouvelle Calédonie*, Éditions Îles de Lumière, Nouvelle Calédonie.
Le Queux, S. 2015, 'Polynésie: les partenaires sociaux au rendez-vous de l'avenir tahitien', *Chronique Internationale de l'IRES*, no. 149, pp. 47–59.
Le Queux, S. and Graff S. 2015, 'Nouvelle-Calédonie: des relations professionnelles politisées dans le prisme du militantisme Kanak', *Chronique Internationale de l'IRES*, no. 150, pp. 25–38.

Leblic, I. 1993, *Les Kanak face au développement: la voie étroite*, Presses Universitaires de Grenoble, Grenoble, France.

Locke, R. and Thelen, K. 1995, 'Apples and oranges revisited: contextualized comparisons and the study of comparative labor politics', *Politics and Society*, vol. 23, no. 3, pp. 337–367.

Mohamed-Gaillard, S. 2010, *L'archipel de la puissance? la politique de la France dans le Pacifique Sud de 1946 à 1998*, PIE – Peter Lang SA, Brussels, Belgium.

Syndex 2010, *Le pouvoir d'achat des: la Nouvelle-Calédonie face à ses inégalités*, Rapport Syndex, Paris, France.

7 Using targeted jobs programmes to support local communities

The case of Indonesia

Emma Allen and John Burgess

Introduction

There has been a long history of public employment programmes to bolster jobs, incomes and local development. The history of such programmes is documented for Indonesia (International Institute for Labour Studies [IILS] 2010) and currently such programmes are known as 'PNPM Mandiri' (Programme Nasional Pemberdayaan Masyarakat/National Community Empowerment Programme). This programme is currently the largest nation-wide poverty reduction programme in Indonesia. PNPM Mandiri covers all sub-districts in Indonesia, and it has been suggested that it has decreased the unemployment rate in rural areas where it is active by up to 1.5 per cent points (World Bank 2010: 168). Targeted public works programmes can be useful in alleviating unemployment, reducing poverty and supporting family incomes (Froy, Giguère and Hofer 2009). In the case of a recession, there is an imperative for countercyclical fiscal measures to support community employment and activity, especially in the context of an underdeveloped private sector and extensive informal and small family business activity (World Economic Forum for Africa 2014). In this chapter, the use of public sector job programmes in Indonesia in 2009 in the aftermath of the global financial crisis (GFC) is analysed.

This chapter provides insights into the effectiveness and efficiency of Indonesia's public employment programmes, in order to develop better understanding of the ability of the government to administer job creation programmes in the context of financial and economic downturn. Particular focus is given to understanding employment quality, the inclusion of vulnerable groups and the social protection function of such programmes. This chapter looks into these issues within the context of the job creation component of Indonesia's 2009 fiscal stimulus package, which used the government's existing programme architecture to provide an automatic stabiliser function and stabilise aggregate demand through channelling additional government budgetary resources to these programmes.

Responding to the global financial crisis

The consequences of the global financial and economic crisis of 2008–2009 began to show signs of penetrating into the Indonesian economy during the latter part of 2008. Economic growth deteriorated from an average of 6.1 per cent points to 5.2 per cent points in the fourth quarter of 2008. Growth projections for the following years were subsequently revised downward, and in 2009, the GDP growth target was set at 4.3 per cent points. Largely due to a declining economic outlook in 2008 (IILS 2010),[1] the Government of Indonesia announced a stimulus package worth IDR 73.2 trillion[2] in January 2009, which was equivalent to 1.4 per cent of GDP (IILS 2010). The fiscal stimulus package was one of the smallest among G20 countries and considerably smaller than the stimulus packages of China, Thailand, Malaysia and Vietnam (IILS 2010). It was financed through unused funds from the previous year's government budget and through raising capital through selling government bonds in the international bond market.

The fiscal stimulus package comprised of three core components that sought to maintain purchasing power, prevent job loss and accelerate local development (Bank of Indonesia 2009). The key instruments that were used included a selection of tax cuts, subsidies and increased spending on infrastructure through a range of government job creation employment programmes. Tax cuts accounted for approximately 77.2 per cent of the package, while infrastructure spending accounted for 16.3 per cent of spending. The composition of this fiscal stimulus package was quite different from other stimulus packages in the region and indicative of Indonesia's priority to maintain purchasing power, stimulate domestic demand and to support the private sector (IILS 2010). By the end of 2009, the government had realised 83.8 per cent of its targeted expenditure and injected an additional IDR 61.4 trillion into the economy (see Table 7.1).

The infrastructure component of the stimulus package was worth IDR 12 trillion and aimed to create an additional 1 million short-term work opportunities through upscaling the budget of a range of existing programmes that were administered across ten ministries (Bank of Indonesia 2009). Each of these programmes was to use a range of labour-intensive and labour-based approaches to invest in infrastructure that would provide short-term work opportunities and stimulate local economic development.

What was important for Indonesia was using this stimulus, not only to respond to the economic downturn, but to increase the resilience of the overall economy and to create jobs (Bank of Indonesia 2009). Therefore, policy makers chose to direct resources to investments that had a high labour-to-capital ratio, including gravel roads, irrigation and flood protection infrastructure investments, which could be implemented through the Ministry of Public Works. Table 7.2 outlines the employment creation targets of the fiscal stimulus package by ministerial allocation (full-time equivalent [FTE] for 12 months). The employment estimates were generated based on best practice assumptions from the implementation of previous programmes (Athmer 2009). For example it was assumed that approximately 30 per cent of the budget for public works programmes would go towards the wages of low and unskilled labourers. The infrastructure component of the fiscal stimulus package was expected to create an additional 1 million short-term

Table 7.1 Composition of the 2009 fiscal stimulus package (IDR '000,000,000)

Fiscal stimulus component	Fiscal stimulus instrument	Budget allocation	Budget realisation	Per cent realisation
Maintain and improve purchasing power	Personal income tax cut	24500.0	19526.7	79.9
	Value-added tax cut	1250.0	828.2	61.4
Prevent employees' contract termination and improve product competitiveness	Employee income tax cut	6500.0	5180.6	79.9
	Corporate income tax cut	19300.0	19300.0	100.0
		2500.0	1006.7	40.27
	Value-added tax cut	2500.0	7.2	0.29
	Tariff import tax cut	4172.8	4157.8	99.64
	Subsidy to state-owned enterprises (SOEs)	500.0	500.0	100.0
Increase investment in labour intensive infrastructure	Public works	6601.2	6433.4	97.5
	Transport	2198.8	2079.7	94.6
	Energy and mineral	500.0	492.4	98.5
	resources	500.0	493.9	98.8
	Public housing	315.0	289.2	91.8
	Trade	650.0	0	0
	Agriculture and fisheries	300.0	253.3	84.4
	Labour and	150.0	149.79	99.9
	transmigration	601.5	601.5	100.0
	Health	120.0	120.0	100.0
	Programme Nasional Pemberdayaan Masyarakat (PNPM)			
	Cooperatives and small and medium-sized enterprises (SMEs)			
Total		73,259.3	61,420.4	83.8

Source: Coordinating Ministry for Economic Affairs (2009), unpublished data.

jobs. In addition, the programme added to essential community infrastructure through investment in key public works and in key services such as health and education.

Due to proactive macroeconomic policies and previous reforms that were implemented after the Asian Financial Crisis, Indonesia was able to exceed its GDP growth target and achieved an average growth rate of 4.5 per cent points in 2009 (IILS 2010). The favourable growth outcomes have been attributed to the large portion of GDP (approximately 58.6 per cent) that is derived from household consumption and a comparatively low dependency on exports, as well as the use of fiscal stimulus to stimulate aggregate demand. The following sections therefore look more closely at the fiscal stimulus programme, particularly the job creation component, in order to understand more about its impacts and effectiveness.

Table 7.2 Estimates of job creation from the 2009 stimulus package

Government ministry/ department	Budget allocation		No. jobs to be created (FTE)
	IDR (in billions)	% of total	
Public works	6601.0	55.3	944,170
Centre	3617.0	30.3	259,375
Regional	2984.0	25.0	684,795
Transport	2198.0	18.4	45,962
Energy and mineral resources	500.0	4.2	N/A
Public housing	500.0	4.2	N/A
Agriculture and fisheries	650.0	5.4	12,450
Labour and transmigration	300.0	2.5	8,300
Health	150.0	1.3	400
Trade	315.0	2.6	5,150
Cooperatives and SMEs	120.0	1.0	5,720
PNPM	601.5	5.0	8,300
Total	11,935.5	100.0	1,030,452

Source: Coordinating Ministry of Economic Affairs (2009), unpublished data.

Evaluating the effectiveness of the public works job programme

To understand the impact and effectiveness of the program, a questionnaire was developed based on surveys previously implemented by the International Labour Organisation's (ILO) Employment Intensive Investment Programme, as well as Indonesia's labour force survey (SAKERNAS) and the national socio-economic survey (SUSENAS). The key issues to be investigated through the questionnaire included:

- *Individual and household characteristics:* demographic composition; educational attainment; savings and debt. This provided insight on the degree to which vulnerable groups were drawn into the programme.
- *Nature of the work opportunity:* the average number of work days per work opportunity; wage range; distribution of work opportunities in the community; source of labour market information. This provided insight into the dynamics of the job creation programme.
- *Recent labour market history:* labour transfer (occupation/sector); recent employment history; previous wage rates; future plans. This provided insight into worker vulnerability and strategies for improving employment outcomes.

Table 7.3 Fiscal stimulus projects by district, budget allocation and project type

District	Water		Human settlement		Roads		Total	
	No.	%	No.	%	No.	%	No.	%
Bekasi	2	2.70	4	5.41	2	2.70	8	10.81
Bogor	1	1.35	6	8.11	14	18.92	21	28.38
Lebak	2	2.70	16	21.62	10	13.51	28	37.84
Tangerang	15	20.27	0	0.00	2	2.70	17	22.97
Total	20	27.03	26	35.14	28	37.84	74	100.00
District	Water		Human settlement		Roads		Total	
	IDR*	%	IDR*	%	IDR*	%	IDR*	%
Bekasi	6250	3.07	2952	1.45	6845	3.36	16048	7.88
Bogor	2500	1.23	12949	6.36	72551	35.61	88000	43.20
Lebak	2432	1.19	29531	14.50	19650	9.65	51614	25.34
Tangerang	21427	10.52	0	0.00	26623	13.07	48051	23.59
Total	32610	16.01	45433	22.30	125669	61.69	203713	100.00

Source: Ministry of Public Works (2009), unpublished data; * denotes IDR'000,000.

The survey was conducted with the direct beneficiaries of the job creation component of the fiscal stimulus that was implemented through the Ministry of Public Works. Baseline data on the programme's beneficiaries was not available, and therefore some retrospective questions were asked in the survey questionnaire. In addition, it was not possible to construct the sample using a 'control' and 'treatment' comparative approach due to resource constraints; therefore, the survey results are reported by looking at differences among beneficiary groups.

Information on the locations of projects funded by the fiscal stimulus was provided by the Ministry of Public Works for four selected districts in two provinces, namely, Banten and West Java. The two provinces were chosen as the development indicators of Banten and West Java tend to lie close to Indonesia's mean. For example, in 2007, the average human development index score for Indonesia was 70.6, with scores ranging between 63.4 and 76.6 in different regions. The scores of Banten and West Java were close to the mean, 69.3 and 70.7, respectively (Bappenas and Badan Pusat Statistik [BPS] 2010).

Project sites to be sampled were selected based on a stratified sampling strategy, which considered project size, project type, funding for local or national levels and geographic location. In total, there were 74 projects across 4 districts that formed the survey population (see Table 7.3). A total of 32 per cent (n = 24) of projects that were funded by the fiscal stimulus within the four districts were included in the survey sample.

Table 7.4 Sample size by district and project type

District	Water	Human settlement	Roads	Total		
	%	%	%	No. of projects	No. in sample	% of sample
Bekasi	8.16	0.47	10.26	5	81	18.88
Bogor	3.03	7.93	38.00	10	210	48.95
Lebak	0.47	0.47	6.99	4	34	7.93
Tangerang	6.99	0.00	17.25	5	104	24.24
Total	18.65	8.86	72.49	24	429	100.00

Source: Author's analysis from data courtesy of the ILO Country Office for Indonesia and Timor-Leste.

The total sample size was 429 (see Table 7.4). The minimum number of workers interviewed per project site was 4, and the maximum number was 21. For projects where activities were ongoing, workers who were present on the worksite were randomly selected. For works that had been completed, local village leaders and/or contractors were contacted in order to access the sample.

Descriptive techniques (cross-tabulations) were used to analyse the survey data. To analyse the level of congruency between the programme's inclusiveness of poor households, population-weighted household income deciles, using Indonesia's national socio-economic survey (SUSENAS) from August 2008 were derived for Java.[3] About 71 per cent (n = 306) of the sample came from the poor median of households in Indonesia, while about 29 per cent (n = 28.67) came from the more affluent median of households. Where appropriate, the data was also analysed by project type and by geographic location in order to explore the differences in participation and programme outcomes. Around 24 per cent (n = 103) of workers came from urban households, and about 76 per cent (n = 326) came from rural households.

Findings from the survey of the fiscal stimulus programme

The fiscal stimulus package (FSP) was designed to provide support to vulnerable groups of the working-age population and to temporarily boost demand in the context of an economic downturn. As the job creation component of the fiscal stimulus package was a crisis response programme that was developed in a relatively short period of time, a clear social target for the receipt of the social assistance was not identified. However, it would be expected that the wage-targeting mechanism of such an initiative would see the majority of the work opportunities going to poorer households or unemployed/underemployed workers.

The following sections analyse the results of the survey conducted with the beneficiaries of the fiscal stimulus package by considering the profile of workers' and their households, the participation of the local community in the project, employment conditions on the project, workers' previous labour market experience and their savings and debt trends.

Profile of the workers' households

The structure of the household, including the size, income and the number of wage-earners are important factors to be considered when assessing the effectiveness and efficiency of programmes with social protection functions. The overall situation of the household in comparison to the average is important, as is identification of where the household is positioned in terms of poverty estimates and income distribution.

In Indonesia in 2009, the poverty line was set at IDR 222,123 per capita per month for urban areas and IDR 179,835 per capita per month for rural areas (BPS 2012). Close to 12 per cent of people in urban areas and about 21 per cent of people living in rural areas fell below this line. Examination of the survey sample by poverty line suggests that approximately 8 per cent of the beneficiaries from urban areas and 17 per cent of beneficiaries from rural areas fell below the national per capita monthly poverty line. Initial comparison of the survey population with national data may lead one to question the initiative's inclusiveness of the poor. However, further examination of the data indicates that many respondents earned only slightly more than the poverty line, suggesting that much of the sample were vulnerable to shocks and susceptible to falling below the poverty line if their main source of income is disrupted.

The average monthly household income for the overall sample was IDR 1,790,123 (ranging between IDR 100,000 and IDR 11,000,000). With an average of 4.69 people per household, the average per capita monthly income for the sample was estimated at IDR 410,818. While the average per capita monthly income of beneficiaries is estimated at close to twice the average monthly per capita poverty line for Indonesia, it is far less than other measures, such as the Indonesian 'decent living needs' (Kebutuhan Hidup Layak – KHL), which forms the basis for determining the minimum wage (Ministry of Manpower and Transmigration [MOMT] 2014). The KHL was created in 2006 and indicates the minimum income that a single worker should earn in order to meet the basic needs, which includes food, clothing, transport and education, among others. It is used as a basis for determining the legal minimum wage by province and is generally set slightly above the minimum wage. The simple national average for KHL was IDR 1,010,372 per month for one worker in 2009 (IDR 917,638 for Banten and IDR 731,680 for Jawa Barat). It is therefore likely that a large number of households included in the sample were vulnerable and poor or near-poor. Households in such situations are particularly vulnerable during economic downturn as they tend to have limited savings and their main sources of income can become disrupted.

Table 7.5 Distribution of survey respondents by household income decile

Decile	Number of survey respondents	Per cent of survey respondents	Accumulative (%)
1 (lowest)	69	16.08	16.08
2	50	11.66	27.74
3	60	13.99	41.72
4	70	16.32	58.04
5	57	13.29	71.32
6	42	9.79	81.11
7	47	10.96	92.07
8	24	5.59	97.67
9	9	2.10	99.76
10 (highest)	1	0.23	100.00

Source: Author's analysis from data courtesy of the ILO Country Office for Indonesia and Timor-Leste.

To analyse distribution and the survey respondents' overall comparative position in society, population-weighted deciles based on household income, where 'Decile 1' represents the poorest 10 per cent of households and 'Decile 10' represents the richest 10 per cent of households, were derived for Java with the assistance of Statistics Indonesia.[4] The household income of the survey respondents was correlated with the population-weighted income deciles for Java to provide an insight on the degree to which jobs created from the fiscal stimulus went to households with different income levels. Analysis of the data by income decile allows for consideration of the survey respondents' overall position in society and provides insights that go beyond poor/non-poor poverty measures outlined earlier.

Table 7.5 shows that many of the jobs created through the job creation component of the fiscal stimulus package went to the poorest households in Indonesia. For instance, 16.1 per cent of survey respondents were from the poorest decile of households, while 71.3 per cent of survey respondents were from the poorest median of households in Java. Analysis through this measure indicates that the jobs created were broadly targeted towards low-income households, that is for every 10 jobs that were created, 7 went to the poorest median of households. This indicates that the intervention was a pro-poor intervention and included some of the most vulnerable households in Indonesia.

It was important for the youth to be included in the fiscal stimulus crisis response programme as labour market experiences during transition from education to the labour force can have an important influence on one's long-term outcomes in the labour market (International Labour Office [ILO] 2013a). Moreover, youth

Table 7.6 Participation of youth by household income

Income group	15 to 29	Above 29	Total
Lower median	41.83	58.17	100.00
Upper median	59.35	40.65	100.00
Average	46.85	53.15	100.00

Source: Author's analysis from data courtesy of the ILO Country Office for Indonesia and Timor-Leste.

unemployment is generally much higher than that of the overall labour force in Indonesia. For instance, in 2009, youth unemployment (15–24 years old) was 22.2 per cent, while unemployment overall for Indonesia was 7.9 per cent. Youth are five times more likely to be unemployed than the general population, and youth account for over 50 per cent of the unemployed population. During times of crisis, youth unemployment can become accentuated, as the number of unemployed people that are competing for the same job becomes greater. In such an environment, youth may be subject to a 'bumping down' effect, as employers choose to hire those with more experience and education, which can worsen their employment prospects.

On average, about 47 per cent of the surveyed beneficiaries were aged between 15 and 29 (see Table 7.6). This indicates that the jobs created from the fiscal stimulus were inclusive of youth. Participants from lower-income households were more likely to be older than participants from higher-income households.

Further consideration should be given to youth targeting and its role in such initiatives, as objectives such as supporting access to employment and reducing poverty may have different target groups. For example in general, the expenditure and consumption patterns of male youth differ from the expenditure and consumption patterns of women with children. Targeting strategies should consider how to optimise outcomes, include vulnerable groups and also take into consideration the spending patterns of those groups, as this will impact on how the initiative benefits households and communities. An initiative that is intended to address structural issues related to poverty will likely have a different target group to a programme that is seeking to provide short-term employment in response to economic downturn.

Notably, none of the survey respondents were women, signifying that women had limited access to the job opportunities created through the fiscal stimulus. In general, women have limited access to jobs in the construction sector, with only 2.4 per cent of jobs within this sector going to women in August 2009 (BPS 2012). Issues of gender inclusiveness in infrastructure investment programmes are therefore likely to be more related to sector-wide structural factors rather than the particular characteristic of the fiscal stimulus initiative. However, the findings of the survey indicate a need to enhance the gender inclusiveness of job creation initiatives, particularly those that are targeted to vulnerable groups and those that have social protection objectives. This is an important point, as transfers to women can strengthen the human and social capital outcomes of development efforts as women's expenditure patterns differ from men (McCord 2004).

While the direct participation of women in the fiscal stimulus package is likely to have been limited, it is important to note that women may have benefited from the spillover effects associated with the programme. Qualitative evidence from construction sites throughout Indonesia indicates that women are often involved in the gathering of local construction materials (stones and sand) and are remunerated on a piece-rate basis for these materials from the procurement allocations in project budgets prior to the commencement of construction works. In addition, local women often provide food vendor services to workers on construction sites during meal breaks. However, the economic viability of women's enterprises that provide small meals in such contexts is unknown but likely to be limited.

Participation of the local community

Infrastructure investment can provide important stimulation for local economic development. The outcomes of such investments can be optimised if local work opportunities go to members of local communities, as the multiplier effects of the investment have more opportunity to circulate within the local economy (ILO 2010). The employment of workers from outside the community/region may dilute the impact of the investment on the local economy due to wages being remitted outside the local area.

Findings from the data set collected indicate that work opportunities funded through the fiscal stimulus did not always go to local labourers. On average, only 33 per cent of jobs went to people from the local village, while 67 per cent of jobs went to people from outside the local village (see Table 7.7). Participants from

Table 7.7 Project location and workers' village of residence

Quintile	From the same village as project		From a different village to project		Total	
	No.	%	No.	%	No.	%
1 (poorest)	55	46.22	64	53.78	119	100
2	36	27.69	94	72.31	130	100
3	33	33.33	66	66.67	99	100
4	18	25.35	53	74.65	71	100
5 (richest)	1	10.00	9	90.00	10	100
Average	143	33.33	286	66.67	429	100

Source: Author's analysis from data courtesy of the ILO Country Office for Indonesia and Timor-Leste.

Table 7.8 Project location and workers' district of residence

Quintile	From the same district as project		From a different district to project		Total	
	No.	%	No.	%	No.	%
1 (poorest)	91	76.47	28	23.53	119	100
2	70	53.85	60	46.15	130	100
3	52	52.53	47	47.47	99	100
4	32	45.07	39	54.93	71	100
5 (richest)	3	30.00	7	70.00	10	100
Average	248	57.81	181	42.19	429	100

Source: Author's analysis from data courtesy of the ILO Country Office for Indonesia and Timor-Leste.

poorer households were more likely to have come from the same village that the project was operating in than participants from higher-income households.

Workers were more likely to have come from the same district (Kabupaten/ Kota) where the project was located; however, on average, 42 per cent of the sample came from outside the district (see Table 7.8). As mentioned, workers from poorer households were more likely to have come from the district where the project was located than participants from better-off households. Possible reasons for non-local labour accessing the employment opportunities may relate to the contractors' recruitment methods, the individual's access to labour market information, limited government engagement with the community and/or lack of local labour supply.

The reasons for use of non-local labour should be seen in light of the objectives of the fiscal stimulus and in light of the role of infrastructure investment in Indonesia. The fiscal stimulus investment intended to increase aggregate demand in order to circumvent an economic downturn; therefore, the main priority was not associated with emphasizing localised economic outcomes. However, consideration should be given to the policy's social protection objectives and the role of local labour and local resources in optimizing outcomes. Adopting eligibility criteria may be a possible strategy for ensuring outcomes are optimised.

In summary, the analysis found that only 58 per cent of workers employed on projects funded by the fiscal stimulus were residents of the district where the project was located. The remaining 42 per cent of workers came from outside the district. Given that the aims of the fiscal stimulus package were to maintain purchasing power, prevent job loss and accelerate development, the programme could have been more effective in achieving its goals if more jobs went to local labour. This is because local labourers tend to consume locally, which in turn stimulates growth in the local economy. Migrant workers tend to remit wages, and therefore, the overall impact of such workers on the local economy tends to be less.

Employment on the programme

Jobs created with funding from the fiscal stimulus package were intended to stimulate the economy and create short-term jobs in order to safeguard against the potential consequences of the economic downturn associated with the global financial crisis of 2008. The work opportunities generated were intended to be short-term jobs that would produce meaningful assets, which could lead to an increase in access to markets and services, thereby supporting improvements in growth and productivity in the longer term. To have achieved this outcome, it would have been important for recruitment practices to have allowed disadvantaged groups access to the work opportunities and for the work opportunities to support consumption smoothing.

Survey respondents were asked how they learned of the job opportunities that were to be created through the fiscal stimulus package. For most of the sample interviewed, the primary source of information regarding this work opportunity came from within their social networks rather than from formal networks (see Table 7.9). Workers from the poorer median of households were slightly more likely to learn about the work opportunity from friends than the more affluent median of households. Similarly, the more affluent median households were more likely to access labour market information from within their family network than poorer households. This reflects research that indicates that access to labour market information and employment opportunities are greatly influenced by the share of people in a person's social environment (MOMT 2009).

It is also interesting to see that workers from the poorer median of households were more likely to learn about the work opportunities from government officials or contractors than more affluent households. This may suggest that a pro-poor targeting strategy was being pursued. However, the high frequency of the use of informal networks suggests a need for further improvements in the sharing of labour market information through local democratic announcement mechanisms, in order to ensure that all members of the communities in which the projects are operating have equal access to employment opportunities. This

Table 7.9 Source of labour market information by household income (%)

Source	Lower median	Upper median	Average
Friend	68.63	65.04	67.60
Family	9.80	17.89	12.12
Government official	10.46	7.32	9.56
Contractor	10.78	8.94	10.26
Other	0.33	0.81	0.47
Total	100.00	100.00	100.00

Source: Author's analysis from data courtesy of the ILO Country Office for Indonesia and Timor-Leste.

may also help to ensure that more of the work opportunities go to workers in the local village or district rather than to workers from outside the local area.

From the time of the announcement of the fiscal stimulus and onwards, the Ministry of Public Works commenced planning processes to facilitate the implementation of the fiscal stimulus. However, the additional funding from the fiscal stimulus package only became available in July 2009 and had to be disbursed and reported on by 31 December 2009. Time needed for contract bidding and procurement meant that most works started in October 2009. Funds from the fiscal stimulus were to be spent by the end of the year, and the additional public holidays in December also limited the number of working days available for completion of works. These factors should be taken into consideration when evaluating the duration of the work opportunities.

Work opportunities funded through the stimulus package had an average duration of 47 days (see Table 7.10). Work on road projects went for a slightly shorter number of days than work on sanitation or irrigation projects. Workers from the poorer median of households tended to have a shorter duration of employment (45 days) than workers from more affluent households (53 days). Workers generally worked for six days per week, for eight hours per day.

The length of the average work opportunity created through the fiscal stimulus package (47 days) exceeds the average duration of work opportunities that are created through other similar programmes. For instance, the Ministry of Manpower and Transmigration's public employment programme provides 20 days of work per project package in 2009 (MOMT 2009). PNPM provided between 10 to 20 days of work for workers under its project during the same time period (Voss 2012). The longer duration of employment, and the associated increased wage–income transfer observed under the fiscal stimulus package, indicates that the programme may have been more effective at providing a social protection function and at maintaining purchasing power for its beneficiaries than other programmes.

While employed on the project, respondents most commonly worked as construction labourers. This reflects general trends within the construction sector, which indicate that approximately 91 per cent of construction sector jobs go to labourers (BPS 2010, MOMT 2009) (see Table 7.11).

Table 7.10 Average length of work opportunity by project type

Project type	Average number of days
Road and bridge works	46.06
Water and sanitation	49.21
Irrigation and water resources	49.81
Average	47.03

Source: Author's analysis from data courtesy of the ILO Country Office for Indonesia and Timor-Leste.

Table 7.11 Occupations in FSP projects and in the construction sector in 2009 (%)

Occupation	Occupations in FSP projects	Occupations in construction sector
Labourer	91.38	91.21
Supervisor	4.90	4.24
Clerical	1.86	1.87
Other	1.86	2.67
Total	100.00	100.00

Source: Author's analysis from data courtesy of the ILO Country Office for Indonesia and Timor-Leste and Baden Pusat Statistik (BPS) 2010.

The majority of workers were paid wages below IDR 50,000 per day. About 18 per cent of workers were paid above IDR 50,000 per day. In comparison, in 2009 the Ministry of Manpower and Transmigration's public employment programme provided a work incentive of IDR 40,000 per day to labourers, and anecdotal evidence from PNPM suggests that the work incentive on this programmes ranged between IDR 30,000 and IDR 50,000 depending on the prevailing local minimum wages in particular districts (MOMT 2009). Therefore, the wages paid to the beneficiaries of the fiscal stimulus were likely to be similar to the work incentives of similar programmes.

The access of poor and vulnerable households to the employment opportunities created through the fiscal stimulus package could have been improved through further efforts on project socialisation within the target areas by government officials. Given the short timeframe for project implementation, the outcome for employment duration was notable, and this suggests that the programme was effective in providing a consumption smoothing function for the beneficiaries of the programme. Most workers were employed as labourers and paid below IDR 50,000 per day, which is consistent with existing general wage trends for labourers within the construction sector.

Labour market experience

Previous economic crises in Indonesia have resulted in the loss of employment in the formal economy and an increase in the number of workers considered to be vulnerable. During and after the Asian Financial Crisis, many formal workers lost their jobs, and subsequently, self-employment in the agricultural and informal economy increased. Due to the structure of the labour market in Indonesia, such trends are not well reflected in unemployment statistics but can be seen in labour shifts between sectors and changes in employment status.

Lack of panel data and the limited number of questions in the labour force survey in Indonesia make it difficult to examine the labour market experience of individuals in terms of mobility, job security and labour market churning. In order to gain insight into the recent labour market experiences of fiscal stimulus beneficiaries, retrospective questions that provide insight into the previous occupation and sector that the respondent worked in were asked. Information about the gap between previous and current employment and plans after exiting the project were also asked. These questions provided information about mobility between sectors and insight on the individual's experience in the labour market.

Most respondents previously worked in the construction or agricultural sector. The most common previous occupations of respondents were as agricultural or construction labourers. Poorer households were more likely to have worked in agriculture, while more affluent households were more likely to have previously worked in construction. About 89 per cent of participants were previously active in the labour market, while close to 11 per cent reported that they were previously not active in the labour market. This may mean that the work opportunities extended by the fiscal stimulus resulted in the opening of opportunities for discouraged workers to (re)enter the labour market (see Table 7.12).

This finding is interesting as it shows that the jobs created through the fiscal stimulus gave opportunities for the poorest households in Indonesia to transition from agricultural to non-agricultural labour markets, where remuneration can be higher. While it is not possible to track the sustainability of this shift in the current study, it would be interesting to understand this occurrence in order to gain insights into whether the work opportunities created by the fiscal stimulus package provided just a 'blip' or a lasting impact in one's labour market experience. Such analysis could also provide insight into how a shift from the primary to the secondary and tertiary sectors can be optimised.

When workers were asked what they would do once work on this project was complete, 61 per cent reported that they would search for new employment, and 31 per cent noted that they would return to their previous employment (see Table 7.13). Only 3 per cent of workers considered starting their own business.

Table 7.12 Previous sector by quintile (%)

Quintile	Not in labour force	Agriculture, forestry, fishery	Construction	Transport/ communication	Other	Total
1 (poorest)	9.24	33.61	29.41	10.92	16.81	100.00
2	6.92	16.15	43.08	10.00	23.85	100.00
3	16.16	15.15	46.46	5.05	17.17	100.00
4	9.86	7.04	49.30	7.04	26.76	100.00
5 (richest)	30.00	0.00	60.00	0.00	10.00	100.00
Average	10.72	18.88	41.49	8.39	20.51	100.00

Source: Author's analysis from data courtesy of the ILO Country Office for Indonesia and Timor-Leste.

Table 7.13 Future labour market activities by household income quintile (%)

Quintile	Job search	Start business	Exit labour market	Continue previous job	Other	Total
1 (poorest)	49.6	1.7	2.5	42.9	3.4	100
2	67.7	4.6	3.8	23.8	0.0	100
3	64.6	2.0	4.0	29.3	0.0	100
4	62.0	2.8	4.2	31.0	0.0	100
5 (richest)	70.0	20.0	10.0	0.0	0.0	100
Average	61.1	3.3	3.7	31.0	0.9	100

Source: Author's analysis from data courtesy of the ILO Country Office for Indonesia and Timor-Leste.

Workers from the poorest quintile were more likely to continue their previous job (in the informal agricultural economy) than other quintiles. Similarly, workers from the better-off quintiles were more likely to look for new employment or start a business than poorer households.

In summary, most respondents previously worked in the construction or agricultural sector. The most common previous occupations of respondents were agricultural or construction labourers. The fiscal stimulus provided opportunities for discouraged workers to re-enter the labour market, with approximately 11 per cent of beneficiaries indicating that they were previously 'not in the labour force' before joining the programme. The jobs created through the fiscal stimulus gave an opportunity for the poorest households in Indonesia to transition from agricultural to non-agricultural labour markets, where remuneration is generally higher.

Most respondents reported that, once the work opportunities on this project were finished, they would either resume job search or their previous self-employment activities. In addition, approximately 25 per cent of beneficiaries indicated that they had given up or reduced alternative labour market activities in order to commit to this work opportunity. Therefore, the programme may have created some minor labour market distortion effects. However, as the majority of workers indicated that the wage on their previous job was higher than the wage on this job, the labour market distortion effects associated with the fiscal stimulus are unlikely to have been purely wage oriented. For instance, participants from the local village may have decided to participate in the programme in order to support asset construction as the new assets provide benefits (in terms of access) to their other economic activities. Furthermore, there was no evidence of deadweight loss (participants gaining jobs that they would have obtained without the programme) or substitution (participants being employed at the expense of others) or displacement (replacement of existing private or public sector workers) due to the fiscal stimulus programme.

Savings and debt

The average rate of savings among survey respondents was generally low, with only 13.5 per cent of the sample reporting that they had savings (see Table 7.14). The likelihood of having savings was much lower for the poorer median of households than the more affluent median of households. When respondents were asked whether their savings had increased since working on the project, more than 80 per cent of workers who had savings reported an increase. However, the overall low rate of workers with savings suggests that the wage income transfer from the project does little to enhance workers' ability to save.

Indonesia currently does not provide unemployment assistance and has only a limited number of other forms of social protection programmes that can support unemployed people of the working-age population. Subsequently, many workers become self-employed in unproductive work in the informal economy in order to cope. Self-employment in the informal economy often does not offer a stable or adequate source of income. Therefore, the ability to save during periods of regular wage employment and the duration of such work opportunities are of high importance.

In summary, as Indonesia has a limited number of programmes that provide support to the working-age population, it is important that the wage income transfer associated with government job creation programmes, such as the fiscal stimulus package, can improve the overall situation of beneficiary households. However, based on the analysis of saving and debt patterns, it is likely that the wage income transfer of the fiscal stimulus was largely used to support the daily consumption needs of households and that the households had limited access to microfinance. As maintaining purchasing power was the main purpose of the fiscal stimulus package, use of the wage income to support daily consumption was desired. However, it is noted that developmental impacts could potentially have been enhanced in the longer term if the income could have contributed to asset accumulation.

Discussion of findings

This survey of the beneficiaries who received the work opportunities from the 2009 fiscal stimulus package investigated factors such as the profile of workers'

Table 7.14 Savings patterns by household income (%)

Income group	Savings	No savings
Lower median	7.84	92.16
Upper median	27.64	72.36
Average	13.52	86.48

Source: Author's analysis from data courtesy of the ILO Country Office for Indonesia and Timor-Leste.

and their households, the participation of the local community in the project, employment conditions on the project, workers' previous labour market experience and their savings and debt trends. The survey provided insights into the ability of the government to quickly upscale government spending and administer employment creation programmes in times of financial and economic turmoil. The survey also shed light on the quality of the jobs that were created and on the degree to which the policy was inclusive of the poor and vulnerable households, which provides important information on the impact and effectiveness of the programme.

The findings of the survey indicate the following:

- Even though no poverty target was specified for the job creation component of the 2009 fiscal stimulus package, about 71 per cent of jobs went to households in the poorest median of households. These findings are similar to previous survey research that looked at job creation programmes during the Asian Financial Crisis and indicates that the work opportunities created from the fiscal stimulus package of 2009 were at least on par with, if not more, inclusive of vulnerable households than the previous crisis response programmes.
- The programme functioned as a social protection programme for low-income households through providing the primary source of income for beneficiary households, while it functioned as a supplementary income support programme for more affluent households.
- The programme was inclusive of youth, which was appropriate given the increased vulnerability that youth experience when entering the labour market in times of economic downturn. The programme was also inclusive of people with a lower educational attainment, with approximately 61 per cent of beneficiaries having a maximum of six years of schooling. However, women had limited access to the work opportunities of the fiscal stimulus package, and therefore further attention should be placed on the inclusion of women, in order to enhance the social protection function of the programme.
- Work opportunities funded through the stimulus package had an average duration of 47 days, which is longer than other similar programmes. The increased employment duration, and the associated increase in size of the wage income transfer, indicates that the programme may have been more effective at providing a social protection function and at maintaining purchasing power for its beneficiaries than other comparable programmes.
- Only 58 per cent of workers employed on projects funded by the fiscal stimulus were residents of the district where the project was located. The remaining 42 per cent of workers came from outside the district. While the aims of the fiscal stimulus package were to maintain purchasing power, prevent job loss and accelerate development, the programme could have been more effective in achieving its goals if more jobs went to local labour.
- Many people learned about the work opportunities funded by the fiscal stimulus package from their social networks, rather than official sources. The

access of poor and vulnerable households to the work opportunities created through the fiscal stimulus package could have been improved through further efforts on project socialisation within the target areas by government officials.

- Most workers were employed as labourers and paid below IDR 50,000 per day, which is consistent with existing general wage trends for labourers within the construction sector. Workers were also likely to accept a lower daily wage on this project than the daily wage that they had received in their previous job, which is indicative of a tightening labour market and reduced access to employment opportunities. This trend supports the justification for implementing a fiscal stimulus package.
- The fiscal stimulus provided opportunities for discouraged workers to re-enter the labour market, with approximately 11 per cent of beneficiaries indicating that they were previously 'not in the labour force' before joining the programme. It also provided work opportunities for workers who were previously unemployed.
- The jobs created through the fiscal stimulus gave an opportunity for the poorest households in Indonesia to temporarily transition from agricultural to non-agricultural labour markets, where remuneration can be higher. However, it is unclear if the fiscal stimulus intervention provided only a 'blip' or a lasting impact on the beneficiaries' labour market experience.

The analysis of the survey data indicates that, given the numerous constraints that government administrators face in preparing and administering a fiscal stimulus programme, the programme was effective and able to support the purchasing power of vulnerable groups. The survey indicated that the government could quickly increase government spending and administer employment creation programmes in times of financial and economic turmoil. Moreover, the survey provided information into the quality of the jobs that were created and on the degree to which the policy was inclusive of poor and vulnerable households.

The major strength of the job creation component of the fiscal stimulus package included the capacity of the government to design and implement a programme that provided employment outcomes that were at least at par with other ongoing government programmes within a constrained time period. The fiscal stimulus package was announced in January 2009, and the funds for implementing the programme only became available to the implementing ministries in late July 2009. Given the time needed for selection of works by location and type, and the time needed for bidding and approval processes, the average length of work opportunity of 45 days is an achievement, specifically in comparison with other programmes that create jobs and invest in village-level infrastructure. However, the outcomes of the fiscal stimulus package could have been strengthened through ensuring the provision of safeguards to improve transparency and socio-economic efficiency. For example the majority of workers learned about the work opportunities of the fiscal stimulus package through social networks; thus, the recruitment process for selecting workers was therefore largely informal.

Moreover, contractors are in a powerful position in that they are able to determine to a large extent who works on their projects.

Therefore, there is a need to increase the transparency of recruitment strategies through enhancing community socialisation processes or through usage of the public employment service, in order to improve access and inclusiveness. It is recommended that information about the projects should be disseminated as widely as possible to local communities through community notices and community meetings, so that people living in the areas where the projects are operating can access the work opportunities equally. A representative from the government could be invited to community socialisation meetings to support the inclusion of women and improve the access of poor and vulnerable households to work opportunities. Improving the socialisation process of the programme may also increase women's access to the programme. This is important as the results of the survey indicate that women did not directly benefit from the work opportunities generated through the fiscal stimulus package. In order for women to derive a greater benefit from the investment, they would need to be included in village meetings on development projects. Barriers related to gender-based occupational stereotypes also need to be addressed. The effectiveness and efficiency of such interventions could be increased if an explicit targeting strategy was adopted.

Due to the need for timely implementation of the fiscal stimulus package, targeting specifications of the job creation programme were limited to creation of a set number of short-term work opportunities. The programme's monitoring and evaluation activities were therefore limited to the tracking of budget realisation and overall job creation. It would be important to strengthen the monitoring and evaluation systems for implementing such programmes. It is important that government investments that contribute to broader socio-economic goals, such as social protection and maintaining purchasing power, are monitored so that future efforts can become more effective and efficient. It is recommended that monitoring systems collect data on infrastructure-related variables and on socio-economic variables. Government administrators should also have budget allocated for effectively monitoring and independently evaluating such programmes.

In order to enhance the impact of a fiscal stimulus programme, an explicit targeting strategy could be adopted to ensure that the investment reaches poor households and vulnerable groups. For instance, the Expanded Public Works Programme (EPWP) in South Africa specifies that 20 per cent of the work opportunities created will go to youth (Expanded Public Works Programme 2005). In addition, 30 per cent of the beneficiaries should be women, and 2 per cent of beneficiaries should be people with disabilities. Projects implemented by the ILO Country Office for Indonesia and Timor-Leste in Aceh and Nias Islands after the tsunami of 2004 have successfully demonstrated that 30 per cent of the work opportunities created in village- and district-level infrastructure investment projects can go to women (ILO 2013b). This sets an important benchmark for similar projects in Indonesia.

The Ministry of Public Works, as well as other ministries in Indonesia, have very limited monitoring and evaluation systems in place that record the progressive spending of budget allocations and progress towards other targets, including job creation. Often reports on targets are based on a comparison of original estimates with project completion reports rather than independent monitoring systems. The job creation targets for individual projects of the fiscal stimulus package were based on an assumption that approximately 30 per cent of the budget for these projects would go towards the wages of low-skilled and unskilled labourers. In order to improve the robustness of these targets, it would be beneficial to validate job creation outcomes more accurately and also to gain insight into other socio-economic variables. Such information could give insights into the effectiveness of the intervention's outreach to disadvantaged groups and into how the investment could be improved in order to enhance poverty reduction outcomes. In this regard, it would be useful to collect data on the inclusion of youth, women and low-income groups. Information on the labour market history of programme beneficiaries would also give insight into labour transfer and the degree to which such programmes are directly or indirectly responding to policy targets or reducing unemployment.

Under the current monitoring and evaluation system, administrative constraints see monitoring reports submitted late and monitoring units without the capacity to maintain data systems or the budget to undertake field monitoring missions. This limits the effectiveness of progressive monitoring activities and the responsiveness of monitoring officers to implementation issues in the field. Once projects are concluded, monitoring activities are handed over to evaluation units who then compare outcomes with planning targets. However, independent evaluation of the socio-economic outcomes of such programmes is rare.

The benefits of job creation include maintaining and developing local infrastructure – constructing and repairing roads and bridges; improving water supply, drainage and sanitation; and maintaining schools and hospitals. These projects all contribute to community capacity building and represent an investment for future development. However, in the context of the GFC and a slowdown in activity, the first concern is that of supporting community jobs and income.

Conclusion

This study has shown that it is possible to administer programmes that seek to create short-term work opportunities through emergency programmes that invest in infrastructure in the context of an economic downturn. The survey research undertaken in this study found that the work opportunities created through Indonesia's fiscal stimulus package of 2009 were inclusive of vulnerable households and provided on average 45 days of work to beneficiaries. The socio-economic outcomes of such programmes could be strengthened in the future through specifying social inclusion targets within policy documents and through investing in both administration and independent monitoring and evaluation systems.

In addition, an ongoing challenge is to ensure the appropriateness of fiscal stimulus and other similar policies, given the situation of the labour market and the persistence of informality, low productivity and limited access to social protection. The challenge is for policy in the future to come to grips with these issues as well as the socio-spatial dimensions of labour market inequalities. The persistence of poor public infrastructure, coupled with extensive labour underutilisation indicates potential for these broad and extensive societal problems to be addressed through an expanded public employment strategy for unskilled workers. Such an approach would seek to address local deficiencies in infrastructure (and could be extended to include social and environmental service), while stimulating localised economic development and drawing the most disadvantaged into the labour market.

Notes

1 The fiscal stimulus package was announced in the lead up to the April 2009 national legislative elections and the July 2009 presidential elections. Incumbent President Susilo Bambang Yudhoyono trumpeted the programmes and his broader stewardship of the Indonesian economy through the 2008 global credit crisis as reasons why he should be elected. Some of Yudhoyono's critics, however, suggest that the programmes amounted to vote buying ahead of the election.
2 Approximately AUD 7.3 billion; IDR 10,000 = Approximately AUD 1.
3 Population-weighted income deciles for Java were provided by BPS.
4 The population-weighted income quintiles for Java were prepared by Statistics Indonesia using the SUSENAS 2008 August survey.

References

Athmer, B. 2009, *The 2009 Indonesia economic stimulus package: potentials and advantages of employment-intensive approaches for infrastructure investments*, ILO Country Office for Indonesia and Timor-Leste, Jakarta, Indonesia (unpublished).

Baden Pusat Statistik 2010, *Labour force situation in Indonesia – August 2010*, KATALOG BPS 2303004, BPS, Jakarta

Bank of Indonesia 2009, *The 2009 revised budget fiscal stimulus programme: mitigating the impact from the global crisis*, Bank Indonesia, Jakarta, Indonesia.

Bappenas and Badan Pusat Statistik 2010, *Resilience in the midst of a global crisis: summary report of qualitative and quantitative assessments of global economic crisis impacts on households in Indonesia*, State Ministry for National Development Planning/Bappenas and Badan Pusat Statistik, Jakarta, Indonesia.

Bappenas and Badan Pusat Statistik 2012, Labourer *situation in Indonesia*, Badan Pusat Statistik, Jakarta, Indonesia.

Coordinating Ministry for Economic Affairs 2009, *Report on the fiscal stimulus package*, Coordinating Ministry for Economic Affairs, Jakarta, Indonesia (unpublished).

Expanded Public Works Programme 2005, *Guidelines for the implementation of labour-intensive infrastructure projects under the Expanded Public Works Programme (EPWP)*, 2nd ed., Government of South Africa, Pretoria, South Africa.

Froy, F., Giguère, S. and A. Hofer (eds.) 2009, *Designing local skills strategies, local economic and employment development (LEED)*, Organisation for Economic Co-operation and Development (OECD) Publishing, Paris, France.

International Institute for Labour Studies 2010, *Indonesia: reinforcing domestic demand in times of crisis*, Studies on growth with equity, International Labour Office, Geneva, Switzerland.

International Labour Office 2010, *Local resource-based approaches for infrastructure investment: source book*, ILO Sub-Regional Office for Southern Africa, Harare, Zimbabwe.

International Labour Office 2013a, *Labour and social trends in Indonesia 2013: reinforcing the role of decent work in equitable growth*, ILO Country Office for Indonesia and Timor-Leste, Jakarta, Indonesia.

International Labour Office 2013b, *Roads to hope*, ILO Country Office for Indonesia and Timor-Leste, Jakarta, Indonesia.

McCord, A. 2004, 'Policy expectations and programme reality: the poverty reduction and labour market impact of two public works programmes in South Africa', *ESAU Public Works Research Project Working Paper*, no. 8, Overseas Development Institute, London, UK.

Ministry of Public Works 2009, *Fiscal stimulus programme and budget*, Ministry of Public Works, Jakarta, Indonesia (unpublished).

Ministry of Manpower and Transmigration 2009, *General guideline for the national public employment programme for 2009*, MOMT, Jakarta, Indonesia.

Ministry of Manpower and Transmigration 2014, *Kebutuhan Hidup Layak di Indonesia, Tahun 2005–2013*, MOMT, Jakarta, Indonesia.

Voss, J. 2012, *PNPM-rural impact evaluation*, World Bank, Jakarta, Indonesia.

World Bank 2010, *National program for community empowerment in rural areas: Indonesia*, World Bank, Washington, DC.

World Economic Forum for Africa 2014, 'Forging inclusive growth, creating jobs', World Economic Forum – Africa Regional Forum, Abuja, Nigeria, 7–9 May 2014.

8 A participatory model of corruption resistance

The case of NGOs in India

Sten Langmann and David Pick

Introduction

Resisting corruption is both desirable and necessary in public sector organisations. This is because it is a fundamental requirement for ensuring the effective delivery of public services and for maintaining public confidence in government. There are number of contemporary challenges in encouraging resistance to corruption. In this chapter, we examine three contemporary challenges for corruption resistance faced by public sector organisations in India. First is the need to take into account the wide variety of situations and contexts that corruption can occur in; second is how to conceptualise it as a process, and third is to identify approaches for public sector organisations that go beyond a simple checklist (Menzel 2007). Progress towards meeting these challenges has been hampered by the elusiveness of a widely accepted definition of public sector corruption. For the purpose of this chapter, we define such corruption as unethical and illegal behaviour by public officials (i.e. serious misconduct and unlawful/corrupt behaviour) (Gottschalk 2012; Newburn and Webb 1999) who pursue their own interests 'through the intentional misdirection of organisational resources or perversion of organisational routines' (Lange 2008: 710).

To conceptualise corruption resistance, we draw on and synthesise existing research and theory in ways that provide an understanding of corruption resistance that is applicable at different levels of analysis. The main aim of this chapter is to explore what a multi-level framework might look like and what range of relevant variables should be incorporated into such a framework in order for research to be conducted to identify internal dynamics and causal pathways of corruption resistance in public sector organisations.

Corruption resistance has become of increased interest in the development and public administration literature, but its definition and use remain uncertain and inconsistent. Moreover, the variation in the scope and scale of perspectives on corruption resistance limits the ability of researchers to develop and test theory. Using an illustrative case example of the efforts of NGOs to build corruption resistance in the Indian public sector, the aim of this paper is to address some of these conceptual limitations associated with the study of misconduct resistance and contribute to an understanding of how capacity for corruption resistance can be built in the context of developing nations. This chapter contributes by synthesising and expanding existing theory and research into an integrative framework for researching, practicing and evaluating corruption resistance.

In this chapter, a definition of corruption resistance is outlined and an exploration of its scope and origins in the literature is presented. A framework for corruption resistance is then explained and illustrated by applying it to a case study of NGOs working in India. The article concludes with a discussion about the implications of the framework for research and practice in corruption-resistance capacity building.

Corruption resistance

In developing the concept of corruption resistance, we employ institutional theory as a foundation for our analysis. Institutional theory draws attention to the environment as a socially constructed context of action that shapes decisions made within organisations (DiMaggio and Powell 1983; Pursey, Heugens, and Lander 2009; Scott 1995) and provides a way of conceptualising organisations as nested systems of individuals, organisations, and political and social structures (Shadnam and Lawrence 2011). Taking such an approach, corruption resistance arises from forces outside public sector organisations' external forces (structures) and from within (agency). There is a body of research that alludes to agency and structure in discussing corruption resistance (e.g. Mulgan and Wanna 2011) and how they combine to establish corruption resistance through the 'the application of values, principles and norms in the daily operations of public sector organisations' as a 'a relative, evolving and culturally defined aspiration' (Evans 2012: 97–98). As such, corruption resistance can then be seen as being, at least in part, 'an ethical consciousness in [an] organisation and in the relationships [employees have] with members of other organisations, private and public' (Menzel 2007: 190) that ensures 'wholeness (stressing consistency), exemplary moral behaviour [and] the quality of acting in accordance with laws and codes' (Huberts and Six 2012: 159).

In this study, we develop the misconduct resistance model proposed by Pick, Issa and Teo (2013) (Figure 8.1) that has its origins in the Organisation for Economic Co-Operation and Development (1998) principles of public sector ethics and Menzel's (2007) two-by-two model of integrity/compliance. Drawing on these perspectives, we conceptualise corruption resistance as having two main elements: one that arises from external forces (structure) and the other from within public sector organisations themselves (agency). According to institutional theory, these forces drive conformity to sets of external (structural) codified anti-corruption principles that work in combination with organisational (agency) policies and practices that ensure public sector organisations are consistently robust in their resistance to corruption.

NGOs and corruption resistance in India

In this study, the typology outlined in Figure 8.1 is applied to examining the role of NGOs in building the capacity of the Indian public sector to resist corruption.

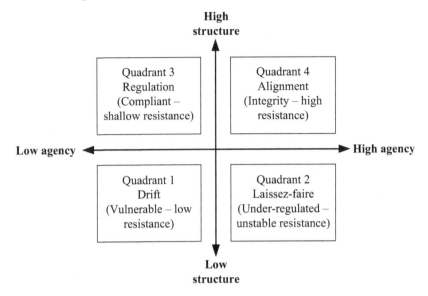

Figure 8.1 A typology of misconduct resistance
Source: Pick et al. (2013).

The situation in India can be characterised as being low in structural influences and low in agency influences, and like many developing nations, resistance to corruption in the Indian public sector is low (Peisakhin and Pinto 2010). India is ranked 85th out of 175 countries on the Corruption Perception Index (Transparency International 2014). This ranking is symptomatic of a deep-seated set of political, organisational, and governance problems in India (Sondhi 2000). Corruption is a way of life, being a daily norm, rather than an exception (Quah 2008) fostered by individual citizens needing to pay bribes out of necessity or to avoid inconveniences (Jenkins and Goetz 1999a).

Building resistance to corruption in India is important partly because the public administration and government organisations are comparatively weak and has changed little over the past three decades. Heidenheimer (1989) identified public-office-centred, market-centred, and public-interest-centred corruption. Jenkins and Goetz (1999b) identified difficulties in obtaining certified copies of government accounts, for example because officials are reluctant to release them, presenting a significant hurdle preventing sustaining an anti-corruption movement, which 'demands enormous attention to substantive detail and frequent and intensive confrontation with authorities' (Jenkins and Goetz 1999a: 42). An increasing number of policy makers and organisations, including NGOs, have taken an interest in increasing the ability of the Indian public sector to resist corruption (Sondhi 2000). This movement is aimed at promoting accountability, fairness, and transparency in the public administration system in India (IMI Konnect 2014). Efforts to increase structural influence include the Right to

Information Act and Lokpal Act in 2013 (IMI Konnect 2014), but they have so far proven to be ineffective for several reasons relating to the low level of agency influences.

There is a lack of political will, referred to as 'the demonstrated credible intent of political actors to attach perceived causes or effects of corruption at a systemic level' (Kpundeh 1998: 92). Political will is an important ingredient in effective anti-corruption efforts. Political leaders must provide the direction in resources, laws, agencies, and punishment against corruption, yet India's lack of political will is manifested in the public perception that its investigative bureau, the Central Bureau of Investigation (CBI), is 'a pliable tool of the ruling party, and its investigations tend to become cover-up operations for the misdeeds of ministers' (Gill 1998: 238). Second, India's anti-corruption efforts are hindered by structural factors, most notably, an unfavourable public policy context, defined by Leichter (1979: 40) as 'a simultaneous interplay of more than one situational, structural, cultural, or environmental influence'. However, India's extreme diversities and disparities on many levels, such as geographical, economic, demographic, and political ones, make it difficult to find strong common denominators (Quah 2008). India's complex four-level administrative structure (central, state, local, and district) makes anti-corruption efforts difficult, as well as governing this on an area of over 3 million km^2 with a heterogeneous population of over 1 billion (Quah 2008). A study by Manzetti and Wilson (2007) reveals that countries with weak democratic structures yield corrupt governments. Therefore, political reforms in those countries are not likely to gather support (Calvo and Murillo 2004), and therefore there is little incentive to reform public administration structures. This generates a common mindset among people, including those in India, that the corruption status quo cannot be changed (Tummala 2002). Therefore, India's development is not founded in and supported by 'blueprints given by the political leadership independently of the civil society, but is often a joint output of the civil society itself' (Sondhi 2000: 4). In spite of efforts to improve structural and agency influences, the situation in India remains locked in Quadrant 1 of the typology (see Figure 8.1).

Corruption resistance capacity building through participation

One major effort to develop the influence of agency is encouraging public participation in mainstream development. This has been a topic of debate since the mid-1970s in an effort to make corruption resistance more effective (Cohen and Uphoff 1980). By the 1980s, community participation became synonymous with cost-and-benefit sharing and project efficiency and effectiveness (Bamberger 1986) but less so with empowerment or capacity building (Cornwall 2002). At that time, participation was pragmatic rather than principled (Cornwall 2008). In India, the work of many anti-corruption activist groups went beyond a 'silent revolution' towards more active involvement and mobilisation of people against corruption (Jenkins 2007). It was Mazdoor

Kisan Shakti Sangathan (MKSS), otherwise known as the Organisation for the Empowerment of Women and Peasants, who fought corruption by engaging the public in corruption investigation and exposure (Jenkins 2007). Furthermore, the MKSS's knowledge-sharing approach of setting up tents in visible spots, presenting government reports, and hearing testimonies by local people transformed ordinary people into citizen-auditors, further establishing a direct link between access to government-held information and corruption resistance (Jenkins 2007). However, structurally, the influence remained weak as MKSS failed to provide support for the development of agency in the form of grass-roots initiatives enabling ordinary people to audit public spending at the local levels, mainly due to those movements having been compromised themselves (Jenkins and Goetz 1999a).

In the 1990s, however, a new approach arose in corruption discussion, leading to a second wave of corruption-resistance capacity-building efforts (Jenkins 2007) in which NGOs played an increasingly important role in corruption resistance (Cornwall 2002; Hulme and Edwards 1997; Sondhi 2000). In the mid-1990s, NGOs and social movements worked to improve anti-corruption by increasing the influence of agency factors in the form of mobilizing citizens to tackle the failure to 'prioritize poor people's concerns' (Jenkins 2007). Enabling voice and participation has become a central method for NGOs to fight corruption and build capacity of informed choices. Civil society, when mobilised effectively, can pressure reforms and governance, 'addressing the state to operate in an accountable, transparent, and responsive manner' (Sondhi 2000: 22). Anti-corruption campaigners especially charted a different course of action by mobilizing ordinary people, where 'excluded individuals could find a collective presence and voice' (Cornwall 2002: 5), focusing on local levels, in which corruption has become a daily routine (Jenkins 2007). However, mainstream participatory approaches became lost in market terminology, for example labelling participants as 'consumers' (Cornwall and Gaventa 2001), altering participation and empowerment to 'stakeholder' and 'ownership' (Cornwall 2002).

Attention was then focused on combining agency and structure in the form of political participation, a move towards a more rights-based approach to participation. Cornwall (2002) argues that the challenge for participation is to understand who is included and excluded in activities and the 'importance of situated invited participation alongside other kinds of spaces that citizens themselves shape and choose', which are critical for both developing capabilities and meaningful engagement. We argue that for public sector organisations to develop and maintain their integrity, as well as advancing corruption resistance in India, it is important to understand the different capacities of public participation in agency and structural terms.

Participation and corruption resistance

The idea of public participation has found strong resonance across a spectrum of organisations including NGOs (Cornwall 2008; Pretty 1995). A good point of departure to discuss participation is its typology, in which Arnstein's (1969) ladder of participation is one of the most widespread concepts. Participation, according to Arnstein (1969), originates from the citizen, drawing on citizen power, tokenism, and non-participation. Citizen power includes citizen control, delegated power, and partnership, whereas tokenism includes consultation, informing, and placation (Arnstein 1969), with tokenism linking closely to the development efforts of giving information as a form of participation (Cornwall 2008). Cornwall (2008) and others criticise the tokenism approach to legitimising decisions, its information exchange providing the illusion of participation, yet showing an expert culture of dominant development organisations, reinforcing elitist, ethnocentric, anthropocentric, and technocentric policy design and action (Hjorth 2003; Hove 2004). Non-participation in Arnstein's (1969) ladder of participation then is closely associated with therapy and manipulation, in a development context often presented in clear-cut ways that define 'what works' and 'what does not work' without addressing contextual circumstances (Torres 2001).

Pretty (1995) classifies participation as ranging from being 'bad' (manipulative and passive participation) to 'better' (functional and interactive) including self-mobilisation. In this way, attention is turned to combining structural resistance to corruption with agency resistance (self-mobilisation) as a form of participation, in which individuals take initiatives (Pretty 1995). Nevertheless, the key point in this participation typology is that self-mobilisation spreads if 'governments or NGOs provide an enabling [structural] framework of support [which] may or may not challenge existing distributions of wealth and power' (Pretty 1995: 1252). For our case example, the key in this approach is the enabling framework by NGOs as a form of structural resistance in promoting self-mobilisation of agency. Note here that both Arnstein's (1969) theory and Pretty's (1995) theory operate on continuums of control by authorities and control by the citizens.

The World Bank refers to this as 'popular participation', defined as participation in which the people who are affected, especially the disadvantaged, choose and influence decisions affecting them (Rudqvist and Woodford-Berger 1996). Popular participation does not just refer to participation of people in 'absolute poverty' but people discriminated on other grounds, such as gender and ethnicity (Rudqvist and Woodford-Berger 1996).

Structural corruption resistance, coupled with a shift in power and control to citizens, occurs at different levels, degrees, or kinds (Rudqvist and Woodford-Berger 1996). Relating this corruption resistance capacity-building efforts of NGOs, a self-mobilising approach to structural resistance provides a spark 'that can lead to popular engagement around particular issues or to changes in attitude among workers or officials' (Cornwall 2008: 274). On the other hand, the most transformational of actions or intentions can fail, if the beneficiaries simply do not take part in it, leading to the importance of investigating participants and who are included in the projects and who are excluded (Cornwall 2008). As Cornwall (2008) rightfully argues, participation is never a seamless process, operating on a realm of contestation, shaping and reshaping actions, based on power and project differences among its actors.

The issue

While we have so far provided an insight into the roles of structural and agency factors in corruption resistance in the form of public participation, there remains a number of theoretical challenges to achieving a greater understanding of the connection between corruption resistance and public participation which need to be addressed.

First, the overall theoretical coverage of participation in relation to corruption resistance is limited. The topics themselves (structure, agency, corruption resistance, participation) have found resonance in the literature, yet the links between these concepts appear largely under-theorised, and no conceptualised framework has been designed yet to illustrate their links of action, reaction, outcomes, and impacts. Second, participation in relation to corruption resistance appears to be largely based on monitoring roles and supervision. The literature summarised the participatory activities of participants being primarily investigative energies and exposure of corruption, as well as sympathy from former bribe-takers in corruption exposure (Jenkins 2007; Jenkins and Goetz 1999a). Third, it appears that the structures in the literature appear to remain the main drivers of corruption resistance, with public participation being secondary to that activity. Cornwall's (2002) explanation of participants becoming stakeholders, perhaps even consumers, suggests that organisations remain the 'gatekeepers' of power, which does not promote citizens to participate in Pretty's (1995) ladder beyond functional participation towards a self-mobilisation approach. Jenkins (2007, p. 68) argues that civil engagement on its own cannot bring about this transformation, 'but flexible alliances that empower people to expose corruption will remain essential to making the Indian state more accountable and competitive politics more inclusive'. We conceptualise this flexible alliance in the form of a participatory structure/agency framework.

Participatory framework for corruption resistance

Based on the literature and emphasis on institutional theory as a foundation for corruption resistance via participation, we propose a participatory framework as a composition of three interconnected components. The first box is composed of drivers, which represent the range of influences internal to organisations that run against corruption. The main driver of an organisation is adaptation, influenced by employee characteristics and citizen drivers. These drivers serve as the foundation for the process of participation, as depicted in the second box. Participation against corruption is achieved via integration (storing and managing information given) and self-mobilisation (acting independently to the organisation with that information). This interplay of integration and self-mobilisation of participation forms a feedback loop back to drivers, potentially improving aspects in the adaptation process. The foundations of drivers for participation lead to a third box, relating to outcomes. In this part of the model, attention is paid to organisational environment (e.g. culture), systems and process outcomes (e.g. policies and practices), and citizen outcomes (e.g. peoples' well-being). Together, the outcomes

Participatory Agency Model:

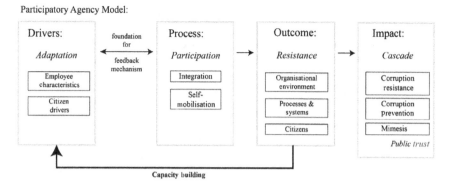

Figure 8.2 Participatory agency model

have potential external impacts (i.e. results relating to broader community concerns) but also in turn have implications for capacity building for corruption resistance. The participatory agency model of corruption resistance is illustrated in Figure 8.2 and will be described in more detail in the following sections.

Our framework incorporates components identified in other frameworks and research but configures them in a way that suggests causal relationships among the components and elements.

Drivers

The first component of the participatory models refers to drivers, which is the starting point of corruption resistance based on the idea of combining structure with agency (see Figure 8.1). Three major influences are evident: adaptation, employee characteristics, and citizen drivers.

The first is adaptation. This refers to the propensity for organisations to reconfigure their composition, plans, policies, and practices in response to and in anticipation of changes in the environment in which they operate (North 1993) and/or to influence situations or problems they face (Emerson, Nabatchi, and Balogh 2012). As such, it represents the ability of individual public sector organisations, managers, and employees to differentiate themselves from other public sector organisations and influence the broader public policy context.

Adaptation is an important element in corruption resistance. In the case of the environment, there are a number of ways that organisations adapt. Public sector managers have an important role in developing and implementing policies and procedures and fostering positive employee orientations to corruption resistance (Lee et al. 2013). In spite of this, there is little research that examines this area. One notable exception is Abbink (2004) who found that staff rotation policies may be a useful tool for developing corruption resistance; however, the research was an experimental laboratory research design providing pointers as to how such policies would play out in practice. There are four mechanisms that managers can deploy: policies and procedures that limit employee freedom of action, a consequence/reward system, educating employees about external requirements, and encouraging attitudes among employees that are amenable to resisting corruption (Lange 2008). The strength of including adaptation, when theorising about corruption resistance is that it draws attention to the idea that agency is not just about organisational control; it is also about how individual employees respond.

When considering agency factors, *employee characteristics* and how they interact with management are important considerations. Gordon, Clegg, and Kornberger (2009: 94) argue that relying simply on ensuring compliance with organisational policies and procedures in public sector organisations is not sufficient because it 'takes power relations for granted . . . rather than understanding them as crucial to the process of making sense of rules and situated contexts' instead focus should be on the day-to-day practices of employees and 'the learned routines of doing things'. In the area of employee characteristics, the demographic profiles of organisations should be considered. Frank, Lambsdorff, and Boehm (2011) report that women are less susceptible to corruption than men in a small, laboratory-based study. While it is not clear how such characteristics impact behaviour in the real world, it does raise the need to take into account the demographic profile of an organisation and the traits of employees. Age and length of service are also important demographic factors in affecting corruption resistance of individual employees. Those that are longer serving and older are more resistant to corruption (Pelletier and Bligh 2006).

Looking more closely at employee characteristics, it is important that organisations have highly professional, well-paid, and motivated employees in order to be corruption resistant (Meagher 2005). More specific research suggests that an important employee characteristic is the psychological contract (PC) that exists between them and their employer composed of salary and promotion prospects, resourcing and equipment, the level of honesty, professionalism and collegiality, and the degree of responsibility employees have for their actions (Kingshott and Dincer 2008). Indeed, 'strong PC, positive corporate society and high citizenship behaviour can work together in reducing the likely incidence of corruption within the public service' (Kingshott and Dincer 2008: 81). To develop such an environment, it is clear that good leadership is important (Kim et al. 2009; Lee et al. 2013). Pelletier and Bligh (2006) take up these themes in their examination of employee perceptions, finding that organisational-level factors and the behaviour of leaders are important in the success of ethics programmes in the public sector. This work is important in that it identifies and connects variables such as employee demographic characteristics to employee reactions in the form of perceptions.

Citizen drivers in this framework describe the essential support from the public towards an NGO and its efforts in corruption resistance. Maxwell, Rosell, and Forest (2003: 1031) rightfully argue that 'citizens' values should define the boundaries of action in a democracy' and therefore also those of organisations. The authors argue, that in a political and policy-setting context, legitimacy and sustainability are dependent on the underlying public values (Maxwell et al. 2003). We argue that the legitimacy and sustainability of corruption resistance is equally dependent on public values and also support. Combining the public's roles as initiators, beneficiaries, taxpayers, and members of a community, their active involvement is vital to the success of an organisation's effort to corruption resistance. We therefore overall propose that the presence of agency drivers is necessary, combined with a public initiative, for corruption resistance to be present.

Process

The process part of our framework highlights the overall importance of participation of citizens in public affairs. We discussed earlier that NGOs since the mid-1990s have utilised investigative energies of the public, as well as focusing on local-level 'routinized corruption', where citizen participation would have the most impact (Jenkins 2007). The overall focus on participation in this framework is then broken down into integration and self-mobilisation.

Integration in this framework describes the process that involves the storing and managing of information that participants receive from the NGO. This information can consist of goals, activities, practices, values, and outcomes, as well as tangible anti-corruption material. These are provided by the previously established agency drivers and serve as a foundation for anti-corruption participation and practices. It is important to note here that motivation by participants is a strong influence in the absorptive capacity of an NGO's agency and determines how willing its members are to learn new things. It also influences the inclination of using that knowledge but also the possibility of rethinking the current methods and philosophies of NGOs, providing a feedback loop from participation to agency.

The integration process serves as a strong catalyst for *self-mobilisation* by participants. We adopt Cornwall's (2008: 272) definition of self-mobilisation, which describes 'people [participating] by taking initiatives independently of external organisations to change systems. Self-mobilisation can spread if government and NGOs provide an enabling framework of support'. This serves two purposes. First, participation no longer serves as a pretence, a token where the people have no actual power, but does challenge existing distributions of power (Cornwall 2008). The participants themselves decide on their methods of implementation, though backed with a framework and suggestions of the underlying NGO. Second, this in turn provides a feedback loop from the participants to the NGOs with suggestions of improvement of delivery of concepts, as well as possible refinement, influencing the adaption within the agency drivers. Our overall argument in the process part of the participatory agency model is that the highest capacity to resist corruption arises when the public is given participation power and self-determination, backed by organisations' frameworks, which are integrated and mobilised by people to resist corruption.

Outcomes

The outcomes of building corruption resistance in NGOs to date have not been well researched. There is much research about *how* to build corruption resistance for example Anechiarico's (2010) work on the effectiveness of anti-corruption agencies in developing and supporting networks. However, there is little research on the outcomes of such activities. There is also research that demonstrates the role of individuals in corruption resistance. This is especially the case when people in organisations resist social pressures that might lead them into misconduct (Pursey, Heugens, and Lander 2009). In our framework, we focus on outcomes that can be discerned in the organisational environment, processes and systems, and citizens, leading to capacity building.

Improvements in the *organisational environment* are an important outcome of enhanced corruption resistance. The key areas are ethical climate, ethical culture, and codes of conduct (Kish-Gephart, Harrison, and Treviño 2010). Since ethical climate and culture are predictors of conduct (Pinto, Leana, and Pil 2008), improvements in these should improve corruption resistance, in particular, the shift from a culture of mistrust to one of trust (Pelletier and Bligh 2006).

Systems and processes that control networks and maintain and improve the effectiveness of NGOs are a significant outcome of enhanced corruption resistance. These create a 'model of bureaucracy and policy formulation that can integrate the reality of personalised relations and social networks whilst ensuring decisions are always made in the interest of the 'the public alone' (Warburton 2001: 235). This is important because it takes into account the issue of contagion. Along with cognitive, emotional, and psychosocial factors, networks contribute to 'the normalization and institutionalization of organizational corruption' (Beenen and Pinto 2009: 284). Effective corruption resistance brings with it organisational designs and practices that not only inhibit corrupt networks but also encourage corruption-resistant networks (Pinto, Leana, and Pil 2008).

For *people* who work in NGOs, as well as participatory citizens outside the organisation, a significant outcome of corruption resistance is reduced ambiguity and uncertainty about what is acceptable and unacceptable conduct. Improved awareness and intuition, coupled with rationalisation and reasoning, facilitates the development of effective approaches that prevent corruption (Murphy and Dacin 2011). Corruption resistance then arises from the ability of organisations to enable employees to recognise dissonance. This provides both NGOs and citizens with the ability to examine and change organisational policies and practices. Cunha and Cabral-Cardoso (2006: 221) argue that, 'for that to occur, conditions must be created for reflection around the normalization process'. A clue to what might be at the core of this 'normalization' is the idea of 'deontic principles' ('acting fairly towards others is a required duty') are associated with an intention to resist corruption (Beugré 2010). While there is research evidence relating to organisational outcomes of corruption resistance (e.g. improved organisational environment, less ambiguity), there is little or no research that examines the outcomes for individual employees. We therefore overall argue that outcomes of corruption resistance include an enhanced organisational environment and a reduction in ambiguity. This is likely to have a positive effect on the overall well-being and both NGOs and participants of anti-corruption movements.

External impacts

The external impacts of the participatory agency model describe the impacts and the cascades that both the NGOs and the participants have on the wider society. We argue that this participatory agency approach impacts corruption resistance and corruption prevention. The two are treated separately here, as corruption resistance aims at reducing existing problems of corruption and corruption prevention sketches efforts to avoid corruption in future transactions among organisations or between organisations and citizens. This provides fertile ground for mimesis, an emulation of anti-corruption practices by either other organisations or citizens.

Corruption resistance and prevention

Corruption resistance in this framework describes the wider effects of resistance, which are explained in the outcome section. Corruption resistance here can be interpreted in both a micro and macro perspective, focusing on the participating citizens, who refuse to pay bribes for services. Corruption resistance in a micro perspective describes the citizens' refusal to pay bribes for individual services. This is resultantly underlined by a mindset of corruption resistance, forming a macro-perspective to resistance, translating this concept into a normative state in which corruption is seen as the 'unusual'.

Corruption prevention on the other hand provides the idea of a prophylactic effect that corruption resistance by the bribe-giver has and is concerned primarily with the bribe-taker. We argue in our framework that resistance of bribe-giving will affect the attitude and mindset of the bribe-taker, countering the urge to take bribes and corruption as a norm for the exchange of services for which the bribe-taker gets paid.

Mimesis

Mimesis or the tendency to imitate is evident in public sector organisations in that they tend to look towards and imitate other public sector organisations (Frumkin and Galaskiewicz 2004). This means that mimetic pressures that come to bear on public sector organisation tend to arise from within the public sector itself. Kim et al. (2009) outline this effect in the development of e-government anti-corruption systems in Korea. Such mimetic forces that encourage corruption resistance may come in the form of model integrity systems formulated in one organisation being adopted sector-wide. We argue that this leads to an overall public trust, extended from citizens to organisations and between organisations, opening up channels for activities in poverty reduction, infrastructure, and services development, to an overall country development.

Public trust

A key impact of corruption resistance is public trust. This is important to the effective functioning of organisations, especially in the public sector, and has thus received a great deal of attention by researchers. Research by Anechiarico (2010) connects corruption resistance to public trust and the overall quality democratic life. This involves public sector organisations 'getting their processes right, treating people fairly, avoiding favouritism and containing corruption' (van Ryzin 2011: 755). Maintaining public trust ensures that citizens have confidence in public sector organisations (Salminen and Ikola-Norrbacka 2010). This trust is developed and enhanced through avoiding negative media coverage (Pelletier and Bligh 2006) and encouraging positive media coverage and achieving accreditation (Pursey, Heugens, and Lander 2009). Accordingly, our proposition in relation to the connection between corruption resistance and public trust is that corruption resistance will positively impact on the levels of trust in public sector organisations held by external actors. We propose that corruption resistance capacity will become greater and more sustainable over time as the outcomes of resistance increase positively impacts on both the public and organisations.

To illustrate this framework practically, we present a case study of an NGO in Chennai, India, which utilises a self-mobilising participatory approach to create awareness of corruption and to counter corruption by campaigning against it and assisting people to engage in resistance misconduct.

Case study

India has witnessed a strong population movement to eradicate corruption, and promote accountability, fairness, and transparency to the large administrative system (IMI Konnect 2014). Both the Right to Information Act and Lokpal Act in 2013 were steps in that direction (IMI Konnect 2014); however, they do not follow up with modifying human behaviour in that system, especially that of the bribe-taker. Enabling voice and participation has become a central method for NGOs and other organisations to fight corruption and build capacity of informed choices. To illustrate this and to support our proposed framework, we present a case study of an NGO fighting corruption and its awareness-based method.

The chosen NGO (NGO 1) is based in Chennai, Tamil Nadu, and its mission is to empower Indians to live corruption-free lives. Their argument is that ordinary people seldom provide resistance when asked by corrupt officials to pay bribes. The organisation stands for avoiding paying a bribe for services that people are entitled to and provides the organisational backing that people resisting corruption are not resisting alone.

The NGO was chosen as a case study for its participatory corruption resistance approach and its effect. The case is unique in that the organisation used a both creative and effective participatory tool for corruption resistance – the Zero-Rupee Note (Figures 8.3 and 8.4), reminding people of their rights and alternative solutions to corruption. The study was conducted in 2012 as part of a larger study to explore different NGO approaches to reduce poverty. A semi-structured interview with the founder and director of the NGO was conducted. The interview was focused on their motivation of corruption resistance and

Figure 8.3 The Zero-Rupee Note – front view

Note: Reproduced with permission.

Figure 8.4 The Zero-Rupee Note – back view

Note: Reproduced with permission.

how the Zero-Rupee Note aids in that vision. The interview was coded in NVivo, as this coding approach is suitable for action research (Stringer 1999) and prioritises the participant's voice and phrases over the interpretation of the researcher.

This, in turn, allows Adler and Adler (1994: 381) to suggest a write-up of veri-similitude, 'a style of writing that draws the reader so closely into subjects' worlds that these can be palpably felt'. We argue that such written accounts produce a higher plausibility and coherence to what the reader might know from his/her own experiences and gives the text a greater sense of authenticity.

The Zero-Rupee Note

NGO 1 claims that corruption widens the gap between rich and poor and empowers only those with capacity to pay. This realisation leads NGO 1 to an ideology that a change in mindset is fundamental in corruption resistance, aiming to empower Indians to love corruption-free lives. The participant said:

> We want to create a new generation of citizens, who will think and act differently towards the problem of corruption. Our objective is . . . to empower the majority of Indians to know how to get their things done without paying bribes.

NGO 1 is actively seeking to change the mindsets of individuals in India via direct empowerment and promoting independence and a 'disconnect' against the system. For that, NGO 1 engages public citizens, as they are directly affected and suffering the most from the unceasing corruption in India. Corruption, in their opinion, affects people both physically and psychologically, linking to disempowerment via an almost volunteered lack of realizing capacities. The participant explained these physical and psychological hardships as follows:

> Citizens cannot get a certificate, cannot get a job, cannot get anything that is related to the government, cannot get anything done in a timely manner, let alone the frustration and the humiliation and the money involved in it.

However, NGO 1 does not only address corruption resistance from a bribe-giver perspective, but also from a bribe-taker perspective. Millions of people in India struggle for a daily income, a livelihood, or a job. The demand for government jobs far outstrips the supply of such jobs. Applicants for jobs are able to buy jobs, making life miserable for poorer people who cannot afford to buy a job The person who bought the job has to take back that investment preferably in the first or second year of the job, which thereafter does not stop but becomes an addictive habit to take bribes and enhance his or her lifestyle.

The approach NGO 1 has chosen is a concept called the Zero-Rupee Note, a larger than a regular Indian Rupee note (see Figures 8.3 and 8.4). On the back of the note is the NGO's main message to not engage in corruption and to consult India's Right to Information Act (2005), to understand their rights and procedures in 'promoting transparency and accountability in the work of every public authority' (Right to Information Act 2005). A legal requirement of the Zero-Rupee Note is to explicitly state that is it not a currency. The Zero-Rupee Note is a concept and tool for NGO 1 to initiate questions and doubt in the bribe-taker's mind as to the purpose of this note and his or her stance in corruption. NGO 1 describes their activities against corruption as follows:

> There is something called the Zero-Rupee Note. It is our device. We started printing it in large numbers and distributing it.

The Zero-Rupee Note is a distributive tool, carried by participants who are resisting corruption. The members of the NGO print this note in large quantities and distribute it to participants via their offices that exist throughout the country, as well as supplying citizens, who participate in the distribution to their friends and family, as well as gathering support for the cause on their own.

The note is given from the NGO to the resisting citizen to the bribe-taker, whenever either corruption occurs in their lives or when they observe corruption. Handing this note to the concerned bribe-taker by the citizen is both a symbol of resistance to pay bribes, as well as a social statement to the bribe-taker not to accept bribes. That the Zero-Rupee Note is larger than normal and made of thin cardboard makes it difficult for the receiving officials to fold the note and hide in their pockets, as well as the note drawing attention from bystanders to the official. The effect of this organised resistance attempt is to change the minds of both the bribe-giver and the bribe-taker. The effect was described by the participant as follows:

> [The Zero-Rupee Note] acts as a change agent and got people their rights immediately without having to argue. The moment you hand the Zero-Rupee Note to the official, they immediately have a change of mind. One is that they are scared, and two, they are uncertain who that person is. At the end, they come to a conclusion that they do not want trouble with the person and get the job done without any bribe.

The outcome of this practice is that people refrain from corruption and break the cycle of the bribe-taker receiving bribes, allowing other people to receive services from that official without taking a bribe. This action is witnessed by bystanders and acts as a catalyst for further distribution of the note, as well as participatory support. The NGO has successfully run on this strategy for five years, its concept having found international recognition including from both the UN and Transparency International, as well as partnering with other NGOs in India.

The Zero-Rupee Note is an effective tool to build capacity in a corruption resistance context in that it is a reminder for people of their rights against corruption and allows for action as a non-violent statement to condemn bribery. It is not a prescriptive tool that directs people in its use but provides a method to utilise in whichever capacity they seem fit. This in turn breaks the cycle of conformity of bribe-giving to bribe-taking, increasing capacity in that it allows its carrier to stand firm for their rights and not paying bribes. As a result, corruption resistance and corruption prevention benefit the resisting party in that the money that was initially required to obtain a service from officials can be used for other things and the frustration and humiliation associated with the process disappears. The note also builds capacity in that it becomes a catalyst for improved access and equity for people depending or relying on public services, for example licensing services or food subsidiaries. Corruption resistance, with the initiative of the Zero-Rupee Note and its associated institutional backing, shapes citizens into monitors of the operation and functioning of public institutions, questioning the status quo of corruption and uncovering alternative methods of functioning.

Conclusion

Drawing from the case study and the three-step participatory agency framework, we argue that corruption resistance is effective with the foundation and method set by a committed NGO, which allows willing people to use and adapt this method in their own ways, self-mobilising and building their own capacities to resist corruption.

We proposed in our framework that agency drivers are the initial step, comprised of adaptation, employee characteristics, and citizen drivers. Our case displays the adaptation process as the development of the Zero-Rupee Note, a method that responds to a belief that corruption can only be resisted if the mind of the participating corrupt citizen is changed. The Zero-Rupee Note became the change vehicle, fostered by NGO 1, having professional and passionate employees with strong commitment to the organisation, often stemming from personal experience, which creates high self-motivation.

The agency setup serves as a foundation to the participation process, in which public citizens integrate the Zero-Rupee Note and distribute the note either with the participating organisation or independently. In either scenario, power is shifted from the organisation to the citizen. Although not apparent in the case study, we argue that this approach creates a feedback mechanism from the participant to the organisation, with suggestions, criticisms, or general reactions, to which the NGO can adapt its framework or approach.

The outcome of this approach is that corruption resistance slowly penetrates different organisational environments and different processes and systems, which before, would have required a bribe to obtain. NGO 1 revealed in the interview that since the inception of the Zero-Rupee Note, it has since been printed in five languages spoken in India and has been widely distributed in those states. The external impacts of this initiative is that corruption resistance efforts carry over to other people, as well as act as a future corruption prevention, with the bribe-taker rethinking his or her attitude towards bribes. We argue that, overall, this will lead to an increase in public trust by the general population, as well as a change in mindset among citizens that corruption is not the status quo.

This research is limited to examining the role of NGOs in enhancing public sector corruption resistance in the context of India using a case study. This means that some care should be taken when generalising from this study. This study has critical and revelatory value (Yin 2009) in that it provides a new contribution to knowledge and theory in corruption resistance in a context that has rarely been studied. In summary, there are three main theoretical contributions. First, this study develops the idea of corruption resistance that takes account of agency and structure. Second, variations in capabilities that public sector organisations have in resisting corruption have been described, and an explanatory framework has been proposed. The usefulness of this framework is demonstrated by applying it to a study of NGOs working for corruption resistance in India.

This study also has practical implications for public sector organisations in their endeavours to enhance corruption resistance. For policy makers and managers, this study provides a useful starting point for the development of cooperative efforts aimed at enhancing the capabilities of the public sector to resist corruption. Both agency and structure are important in such efforts, this means that public participation must take into account contextual factors to make corruption resistance personally relevant to those it affects (Warburton 2001). In particular, political will is required on the part of policy makers to develop behavioural norms, cooperating with outside organisations such as NGOs who can bring ideas from other jurisdictions. Allowing some 'bottom-up' development of procedures and practices are also essential elements in building the capacity of public sector organisations to resist corruption. Corruption resistance in relation to capacity building therefore has positive impacts on the operation and functioning of institutions. Strengthening corruption resistance in the distribution of goods and services improves access and equity of citizens in relation to those. Institutions therefore are able to provide goods and services to citizens more efficiently, increasing their capacity to serve as well as promoting accountability, fairness, and transparency in the public administration system in India. This, in turn, becomes a starting point for integrity within the public sector and political leadership, in which the modus operandi of public institutions shifts away from corruption as the status quo.

References

Abbink, K. 2004, 'Staff rotation as an anti-corruption policy: an experimental study', *European Journal of Political Economy*, vol. 20, no. 4, pp. 887–906.

Adler, P.A. and Adler, P. 1994, 'Observational techniques', in N.K. Denzin and Y. Lincoln (eds.), *Handbook of qualitative research*, Sage Publications, Thousand Oaks, CA, pp. 377–392.

Anechiarico, F. 2010, 'Protecting integrity at the local level: the role of anti-corruption and public management networks', *Crime, Law and Social Change*, vol. 53, no. 1, pp. 79–95.

Arnstein, S.R. 1969, 'A ladder of citizen participation', *Journal of the American Institute of Planners*, vol. 35, no. 4, pp. 216–224.

Bamberger, M. 1986, *The role of community participation in development planning and project management*, World Bank, Washington, DC.

Beenen, G. and Pinto, J. 2009, 'Resisting organizational-level corruption: an interview with Sherron Watkins', *Academy of Management Learning and Education*, vol. 8, no. 2, pp. 275–289.

Beugré, C.D. 2010, 'Resistance to socialization into organizational corruption: a model of deontic justice', *Journal of Business and Psychology*, vol. 25, no. 3, pp. 533–541.

Calvo, E. and Murillo, M.V. 2004, 'Who delivers? Partisan clients in the Argentine electoral market', *American Journal of Political Science*, vol. 48, no. 4, pp. 742–757.

Cohen, J.M. and Uphoff, N.T. 1980, 'Participation's place in rural development: seeking clarity through specificity', *World Development*, vol. 8, no. 3, pp. 213–235.

Cornwall, A. 2002, 'Locating citizen participation', *IDS Bulletin*, vol. 33, no. 2, pp. i–x.

Cornwall, A. 2008, 'Unpacking 'participation': models, meanings and practices', *Community Development Journal*, vol. 43, no. 3, pp. 269–283.

Cornwall, A. and Gaventa, J. 2001, 'From users and choosers to makers and shapers repositioning participation in social policy', *IDS Bulletin*, vol. 31, no. 4, pp. 50–62.

Cunha, M.P.E. and Cabral-Cardoso, C. 2006, 'Shades of gray: a liminal interpretation of organizational legality-illegality', *International Public Management Journal*, vol. 9, no. 3, pp. 209–225.

DiMaggio, P.J. and Powell, W.W. 1983, 'The iron cage revisited: institutional isomorphism and collective rationality in organizational fields', *American Sociological Review*, vol. 48, no. 2, pp. 147–160.

Emerson, K., Nabatchi, T. and Balogh, S. 2012, 'An integrative framework for collaborative governance', *Journal of Public Administration Research and Theory*, vol. 22, no. 1, pp. 1–29.

Evans, M. 2012, 'Beyond the integrity paradox–towards 'good enough' governance?', *Policy Studies*, vol. 33, no. 1, pp. 97–113.

Frank, B., Lambsdorff, J.G. and Boehm, F. 2011, 'Gender and corruption: lessons from laboratory corruption experiments', *European Journal of Development Research*, vol. 23, no. 1, pp. 59–71.

Frumkin, P. and Galaskiewicz, J. 2004, 'Institutional isomorphism and public sector organizations', *Journal of Public Administration Research and Theory*, vol. 14, no. 3, pp. 283–307.

Gill, S. 1998, *The pathology of corruption*, HarperCollins Publishers, New Delhi, India.

Gordon, R., Clegg, S. and Kornberger, M. 2009, Embedded ethics: discourse and power in the New South Wales police service', *Organization Studies*, vol. 30, no. 1, pp. 73–99.

Gottschalk, P. 2012, 'White-collar crime and police crime: rotten apples or rotten barrels?', *Critical Criminology*, vol. 20, no. 2, pp. 169–182.

Government of India 2005, *Right to Information Act*, Act 22 of 2005, 15 June 2005.

Heidenheimer, A.J. 1989, 'Perspectives on the perception of corruption', in A.J. Heidenheimer, M. Johnston and V.T. LeVine (eds.), *Political corruption: a handbook*, Transaction Publishers, New Brunswick, NJ, pp.149–163.

Hjorth, P. 2003, 'Knowledge development and management for urban poverty alleviation', *Habitat International*, vol. 2, no. 3, pp. 381–392.

Hove, H. 2004, 'Critiquing sustainable development: a meaningful way of mediating the development impasse', *Undercurrent*, vol. 1, no. 1, pp. 48–54.

Huberts, L.W. and Six, F.E. 2012, 'Local integrity systems', *Public Integrity*, vol. 14, no. 2, pp. 151–172.

Hulme, D. and Edwards, M. (eds.) 1997, *NGOs, states and donors: too close for comfort?*, Macmillan, London, UK, pp. 3–22.

IMI Konnect 2014, *India against corruption: IMI Kolkata holds a seminar*, International Management Institute, Kolkata, India, viewed 2 December 2014, <https://imi-k.edu.in/images/IMIData/pdf/Web_IMI-K_March-2014_29-03-2014_protected2.pdf>.

Jenkins, R. 2007, 'Civil society versus corruption', *Journal of Democracy*, vol. 18, no. 2, pp. 55–69.

Jenkins, R. and Goetz, A.M. 1999a, 'Accounts and accountability: theoretical implications of the right-to-information movement in India', *Third World Quarterly*, vol. 20, no. 3, pp. 603–622.

Jenkins, R. and Goetz, A.M. 1999b, 'Constraints on civil society's capacity to curb corruption lessons from the Indian experience', *IDS Bulletin*, vol. 30, no. 4, pp. 39–49.

Kim, S., Kim, H.J. and Lee, H. 2009, 'An institutional analysis of an e-government system for anti-corruption: the case of OPEN', *Government Information Quarterly*, vol. 26, no. 1, pp. 42–50.

Kingshott, R. P. and Dincer, O. C. 2008, 'Determinants of public service employee corruption: a conceptual model from the psychological contract perspective', *Journal of Industrial Relations*, vol. 50, no. 1, pp. 69–85.

Kish-Gephart, J. J., Harrison, D. A. and Treviño, L. K. 2010, 'Bad apples, bad cases and bad barrels: meta-analytic evidence about sources of unethical decisions at work', *Journal of Applied Psychology*, vol. 95, no. 1, pp. 1.

Kpundeh, S. J. 1998, 'Political will in fighting corruption', in S. Kpundeh and I. Hors (eds.), *Corruption and integrity improvement initiatives in developing countries*, United Nations Development Programme, New York, NY, pp. 91–110.

Lange, D. 2008, 'A multidimensional conceptualization of organizational corruption control', *Academy of Management Review*, vol. 33, no. 3, pp. 710–729.

Lee, H., Lim, H., Moore, D. D. and Kim, J. 2013, 'How police organizational structure correlates with frontline officers' attitudes toward corruption: a multilevel model', *Police Practice and Research*, vol. 14, no. 5, pp. 386–401.

Leichter, H. M. 1979, *A comparative approach to policy analysis: health care policy in four nations*, Cambridge University Press, Cambridge, UK.

Manzetti, L. and Wilson, C. J. 2007, 'Why do corrupt governments maintain public support?', *Comparative Political Studies*, vol. 40, no. 8, pp. 949–970.

Maxwell, J., Rosell, S. and Forest, P. G. 2003, 'Giving citizens a voice in healthcare policy in Canada', *British Medical Journal*, vol. 326, no. 7397, pp. 1031–1033.

Meagher, P. 2005, Anti-corruption agencies: rhetoric Versus reality', *The Journal of Policy Reform*, vol. 8, no. 1, pp. 69–103.

Menzel, D. C. 2007, *Ethics management for public administrators: building organizations of integrity*, M. E. Sharpe, New York, NY.

Mulgan, R. and Wanna, J. 2011, 'Developing cultures of integrity in the public and private sectors', in A. Graycar and R. G. Smith (eds.), *Handbook of global research and practice in corruption*, Edward Elgar Publishing, Cheltenham, UK, pp. 416–428.

Murphy, P. R. and Dacin, M. T. 2011, 'Psychological pathways to fraud: understanding and preventing fraud in organizations', *Journal of Business Ethics*, vol. 101, no. 4, pp. 601–618.

Newburn, T. and Webb, B. 1999, 'Understanding and preventing police corruption: lessons from the literature', *Police Research Series*, no. 110, Policing and Reducing Crime Unit, Research, Development and Statistics Directorate, London, UK.

North, D. C. 1993, 'Five propositions about institutional change', *Economics Working Paper Archive*, Washington University, St Louis, MO.

Organisation for Economic Co-Operation and Development 1998, *Principles for Managing Ethics in the Public Service*, The Organisation for Economic Co-Operation and Development, Paris, France.

Peisakhin, L. and Pinto, P. 2010, 'Is transparency an effective anti-corruption strategy? evidence from a field experiment in India', *Regulation and Governance*, vol. 4, no. 3, pp. 261–280.

Pelletier, K. L. and Bligh, M. C. 2006, 'Rebounding from corruption: perceptions of ethics program effectiveness in a public sector organization', *Journal of Business Ethics*, vol. 67, no. 4, pp. 359–374.

Pick, D., Issa, T. and Teo, S. 2013, 'Misconduct resistance: the management of restricted drugs in the Western Australian public health service', proceedings of 2013 British Academy of Management Conference: Managing to Make a Difference, Liverpool, UK, 10–12 September 2013, viewed 30 November 2014, <http://aut.researchgateway.ac.nz/handle/10292/6644>.

Pinto, J., Leana, C. R. and Pil, F. K. 2008, 'Corrupt organizations or organizations of corrupt individuals? Two types of organization-level corruption', *Academy of Management Review*, vol. 33, no. 3, pp. 685–709.

Pretty, J. N. 1995, 'Participatory learning for sustainable agriculture', *World Development*, vol. 23, no. 8, pp. 1247–1263.

Pursey, P. M, Heugens, A. R. and Lander, M. W. 2009, 'Structure! agency! (and other quarrels): a meta-analysis of institutional theories of organization', *Academy of Management Journal*, vol. 52, no. 1, pp. 61–85.

Quah, J. S. 2008, 'Curbing corruption in India: an impossible dream?', *Asian Journal of Political Science*, vol. 16, no. 3, pp. 240–259.

Rudqvist, A. and Woodford-Berger, P. 1996, *Evaluation and participation: some lessons*, Swedish International Development Cooperation Agency, Stockholm, Sweden.

Salminen, A. and Ikola-Norrbacka, R. 2010, 'Trust, good governance and unethical actions in Finnish public administration', *International Journal of Public Sector Management*, vol. 23, no. 7, pp. 647–668.

Scott, W. R. 1995, *Institutions and organizations*, Sage Publications, Thousand Oaks, CA.

Shadnam, M. and Lawrence, T. B. 2011, 'Understanding widespread misconduct in organizations', *Business Ethics Quarterly*, vol. 21, no. 3, pp. 379–407.

Sondhi, S. 2000, 'Combating corruption in India', paper presented at the XVIII World Congress of International Political Science Association, Quebec City, Canada, 1–5 August 2000.

Stringer, E. T. 1999, *Action research*, 2nd ed., Sage Publications, Thousand Oaks, CA.

Torres, R. M. 2001, 'Knowledge-based international aid: do we want it, do we need it?', in W. Gmelin, K. King and S. McGrath (eds.), *Knowledge, research and international cooperation*, University of Edinburgh, Edinburgh, UK, pp. 103–124.

Transparency International 2014, *2014 Corruption Perception Index*, Transparency International, Berlin, Germany, viewed 30 November 2014, <www.transparency.org/cpi2014>.

Tummala, K. K. 2002, 'Corruption in India: control measures and consequences', *Asian Journal of Political Science*, vol. 10, no. 2, pp. 43–69.

van Ryzin, G. G. 2011, 'Outcomes, process and trust of civil servants', *Journal of Public Administration Research and Theory*, vol. 21, no. 4, pp. 745–760.

Warburton, J. 2001, 'Corruption as a social process: from dyads to networks', in P. Larmour and N. Wolanin (eds.), *Corruption and Anti-Corruption*, ANU E Press, Canberra, Australia, 221–237.

Yin, R. K. 2009, *Case study research: design and methods*, 5th ed. Sage Publications, London, UK.

9 A chronicle of Indigenous entrepreneurship, human development and capacity building in east Arnhem Land of Australia

Cecil Arthur Leonard Pearson and Yi Liu

Introduction

An increasingly accepted view is that successive Australian government policies have not effectively promoted Indigenous economic development. An early
attempt to engage Indigenous Australians in commercial aspirations was the
establishment of the Commonwealth Capital Fund for Aboriginal Business in
1968 (Smith 2006). By the early 1970s, during the installation of the policy construct of self-determination, Australian government agencies provided finance
for Aboriginal enterprises. Almost two decades later, legislation was passed in
1989 by the Commonwealth government to establish the Aboriginal and Torres
Strait Islander Commission (ATSIC) for administrating a range of Aboriginal
programmes (Anderson 2007). More recent evidence of the Australian government's commitment to developing business and employment opportunities for
Indigenous people was the establishment of Indigenous Business Australia in
2001 as well as a number of Indigenous-specific programmes (Australian Government 2007). Fuelling the political momentum supporting the agenda in
Aboriginal affairs are the two goals of reducing Indigenous unemployment and
poverty. Over time, there have been numerous audits of government interventions and programmes for solving Indigenous community problems (Altman,
Biddle, and Hunter 2005; Australian Government 2010; Hughes and Warin
2005; Hunter 2009; Pholi, Black, and Richards 2009), and these investigations
have consistently found that Indigenous people are the most socially disadvantaged in Australia.

Extensive documentation discloses that Indigenous Australians experience
substantial labour market exclusion relative to other Australians. Emerging from
the literature are the economic and social consequences of weak labour market engagement and marginal self-employment that present as lower household
incomes, poorer health, unsanitary living conditions and a greater likelihood of
dependence on welfare payments (Australian Government 2010; Giddy, Lopez,
and Redman 2009; Hunter and Gray 2012). A concerted effort reveals precarious Indigenous employment has many caveats for disengagement from the
labour market with the three most frequently ascribed to Australian Aboriginals

as (1) education, (2) spatial mismatch job to residence, and (3) cultural attachment (Altman 2009; Biddle 2010; Hunter 2010). Strong cultural continuities are a central thread of these identified elements.

There is diversity between the Australian social ethos of employment and the Indigenous inclination to work. Biddle (2010: 176) writes 'the incentive or inclination to undertake work in the wage economy is lower for Indigenous compared to non-Indigenous Australians'. The forces manifesting as disinclination to meaningful employment are particularly dominant in extremely remote and regional localities. These settlements are often beyond viable markets and are where the community norms are aligned with wildlife harvesting as well as spiritual and religious connections to ancestral lands (Altman 2003; Biddle, Taylor, and Yap 2009; Trudgen 2000). In these settings, formal education is considerably less important than family attachment, moving to another job location leads to geographic isolation and an absence of cultural attachment is to live in an unknown world (Yunupingu 2009). Indigenous aspirations are incompatible with traditional business ideals of the commercial world, and a lineage of Australian government Indigenous development policies has not fostered a prosperous and vibrant Indigenous entrepreneurial sector (Jordan and Mavec 2010; Muir 2011).

Mainstream solutions to entrepreneurial development are unlikely to find traction in Indigenous society. Aboriginal cultural protocols on tribal ancestral homelands have strong connections to community norms of behaviour 'that are inconsistent with maintaining employment' (Gray and Hunter 2005: 387). Welfare dependence, humbugging (i.e. dominant seniors appropriating assets and resources from family and clan members) in a mutually obligated kin-based network (Altman 2002; Worsley 1955), and policies, including wage subsidies as the principal source of income (Brown 2009; Uniting Justice 2011), significantly discourage participation in the mainstream labour market. Unemployment becomes exacerbated when Indigenous people live in remote and regional settings where there is a lack of meaningful work opportunities. Nevertheless, when power replaces powerlessness, the structural sources of inequality are transformed to displace insecure or precarious models of unemployment, a notion demonstrated in pace and change within this chapter.

Mainstream Australian society has shaped the direction of Indigenous entrepreneurship. In spite of a prodigious body of evidence of major differing characteristics between the Indigenous community and the dominant Australian society (Altman 2002, 2009; Foley 2006; Johns 2011; Trudgen 2000), Australian governments and a wide sector of academia have consistently cited a lack of appropriate governance mechanisms in Aboriginal entrepreneurship (Indigenous Business Review 2003; McDonnell 1999; Furneaux and Brown 2008; Russell-Mundine 2007). Paradoxically, notwithstanding a range of political views, a lack of stringent commercial diligence by ATSIC, the dominant Indigenous Commonwealth government business financier, led to the abolition of the agency in 2004 by the Howard Coalition government (Anderson 2007; Maddison 2008). Limited research on Australian Indigenous entrepreneurship reveals a growing geographic and sector spread of successful Aboriginal enterprises (Foley 2003;

Hunter 2013; The Parliament of the Commonwealth of Australia 2008), which lacks dynamism despite small pockets of intense activity (Australian Government 2009; Wood and Davidson 2011). Inherent in this landscape are issues of power and control clearly demonstrated by the historical endeavour of the Yolngu clans of east Arnhem Land of the Northern Territory (NT) of Australia.

In this chapter, a theoretical foundation for capacity building and development on the Gove Peninsula is presented. Practical aspects are given by a historical account revealing the local Indigenous Yolngu people, who are the first Australians, had been engaged in entrepreneurial venturing long before the First Fleet sailed into Botany Bay in 1788. Connections are also made with an obligation to balance social, political, environmental and economic dimensions to draw a salient conclusion that developing capacity building in emerging societies in the Asia Pacific region has been interpreted too narrowly.

Contemporary Yolngu community capacity building

In their long history, the Indigenous Yolngu people have consistently engaged in entrepreneurial activity. The more precise written records disclose the coastal Yolngu people were the first Australian international business consortium, a position they held for over 300 years until government policy terminated venturing with the Macassan sailors (Ivory 1999; Russell 2004). Australian government intervention was to have two further major influences on Yolngu capacity building. First, in 1911 when the Methodist Church was allowed to establish coastal mission stations, there was opportunity for the Yolngu to engage in agrarian pursuits including a soft wood timber industry that flourished for 50 years (Shepherdson 1981; Pearson and Helms 2012a). In this arrangement, there was community capacity building but scant opportunity for Indigenous self-employment as the church was in control.

The second set of government initiatives was connected with mining and the announced policies and legislation have unexpectedly led to entrepreneurial control by the Yolngu people. When the 2011 Land Use Agreement (LUA) was ratified at Yirrkala by Prime Minister Julia Gillard, the Yolngu Traditional Land Owners assumed power and control. Within six months, the local Yolngu people had responsibly installed an education–vocation programme as the precursor to extraordinarily founding Indigenous entrepreneurial dealings and extensive community capacity building on the Gove Peninsula. This region, and the locations mentioned in the chapter, is presented as Figure 9.1.

Historical foundations

Australian Indigenous communities developed capacity building long before the arrival of the First Fleet in 1788. Anthropological records indicate Indigenous Australians swept down from southern Asia crossing a land bridge some 50,000 years ago, and this oldest continuous national society has survived by retaining strong social and economic connections with the country (Blanch

Figure 9.1 The Gove Peninsula on the Northern Territory and places of interest

2008; Suter 2003). Maintaining natural resource management actions compelled the Aboriginal people to trade among themselves for thousands of years. Indeed, in their book *The World of the First Australians: Aboriginal Traditional Life Past and Present*, Berndt and Berndt (1999, p. 494) state that 'bartering centres were established', a necessity for the consumption of perishable foods in the absence of refrigeration. Undoubtedly, these sustainable concepts of traditional Aboriginal society provided sound foundations for building economic trading relationship with European voyagers (Worsley 1955).

The historical records frequently reference contact between the Yolngu people and seafarers. There is some suggestion that the Chinese sailed to the northern waters prior to the extensive trade with the Macassans who visited annually from the Celebes (now Sulawesi) by the northern monsoonal winds (November) to return six months later (March) by the south east trade winds (Russell 2004). A long-standing period of capacity development for 300 years is evidenced in written records, residual artefacts, words in the contemporary Yolngu language, and the addition of tamarind trees to the local flora. The Macassans sought vast quantities of trepang (sea cucumber), pearls and pearl shell, turtle shell as well as timber for their *paus* (sailing vessels), which were traded for tobacco, cloth, axes, steel for spearheads, and items associated with ritual and religious importance (Rose 1987). The exchange process was supplemented with labour productive capacities as highlighted by Worsley (1955: 3).

> The work which the aborigines performed ranged from diving for trepang, smoking and curing the sea-slug, to fishing, building smoke – houses for curing, cutting firewood and digging wells.

In 1907, the developed investment business and community capacity building collapsed when the South Australian government, then responsible for the Northern Territory, blocked the economic growth and employment opportunities by cancelling fishing licenses.

During the period of economic capacity building with the Macassans, a number of other notable early voyagers visited the region. Willem Janszoon visited and had contact with the Yolngu people in 1605 when sailing the *Duyfken*. In 1623, the Dutch explorer Jan Carstenzoon, Captain of the *Pera* and William Joosten Van Colster, Captain of the *Arnheim*, were commissioned by the Dutch East India Company to sail from Amboyna to explore the land sighted by Janszoon. After sailing down and up the east coast of the Gulf of Carpentaria the *Pera* returned to the Celebes while Van Colster travelled westward across the top of the Gulf. When Van Colster sighted land at the tip of the west coast of the Gulf, he named it after his ship (Thomson 2010), and today that land is known as Arnhem Land. During his circumnavigation of Australia in the *Investigator*, Captain Matthew Flinders encountered a large fleet (1,500) of *paus* near Melville Bay in 1803. A detailed account of the meeting with the fleet commander, Pobassoo, and his trade activities with the Yolngu people is provided in the log of the *Investigator*. Although the frequent contacts with Western European seafarers with their advanced technology had no apparent radical change on Yolngu society, the Yolngu–Macassarese period of capacity building had secured a tangible expression in the regional culture. When the *paus* sailed away, the last vision was the sails, and the Yolngu people assumed they were returning to the gods of the spirit world. Today Yolugu burial sites or where death has occurred from a vehicle accident are adorned with large, sail-like flags to make connections with the spirit world.

Methodist church influence on Yolngu capacity development

The Australian colonies and territories federated in 1901, and a decade later, Commonwealth action initiated a profound impact on the capacity development of future Yolngu society. In 1911, the Australian Federal Government assumed responsibility for the NT, including the welfare of the Indigenous people, and within a year, an interdenominational Committee of Churches, having an explicit interest in the wellbeing of Australian Aboriginal Missions, was formed in Melbourne (McKenzie 1976). Negotiations were held with Commonwealth government representatives in 1913, and subsequently, the Reverend James Watson was commissioned by the Methodist Overseas Mission Board to establish a church mission in Arnhem Land. The Reverend Watson sailed to Darwin; with government representatives, he travelled to the northern Bathurst and Melville Islands and then returned to Darwin. With Indigenous guides, Watson forayed well to the southeast of Darwin and then further east and finally to the Goulburn Islands, which were the western boundary of Arnhem Land. The Reverend Watson returned to Melbourne to tender his report, and in 1916, he established the first Aboriginal Church mission on South Goulburn Island. The remote mission provided religious, medical, and physical sustenance to the congregated Indigenous people, who for survival of the settlement had to transition from hunter-gatherers to new dependency life skills of agrarian competencies for food production, basic constructing abilities for shelters, and fundamental engineering activities. Traditional lifestyles were being eroded to be replaced with community capacity development, but more radical change was approaching.

A central contribution to the advancement of Yolngu capacity building is to be found in the fascinating lives of Harold and Ella Shepherdson. These two enigmatic figures, who came from disparate backgrounds, hold a distinguished place in modern Australian history for their contribution to reframing contemporary Yolngu community capacity development. The Reverend Harold Urquhart Shepherdson was a qualified engineer, who was born in Bunbury, Western Australia, while Ella was born in Edinburgh, Scotland, in 1913 and immigrated to Adelaide with her parents. Harold and Ella met at the Payneham Methodist Church and, when engaged, decided to do missionary work, which was to realign their life and the development of Indigenous communities in the NT. The church arranged for Harold to work at a country timber mill and for Ella to complete a six-months nursing course. More staggering is that, at another location in Adelaide, the Christian Endeavour Society had initiated fund raising to purchase a sawmill for an NT mission. When married in October 1927, Harold and Ella travelled by rail to Sydney, then to Darwin by ship, and then by a lugger to the remote Methodist Milingimbi Mission, where they arrived on 28 April 1928. The mill had preceded them.

After arrival at Millingimbi, the Reverend Shepherdson assembled the 5-foot diameter blade mill and organised a supply of logs. Milingimbi was devoid of suitable trees, but with Indigenous labour and the employment of 50 feet luggers, logs could be obtained from the forests on Elcho and Howard Islands. The trees were cut down by Indigenous men, and in a team of ten men using a whim, the logs were dragged to the shore where they were lashed to 50-foot luggers and shipped to Milingimbi. In her book, *Half a Century in Arnhem Land*, Ella Shepherdson (1981) left a magnificent legacy of black-and-white photographs as well as text to comprehensively record the operations. Milling at Milingimbi with the soft wood cypress pine *(Callitris intratropica)*, which is resistant to termites, the indefatigable predators of other timbers, was the beginning of a capacity-building timber-merchandising industry in east Arnhem Land that was to last half a century.

Fighting between Japanese trepangers and Yolngu warriors at Caledon Bay expanded the mission network as well as meaningful timber production at Milingimbi. When Yolngu women were severely mistreated by the Japanese sailors in 1933, five of them were killed by Indigenous men. The response by the Methodist Church was to establish a mission at Yirrkala and in 1936, a lugger arrived from Milingimbi with milled timber and two Yolngu carpenters, who constructed a manse and store room for the Reverend Wilbur Chaseling and his wife. Operations continued at Milingimbi as the onset of the Great Depression curtailed expansion of the mission network to Elcho Island where the land was more suitable for agriculture and where there was higher quality water, a better anchorage, and plentiful stands of millable timber. But within six years, international events were to trigger sustainable economic growth, a substantial reduction in community poverty, and greater productive capacity at Elcho Island.

The Second World War seeded a continuing development of Yolngu timber-related capacity building. During the 1940s, the Japanese military began to give increasing attention to northern Australia, and on Thursday, 19 February 1942, Darwin was bombed. The Australian government had constructed a number of airstrips in the NT, and the Milingimbi airport was close to the mission buildings. When squadrons of Beaufighters and Spitfires were assigned to Milingimbi, the Methodist Church appreciated the imminent danger to the mission church, hospital, school, and other buildings (which were bombed later), and the Reverend Harold Shepherdson was instructed to vacate the region. Thus, on Monday, 3 August 1942, the mission's personnel departed on the lugger *Larrpan* for Elcho Island.

Establishing the Methodist mission on Elcho Island extensively intensified Indigenous community capacity. On Milingimbi, the milling operations were in the open and subjected to inclement weather, but at Elcho Island, the sawing equipment and huge quantities of boards, planks, and slabs of timber were beneath the roof an expansive structure. A range of construction materials were scavenged from what had been left by the Napha Petroleum Mining Company that had gone into liquidation on Elcho Island in 1931. Also, a tractor that had been restored and used on Milingimbi had been shipped back to Elcho Island for pulling logs to the milling operations as the tractor operations were quicker and replaced the 10-man team that had manually pulled a log. Within a relatively short time, a church, a new hospital, a large house for the Shepherdson family, and community dwellings attested to the strength of the capacity development of the settlement. After the close of the war, great use was made of the cypress pine from Howard and Elcho Islands as the structural timber was used across northern Australia. In fact, the consumption was so high that, in 1964, Russell Beazley and a team of Indigenous men commenced a reforestation programme, but the demand for the product had peaked. Political, social, and technical advancements were taking place.

In 1969, the Methodist Church established the last mission on the mainland of east Arnhem Land. The mission was on the edge of a large lake of fresh water that had been sighted by two senior missionaries in 1935. When flying from Milingimbi to Yirrkala in a Miles Hawk, the Reverend T. T. Webb (wife Eve), and the pilot the Reverend H. Shepherdson (wife Ella) named the lake after their wives. Today, there is an Aboriginal settlement named Gapuwiyak on the edge of Lake Evella.

For a short, time Gapuwiyak had a modest capacity development sustained by a timber industry. A mill was established to cut logs from the surrounding forest, but modern building materials of bricks, fibro, and steel as well as chemicals to combat the termite threat were arriving by barge via the Buckingham River and then by motor trucks. Capacity development was reinvigorated in 1981 by supplying 8-inch diameter cypress pine logs to Kuri Bay in Western Australia for the Paspaley Pearling Company, but this industry was overtaken with plastics by 1983.

Today Gapuwiyak is an Aboriginal community reliant on welfare, government services, and subsidised community work. While substantial enterprises built by the missionaries over 50 years were in decline during the 1970s, for the next four decades, a sea change in community capacity development, driven by unlikely bedfellows of past war events, Indigenous land rights, and Australian mining, was arising – like the mythical phoenix.

Military activity, mining and indigenous land rights

Building a military airstrip in the savannah forest in northeast Arnhem Land unleashed an extraordinary train of events. The momentous reframing of the Australian genre of political history began when the Number 8 Mobile Works Squadron was assigned the task of constructing a 5,000-foot airstrip near Yirrkala between August 1943 and July 1944 (Defence 1978), but because gravel was unavailable, high-grade bauxite ore was used. Even the name of the region (Gove Peninsula) and the new airport (Gove) has geographical prominence, being in recognition of Sergeant William Julius Henderson Gove, who was killed while flying a Hudson bomber at Rabuma Island (near Milingimbi) on the 20 April 1943 (Pretty n.d). Events with greater destiny for capacity building originated in 1951 when the Australian Federal Government reserved the bauxite deposits, and in 1954, British Aluminium began a programme of exploration in the region around Melville Bay (Crough 1985). There was some contemporary capacity building for Yolngu people who worked as a drilling team under the control of Klaus Helms. By 1958, reserves of 50 million tonnes (mt) had been identified to be extended to 166 mt (Raggatt 1968), and the deposits attracted investors who in 1956 formed a group of Australian companies to establish the Northern Australian Bauxite and Alumina Company (NABALCO). Other international companies that had been involved with the Gove Peninsula exploration were more attracted to the world's largest bauxite deposits at Weipa in northern Queensland. The mineral exploration activities had been occurring on Aboriginal land mainly adjacent to the Yirrkala mission, the Yolngu people had not been consulted, and their opposition was beginning to rise.

The Yolngu people displayed dissatisfaction with the decision by the Australian federal government to excise 140 square miles from the Arnhem Land Reserve (Aboriginal) for mining. In 1963, the Yolngu clans presented the Bark Petition to the parliament in Canberra on 14 August, but the Australian government deemed a mine and a refinery were in the interest of regional capacity development (Brody 2011; Drill Hall Gallery and Buku-Larrngay Mulka Centre 1999). In 1968, a new town and supporting infrastructure were designed to occupy a number of special leases (The Gove Bauxite Development 1968; Pearson 2012a). The extent of resentment by the Yolngu clan continued to culminate as a challenge in the Darwin Supreme court in 1970–1971 (Blackburn and Leslie 1971), but the case was lost, and the mining operations continued. The introduction of alcohol led to severe social dislocation of the Indigenous community to heighten Yolngu grievances, and in the mid-1970s (Altman 2003), the Elders led the clans back to their homelands.

Before the exodus of Yolngu people from the Yirrkala mission and the other nearby Indigenous settlements, there had been growing capacity development in the Nhulunbuy region. An extensive influx of non-Indigenous construction workers for the townsite, mine, and refinery projects provided a consumptive market for the Yolngu people. Visual records that were provided by the anthropologist Ian Dunlop (1996) illustrate Daymbalipu Munugurr operated a family business of collecting oysters from mangrove roots in Daliwuy Bay 10 km south of Yirrkala. The produce was sold to the kitchens at the tent city next to the airport and the H block accommodation adjacent to the refinery site. These two establishments were the initial places of residence for a workforce estimated at some 4,000 non-Indigenous construction workers. Narritjim Maymura, the Yolngu master artist, established a rudimentary studio at Yirrkala where Yolngu women were employed to prepare paintings, sculptures, necklaces, and other forms of art that was sold to a growing body of non-Indigenous workers (Dunlop 1995). In a relatively short time, a large population of multinational, non-Indigenous workers provided impetus for local Yolngu capacity development.

Yolngu capacity building escalated with infrastructure construction at Nhulunbuy. A number of Indigenous men were employed in low-skilled construction and civil engineering work at the mine and refinery sites. The intensity of construction created a need for bricks, and several Yolngu men were employed in a sand cement brick-making factory operated by Yirrkala Business Enterprises (YBE), but when the demand for bricks declined, the work force was dismissed. There were also jobs for Yolngu women who worked in an industrial laundry where they washed and ironed linen for the non-Indigenous workforce who were accommodated at Gove House. By the mid-1970s, when the clans returned to their homelands, these women left their employment. Cousins and Nieuwenhuysen (1984) claim that, by the close of 1982, NABALCO was not employing any Yolngu people in the mining and refining operations. In a relative few years, the Yolngu capacity building had collapsed, but resentment for land acquisition continued to simmer and foster the Indigenous land rights movement.

The 1960s were the beginning of the golden years for mining corporations in Australia, but by the 1980s, the ostracism of Indigenous people was being confronted. In the Pilbara of Western Australia during the mid-1960s, Hamersley Iron was re-profiling mountains of iron ore, but two decades later at Noonkanbah in northern Western Australia, the oil drillers had to be escorted by police through the gauntlet of Indigenous protesters and conservationists (Kolig 1987; O'Lincoln 1993; Thomson 1983). Gaining currency in Australia was a mood for change from the anachronistic notion of *terra nullius* – land belonging to no one – established in 1788 at the commencement of British colonisation. In the 1980s, a majority of Australian citizens were rejecting the doctrine of tenure of acquisition of the nation by sovereignty of the Crown, and the populous now promoted a human rights perspective with a concern for Aboriginal interests.

Foremost in the minds of many non-Indigenous Australians were opinions about the sacredness of the environment and mining in national parks, kindled with government intentions to extend uranium mining in the NT World Heritage site of the Kakadu National Park (Hamilton 1996; Hintjens 2000). Mass rallies in the streets of Australian cities were responses reflecting community challenges to capitalistic colonial assumptions interlocking with Indigenous rights and environmentalism, which engendered a momentum for corporate social responsibility. Mining corporations were to become controversially and unavoidably involved in community engagement, but in less than a decade, radical change would oblige the miners to enter the Aboriginal world. The notion of *terra nullius* was made redundant on 3 June 1992. In a landmark case, Eddie Mabo, David Passi, and James Rice – all Merian People – contested in the High Court of Australia the action of the Queensland government to annex the Murray Islands in the Torres Strait in 1879. The High Court found the Murray Islands belonged to the Merian People.

The 1992 *Mabo* decision began to have wider implications in the context of Australian property law. In the following year, the Labour Federal Government introduced the Native Title Act 1993. This legislation set in place procedures for dealing with Native Title claims, and it had a retrospective clause to validate the interests of non-Indigenous landholders. The retrospective condition was agreed to by Indigenous groups in exchange for guaranteed rights to negotiate Land Use Agreements (LUAs). Native Title has given the Yolngu people extraordinary capacity-building potential.

Leveraging indigenous capacity development

The initial Nhulunbuy 42-year LUA was a colonial-administered, commercial arrangement between the Australian government and influential mining companies. Recognition of the Aboriginal people was broadly benevolent and administrated as ad hoc philanthropic practices within state-sanctioned regulatory regimes (Coronado and Fallon 2010). Harvey and Brereton (2005) explain why Aboriginal people are overlooked in the Australian mining sector when they state that, although community interaction is unavoidable, it is secondary to the primary objective of running the mining operations. But, in fairness to NABALCO, the Yolngu people did not possess the qualifications, certification, or contemporary work skill sets identified and demanded by the Australian Federal and State Government mining regulators. Creating an opportunity for the local Yolngu people to be employed in the Nhulunbuy operations was exercised by installing an education vocation scheme that operated close to the large Indigenous settlement of Yirrkala.

Educational – vocational arrangements

The tripartite initiative between YBE (Y), NABALCO (N) and the Australian Federal Government to install an Operator (O) Training (T) School (S) for Yolngu men created YNOTS. This 30-week course, which commenced in 2000, was to train men to become moveable machine operators (haul trucks, excavators, endloaders, graders, bulldozers) and graduate with a Certificate II in opencut mining. Instruction was given on a mining lease 22 km from Nhulunbuy and 7 km south of the Gove airport. In the second year, the scheme was expanded to include a number of modules of literacy, numeracy, communication and management-related content as well as opportunity for Yolngu women. Paradoxically, the considerable capacity development in the Yolngu community over seven years that was attributed to YNOTS led to the abandonment of the scheme.

In 2004, the new mining operator was Alcan Gove, and the company began a massive expansion of the refinery. The design capacity in 1968 was 0.5 million tonnes per annum (mta), in 2004, it was 1.9 mta, and the proposal was for 3.8 mta by 2007 to secure sustainable economic capacity development for the region. Extensive, temporary, fully messed accommodation was provided at Nhulunbuy for a workforce of over 2,000 people as it was estimated the project would require 35 million hours and consume US$2.5 billion over 4 years. At that time, it was promoted as the biggest industrial project ever to be undertaken in Australia.

Even before the refurbishment commenced, it was recognised that the new workforce would be insufficient. Consequently, YNOTS transitioned from an education–vocation scheme to an employment initiative. The Yolngu employees upgraded the 17-km conveyor belt from the mine site to the refinery; they undertook stevedoring and worked on a variety of civil construction tasks. Arriving at the port from southern Asia were 630 preassembled modules each of 4,000 tonnes that had to be placed at the refinery site. There were also some 18,000 tonnes of steel and 120 km of variously sized pipes to be unloaded and taken to work areas (Alcan Gove 2008). The project was completed in December 2007, and now the YNOTS personnel were highly skilled, and their newfound employability capacity made them very attractive to YBE. Thus, YBE had little interest in continuing the YNOTS education–vocation scheme. Moreover, the new mining operator wanted to divest from the NABALCO experiment as a new skill set focus was required. These aspirations gave birth to the Arnhem Learning Education Regional Training (ALERT) scheme.

The ALERT is an Indigenous education–vocation programme. This scheme, which commenced in July 2007, has been comprehensively evaluated and reported extensively in the literature (Daff and Pearson 2009, 2010; Pearson 2012b; Pearson and Daff 2008, 2011, 2013). Superficially, there are three stages of administration and achievements. First, for the first two years, about one-third of the participants graduated and worked in mainline jobs mostly in the community while some two-thirds of the participants withdrew to their remote homelands. Second, from the latter half of 2009, when fully messed accommodation could be provided by the mining company, the catchment area was expanded beyond the Gove Peninsula. Applicants beyond the Gove Peninsula arrived with higher English literacy and numeracy competencies than the local Yolngu people and acquired greater capacity development as reflected in 29 per cent (50 of 175) of them obtaining mainline positions in the Australian mining sector and 19 per cent being employed in sustainable jobs in local Indigenous organisations or in the private and government sectors in Australian states other than the NT (Pearson and Daff 2013). Last is an emerging, expanding stream of Yolngu graduates with different aspirations that were limited in the educational–vocational programmes before ratification of the historical LUA at Yirrkala on the 8 June 2011 by then Prime Minister Julia Gillard. Today, there is a more prevailing cultural awareness reconciliation dimension to the scheme.

Section 11 of the LUA delineates specifications of employment and training. Specifically, section 11.2 states the clans of the Traditional Land Owners (Gumatj, Rirratjingu and Galpu), in consultation with the mining corporation, are to develop a regional employment and training strategy for Aboriginal people of northeast Arnhem Land. On Thursday, 1 December 2011, a Working Group comprised of representatives of the Gumatj and Rirratjingu clans as well as the mining corporation met and identified the key elements of an Indigenous education and vocation programme.

There were two primary objectives of the regional employment strategy. First, a major objective was to commence the programme as soon as possible. Thus, the programme was named Ralpa because when the word is translated from the mother tongue, it means 'to get things done quickly'. Second, a central focus was to identify the types of jobs with skill sets that could be learned relatively quickly and work as a medium connecting with the spiritual dimensions of Yolngu society. A most significant feature of the Yolngu system is a holistic concept of all things within the universe (Brody 2011; Stanner 1979) and an alignment with their heritage of custodians of the land green type jobs (environmental, conservation) 'to provide working conditions that are sympathetic with the needs and preferences of the Indigenous workers' (Hunter 2013: 16), which were the universal choice of the Working Group.

The Working Group also formulated the programme's pedagogy. Morning sessions were designed to deliver job-related material at the mining company training centre or technically relevant skill development at the Nhulunbuy Technical and Further Education (TAFE) premises. For instance, teaching in job management, safe working issues, and personal hygiene and visits by employers were reinforced by instruction in carpentry, painting, sheet metal working, and welding at the TAFE buildings prior to lunch. In the afternoon, trainees visited work sites and during the first week began working on community projects. As the programme advanced, the work became more specialised, and while there was a core of general material to be learned, each Ralpa programme was tailored for the likely vocations of the graduates. For example the women were given instruction in food preparation and retail operations as they were likely to be working in the coffee shop or the community store. In contrast, the men were destined to mill logs, to construct or maintain houses, or to work on the cattle station so their learning programme would be aligned in these vocations. At the beginning of a Ralpa programme, meaningful jobs were identified, and candidates were able to focus on likely future careers.

A Ralpa programme was integrated with pastoral care. All candidates were transported from their homes to the training centre and returned to their community at the end of the day. All meals were provided as well as work clothes that the trainees washed in industrial machines before departing for home so they had clean clothes for the following workday. The programme was for eight weeks, six hours a day, and four days a week, leaving three days for hunter-gatherer pursuits or cultural activities. At the close of the programme, there was a formal, catered graduation ceremony attended by family and community Elders as well as local dignitaries. In the following week, the graduates began working in sustainable jobs, but the programme deliverers continued to engage in supporting, nurturing mechanisms with the new employees and their employers. The Ralpa trainees were paid at casual rates during their programme.

Table 9.1 shows a summary of the Ralpa programme outcomes. Some 68 per cent (64 of 93) of the trainees graduated and were placed in a mainline job, and for most of the employees, this was the first time they had ever been sustainably employed in paid work. Dismissals were for continual absence or being unfit for work (e.g. substance abuse). The item 'Town' represents a workforce that was contracted to maintain gardens and undertake various tasks for the 800 Nhulunbuy properties owned by the mining corporation. Nhulunbuy is a 'closed' town (Pearson 2012a).

The content of Table 9.1 is remarkable for an array of features. First, because of logistic restrictions, there were two Ralpa programmes a year, and each one had a nominal 15 candidates. Second, the short duration of the programme limited the number of nationally recognised courses that could be undertaken, but most graduates with functional English literacy and numeracy competencies completed four subjects accredited by the Australian Qualifications Framework. Third, few of the women completed the subjects as most were English illiterate and innumerate preferring to speak in their mother tongue. Nevertheless, they enthusiastically learned the health and safety features for meat processing, retailing, and horticulture jobs, and their graduation certificates acknowledged their achievements. Fourth, English reading ages were assessed with national tests (Burt Reading Test 1974; Shearer, Cheshire and Apps 1975), and a sample of 33

Table 9.1 Ralpa employment attainment
(31 January 2012 to 2 May 2014)

Employment attainment	Number
Employment focus	
Timber milling/carpentry	21
Indigenous organisations	5
House carpentry maintenance	3
Health	5
Horticulture	9
Town	10
Retail	8
Cattle station	3
Total	64
Losses	
Withdrew or dismissed	26
Custodial	3
Total	29

Note: A total of 21 potential candidates nominated by their communities were found to be medically unfit or disinclined to enter a Ralpa programme.

Ralpa applicants (excluding the non-English-speaking candidates) had a reading age of 6.2 years with comprehension a nominal 2 years less. English literacy and numeracy skills are valuable assets in the workplace, but in Indigenous, bilingual work settings, such deficits do not prohibit vocational attainment.

The content of Table 9.1 reveals dimensions of capacity development. In a relatively short period of two and a half years, there was a reasonable growth in academic achievement and employment opportunity capacity. More remarkable is that these achievements have been attained by Indigenous people, who have seldom worked in mainline paid work and, hence, have been wedded to welfare. Improving the employment prospects of Indigenous community members can facilitate embedding this resource into existing social structures to yield sustainable benefits for the common good (Peredo and Chrisman 2006). Robust evidence of recent vocational development in Indigenous communities (on the Gove Peninsula) with interests in cultural and environment preservation is demonstrated by recent prominent Yolngu accomplishments and particularly how they have accelerated with the availability of the skilled Ralpa labour force.

Capacity and community development

During the early 2000s, the Gumatj Corporation was operating a cattle farm at Garrathiya funded from mining royalties. Hardwood planks and boards were needed for the tops of tank stands, verandahs, and general construction, but importing building timber to Nhulunbuy was cost prohibitive. Galarrwuy Yunupingu, the clan leader, who negotiated with the Jack Thompson Foundation, and John Moffin (Territory 2008) went to Garrathiya to show Yolngu men how to harvest NT stringy bark (*Eucalyptus tetrodonta*) trees, which were plentiful on their ancestral land, and gave instruction how to mill the logs to timber with a Lucas Mill. By 2008, these men and others under instruction, were building a three-unit accommodation block (kitchen, sleeping quarters, and ablution/toilet) for additional Indigenous staff to profitably work at the cattle station. In fact, three participants of the inaugural ALERT programme withdrew and moved to Garrathiya.

The greater vision to provide fresh beef products to Indigenous communities on the Gove Peninsula was to underpin a rash of capacity building. Cattle yards were constructed 10 km north of Garrathiya where stock could be herded for testing the fitness of the meat of 350 Braham cattle for human consumption. By 2009, a point had been reached where further accommodation was to be built at Garrathiya, which occasioned Galarrwuy Yunupingu to create partnerships with three Tasmanian organisations. Withdrawals from the ALERT programme had a positive aspect as these men were to become a pool of available labour to the Gumatj Corporation. The integration of these two attributes resulted in a watermark in Indigenous capacity building on the Gove Peninsula.

Construction of a bunkhouse at Garrathiya to accommodate five men began in mid-2009. On the morning of 25 May, the first author was on site to observe the placement of the first galvanised steel stump. Returning on the morning of 7 August to the official opening, it was surprising to find the remote site occupied by a great number of motor vehicles and over 100 people. There were several TV crews as well as reporters from regional and national newspapers all with the express purpose of recording the construction efforts and to report the unfolding event of the ceremony. In addition, there were politicians from the three levels of Australian governments, local dignitaries, and prominent stakeholders such as Jack Thompson as well as representatives of the Tasmanian partners and, importantly, the pool of Indigenous men, who had milled the 20 tonnes of timber and built the bunkhouse. Comprising this pool was the Indigenous workers, who had been guided by two supervisors from Fairbrother Builders, the largest Tasmanian construction group. Also present was the milling team of ten Indigenous men (Pearson and Helms 2010a), who had harvested selected trees and milled the logs to produce the construction timbers under the watchful leadership of a representative from Forestry Tasmania. The building had been designed by the architectural department of the University of Tasmania that had provided the construction drawings. This building was the first in the NT to be designed to Western architectural standards and built with timber milled by Indigenous people and constructed by Yolngu workers. Creating the building acclaims a distinguished level of capacity building.

Partnerships and a degree of productive enthusiasm extended the capacity building in 2010. At Dhanaya on the shore of Port Bradshaw, a five-room house was constructed (Pearson and Helms 2010b). The architectural Tasmanian Partners prepared the construction plans, and Fairbrother Builders provided on site supervisors for the life of the project, while Forestry Tasmania, for the last time, supervised the milling teams in the savannah forests. In fact, the supervisor told the first author there was 'nothing more to teach these guys so I am going home tomorrow'. Verandahs were built on a number of houses at Gunyangara, other community infrastructure was being built (e.g. perimeter log rail barriers to the new football ground), and timber was flowing to the Gumatj timber shop. A notable endeavour was the construction of five boardroom tables that were sold for a considerable profit (Pearson and Helms 2011). All of this work was being undertaken by a steady stream, small in number, of Indigenous male graduates from the ALERT programme, but within a few months, the intensity of capacity building would explode.

The first Ralpa programme commenced on 30 January 2012 with 15 Yolngu men, and 12 graduated. All of the graduates completed four accredited courses that were delivered by staff from Charles Darwin University. Following graduation, seven of the men began employment at the Dhupuma industrial site where they mill logs to a range of sections of structural timber. The logs are cut from the new mining lease by a separate team of Ralpa graduates. Today the original Ralpa graduates still work in their chosen career being transported to and from the site where they operate Lucas Mills (2), chain saws (5), or the more sophisticated Mahoe saws (2). By mid-2012, ALERT and Ralpa had become Indigenous community brands, and the Indigenous women had been agitating for some time to be involved in training with work opportunity. As remarked by Gayili Yunupingu Marika, 'For some time Yolngu women had been stepping up. They operate the cottage industry within 200 km of Yirrkala. Some of them are today international artists in their own right'. But many of the women Ralpa advocates from Birritjimi, Galupa, and Gunyangara had children. Moreover, it was unlikely the women would be attracted to the careers chosen by the men. These issues provoked a new stream of capacity development.

A vast growth in community capacity development emerged during 2012 that continues to expand. At Gunyangara, the building of a transitional school had been meandering, but the urgency of having the school operational by the 14 May 2012, when the women were to commence their training, accelerated community social capacity endeavours. Men from previous ALERT programmes, some from the first Ralpa initiative as well as community women, who came to help with the painting, ensured the buildings were completed to meet the deadline (Pearson, Helms, and Daff 2014; Yunupingu 2014). The Indigenous women named their programme Goyurr, which translates as 'a journey'. However, the places where these women would work after graduation accelerated a range of other projects. The intention was that trained Indigenous women would be required to work in the Mungurr Community Council, the horticulture nursery at Gunyangara, and local Indigenous organisations (Dhimarru, Bunuwal, Miwatj Health); however, other opportunities were created by the Indigenous leaders. A community store that opened on 5 July 2013, a coffee shop about a month later, and a display room adjacent to the carpentry shop were built on the expansive grounds of the Gunyangara horticulture gardens. These facilities were built mainly with timber milled at the Dhupuma site, and these buildings created job positions for the Goyurr graduates.

A vision of self-sufficiency in capacity building was rapidly evolving. On 18 September 2013, when sitting outside the Gunyangara coffee shop in the company of Klaus Helms, the CEO of the Gumatj Corporation, and Galarrwuy Yunupingu, the Gumatj Clan leader, the capacity-building situation on the Gove Peninsula was summarised by the Indigenous statesman.

> My vision was there was plenty to share. My people need to eat and one way was with fresh meat. Thus, the idea of the cattle station at Garrathiya, the building of the accommodation, the abattoir for slaughtering and storage of the chilled meat, and transporting of carcasses to the cutting rooms at the crocodile farm. Now the bakery makes pies with our meat that we sell in our community store.

Further afield at Garrathiya, an abattoir was built. In April 2012, the first author visited Gunyangara to observe the initial stage of construction. Also on site were three representatives of the NT Department of Resources, who visited to give periodic guidance to ensure the structure construction adhered to hygiene regulations. Nominally two cattle are slaughtered each week. The magnificent obsession of Galarrwuy Yunupingu is being realised by the wealth of community capacity development. Nevertheless, there are also blemishes to acknowledge.

Seldom do Indigenous people subscribe to the wage economy or commercial tenets of the dominant mainstream economy. The 64 Ralpa graduates nominated in Table 9.1 as having employability status are unlikely to regularly present for work. Exceptions are the seven Indigenous men who work at the Dhupuma industrial site, the team who work on the town house lots, the cattle station workers, the ladies who work at the Gove Hospital, and those who work in Nhulunbuy Indigenous organisations (Bunuwal, Buku Larrnggar Mulka Art Centre, Dhimurru, Laynhapuy Homelands, Miwatj Health, Mungarr Community Council). Most Indigenous people are obliged to vacillate between work and customary cultural functions. Clan members are bound to attend cultural days and initiation ceremonies and undertake intellectual development by memorising clan laws, dances, songs, and the Dreamtime Stories. Moreover, in the wet season, the roads become impassable while the water courses and rivers cannot be traversed for, even with low flow rates, the numerous crocodiles make the sites extremely dangerous. Consequently, it is practical that the contract operations and the employment of Indigenous people, who would work in the savannah forest, are suspended.

Cultural forces underpin patterns observable in frameworks of working in the regulated market economy. Indigenous small business has magnetised a great deal of academic interest revealing a range of barriers (Russell-Mundine 2007), misconceptions, and ambiguous shortcomings (Foley 2007) despite considerable commitment by successive Australian governments to broker better outcomes such as a reduction in poverty and an improvement in wellbeing (Hunter 2013). Australian Indigenous small business found value creation through the pillars of social entrepreneurship with prominent features of family binding, social capital, high levels of membership reciprocity, and densely interlocked kin-based blood lines of relationships (Pearson and Helms 2012b). These frameworks are distinctly different to fundamental Western principles of profit for a singular identity or small group of stakeholders and the promotion of dimensions like sales growth or market share (Kukoc and Regan 2008). Indigenous social entrepreneurship is undertaken for the common good of the community; wealth is viewed as a commodity and not as funding future prosperity; and the venture is undertaken to transform the economic, social, and ecological circumstances of the group (settlement, community), not the individual (Jones 2007; Pearson and Helms 2013). Understandably, the well-intentioned endeavours of Australian government agencies emphasising adherence to governance and compliance to regulatory requirements have yet to successfully leverage capacity building in Indigenous enterprise framed with disparate cultural sensitivities.

An extremely ambitious capacity-building initiative is being established on the Gove Peninsula by the Yolngu residents. The catalyst for creating the Gulkula Mining Company, which has recently submitted an exploration license and a mine management plan to the relevant Australian government agencies, is the $2.4 million funding within the LUA with Rio Tinto (Dunlevie 2014). Features of the proposal are the construction of a new training school for Indigenous people of the NT, who as graduates will mine the Dhupuma Plateau. Also the Indigenous Gumatj Clan will own and operate the business, which is scheduled to commence in 2015. A mining operation of this proportion will open new avenues for Indigenous employment and create community productive capacity to a level not previously experienced in Australia.

Conclusion

Historically, Yolngu capacity development is portrayed as a function of how autonomy and dependency are exercised. Anthropological evidence and the written records in the logs of ships of visiting seafarers to northern Australia long before the federation of the Australian colonies show Yolngu people autonomously created extensive levels of capacity building. With the onset of federation and the establishment of the Church missions, greater restrictions, and higher dependency were placed on the lives of Yolngu people, who congregated at these coastal settlements. The outcome was a different type of controlled capacity development. When the miners came to the Gove Peninsula in the 1960s, they brought with them notions on how the Yolngu people should adapt (be controlled) to Western-style education and the national wage-earning economy. Faced with intense levels of dependency and minimal autonomy, most of the Yolngu clans returned to their remote ancestral homelands. Ratification of the new LUA in mid-2011 by the Australian Prime Minister enacted a renaissance in Yolngu control in the direction of education and vocation. For the first time in over 50 years, the Yolngu Elders have been able to install education systems with Indigenous-related epistemology and pedagogy. Now the Yolngu community leaders select the Ralpa participants, not the mining company. The recently acquired level of autonomy through the LUA is enabling the Yolngu people to care for customary responsibilities of their extensive land and sea estates by creating forms of economic development to build the capacity of their communities.

Australian Indigenous society has frequently been depicted as fragmented and excluded from the mainstream national economy. A large body of literature has constantly debated that Australian Indigenous policy has failed the Aboriginal community by establishing abounding deprivation and misery with reliance on welfare. Calls have been made for greater social inclusion to working, capitalist Australia as a pathway movement away from the deficit environment of a disadvantaged society. However, the strong cultural identity that is particularly prevalent in regional and remote Australia as well as to some extent on the fringes of larger towns and centres cannot be ignored.

A notion that Indigenous Australians will realign mindsets with 50,000 years heritage warrants revisitation. The core issue is not whether Aboriginal people can embrace a market economy, for they have demonstrated such capacity, but in what framework. A solution may be found in the cross culture management literature that entertains how individual divergent behaviours (to the mainstream society) are influenced by the convergent forces of the dominant institutions, rules, and societal values. Popularised in the current works is the perspective of a value system of crossvergence, a synergistic state resulting from the blending of the divergent and convergent elements. What is likely to have triggered the onset of crossvergence in past and present eras of Yolngu with the concomitant intensification of community building are the dimensions of opportunity and leadership. The major challenge for contemporary Australian Indigenous society is to find these features in their life–working mechanisms. Sobering is that few Australian Indigenous communities have been able to re-evaluate their core beliefs and deep-rooted ancient values to make them relevant in contemporary national and international forums.

References

Alcan Gove 2008, *Alcan Gove third stage expanson project review: a historical account of one of Australia's biggest industrial developments*, Alcan Gove, Nhulunbuy, Australia.

Altman, J.C. 2002, 'Indigenous hunter – gatherers in the 21st century: beyond the limits of universalism in Australian social policy', in T. Eardley and B. Bradbury (eds.), *Competing visions: refereed proceedings of the National Social Policy*

Conference 2001, Social Policy Research Centre, University of New South Wales, Sydney, Australia, pp. 35–44.

Altman, J.C. 2003, 'People on country, healthy landscapes and sustainable indigenous economic futures: the Arnhem Land case', *The Drawing Board: An Australian Review of Public Affairs*, vol. 4, no. 2, pp. 65–82.

Altman, J.C. 2009, 'Beyond closing the gap: valuing diversity in Indigenous Australia', *CAEPR Working Paper*, no. 54, Centre for Aboriginal Economic Policy Research, The Australian National University, Canberra, Australia.

Altman, J.C., Biddle, N. and Hunter, B.H. 2005, 'A historical perspective on Indigenous socioeconomic outcomes in Australia 1971–2001', *Australian Economic History Review*, vol. 45, no. 3, pp. 273–295.

Anderson, I. 2007, 'The end of Aboriginal self-determination?', *Futures*, vol. 39, no. 2/3, pp. 137–154.

Australian Government 2007, *Australian now*, Department of Foreign Affairs and Trade, Canberra, Australia.

Australian Government 2009, *Indigenous small business owners in Australia*, Australian Taxation Office, Canberra, Australia.

Australian Government 2010, *Closing the gap: Prime Minister's report 2010*, Commonwealth of Australia, Canberra, Australia.

Berndt, R.M. and Berndt, C.H. 1999, *The world of the first Australians: aboriginal traditional life past and present*, Aboriginal Studies Press, Canberra, Australia.

Biddle, N. 2010, 'Proximity to labour markets: revisiting Indigenous employment through an analysis of census place of work data', *Australian Journal of Labour Economics*, vol. 13, no. 2, pp. 175–189.

Biddle, N., Taylor, J. and Yap, M. 2009, 'Are the gaps closing? – regional trends and forecasts of Indigenous employment', *Australian Journal of Labour Economics*, vol. 12, no. 3, pp. 263–280.

Blackburn, R.A. and Leslie A.J. 1971, *Milirrpum v. Nabalco Pty Ltd and the Commonwealth of Australia: (Gove Land Rights Case): a claim by Aborigines that their interests in certain land had been invaded unlawfully by the defendants. Judgment of the Honourable Mr. Justice Blackburn*, Law Book Company, Sydney, Australia.

Blanch, S. 2008, 'Steps to a sustainable northern Australia', *Ecological Management and Restoration*, vol. 9, no. 2, pp. 110–115.

Brody, A.M. 2011, *Larrakitj: the Kerry Stokes collection*, Australian Capital Equity Pty, West Perth. Australia.

Brown, J. 2009, 'What's next for welfare-to-work?', *Issue Analysis*, no. 117, pp. 1–15.

Burt Reading Test 1974, *Burt reading test, revised*, University of Glasgow, The SCRE Centre Research in Education, Scotland.

Coronado, G. and Fallon, W. 2010, 'Giving with one hand: on the mining sectors treatment of Indigenous stakeholders in the name of CSR', *International Journal of Sociology and Social Policy*, vol. 30, no. 11/12, pp. 666–682.

Cousins, D. and Nieuwenhuysen, J. 1984, *Aboriginals and the mining industry: case studies of the Australian experience*, George Allen and Unwin, North Sydney, Australia.

Crough, G.J. 1985, *The history and contractual arrangements of the Gove bauxite/alumina project in the Northern Territory of Australia*, The Transnational Corporations Research Project, University of Sydney, Australia.

Daff, S. and Pearson, C.A.L. 2009, 'Indigenous employment: the Rio Tinto Alcan initiative in Northern Australia', *The Journal of Contemporary Issues in Business and Government*, vol. 15, no. 1, pp. 1–20.

Daff, S. and Pearson, C.A.L. 2010, 'Realising the capacity of Yolngu Aboriginals: an educational vocational scheme underpinned with family support', *Journal of Australian Indigenous Issues,* vol. 13, no. 1, pp. 3–18.

Defence 1978, *Letter from Department of Defence,* Held in the Special Closed Reserve of the Nhulunbuy Library, Nhulunbuy, Australia.

Drill Hall Gallery and Buku-Larrngay Mulka Centre 1999, *Saltwater: Yirrkala bark paintings of sea country: recognising Indigenous sea rights,* Buku-Larrngay Mulka Centre in association with Jennifer Isaacs Publishing, Neutral Bay, New South Wales, Australia.

Dunlevie, J. 2014, 'Rio Tinto – funded training centre to help Aboriginal miners', *ABC News,* viewed 2 August 2014, <www.abc.net.au/news/2014-08-02/rio-tinro-funded-miner-training-centre-in-arnhem-land-nt/5643240>.

Dunlop, I. 1995, *Pain for this land,* The Yirrkala Film Project, Pyrmont, New South Wales, Australia.

Dunlop, I. 1996, *Baniyala – 1974,* (DVD), The Yirrkala Film Project, Pyrmont, New South Wales, Australia.

Foley, D. 2003, 'An examination of Indigenous Australian entrepreneurs', *Journal of Developmental Entrepreneurship,* vol. 8, no. 2, pp. 133–151.

Foley, D. 2006, 'Indigenous Australian entrepreneurs: not all community organisations, not all in the outback', *CAEPR Discussion Paper,* no. 279, Centre for Aboriginal Policy Research, The Australian National University, Canberra, Australia.

Foley, D. 2007, 'Do we understand Indigenous entrepreneurship?', paper presented at the 20th SEAANZ Conference proceedings, Manukau City, New Zealand, 23–26 September 2007.

Furneaux, C.W. and Brown, K.A. 2008, 'Australian Indigenous entrepreneurship: a capital – based view', *International Journal of Entrepreneurship and Innovation,* vol. 9, no. 2, pp. 133–144.

Giddy, K., Lopez, J. and Redman, A. 2009, *Brokering successful Aboriginal and Torres Strait Islander employment outcomes: common themes in good-practice models: literature review,* National Centre for Vocational Research, Adelaide, Australia.

The Gove Bauxite Development 1968, *Feasibility report – supporting volume VI, town,* Nabalco, Sydney, Australia, and Zurich. Switzerland.

Gray, M. and Hunter, B.H. 2005, 'The labour market dynamics of Indigenous Australians', *Journal of Sociology,* vol. 41, no. 4, pp. 386–405.

Hamilton, C. 1996, 'Mining in Kakadu: lessons from Coronation Hill', *The Australian Institute,* vol. 9, pp. 1–19.

Harvey, B. and Brereton, D. 2005, 'Emerging models of community engagement in the Australian minerals industry', proceedings of the United Nations Conference on Engaging Communities, 14–17 August, Brisbane, Australia, pp. 1–15.

Hintjens, H. 2000, 'Environmental direct action in Australia: the case of Jabiluka Mine', *Community Development Journal,* vol. 35, no. 4, pp. 377–390.

Hughes, H. and Warin, J. 2005, 'A new deal for Aborigines and Torres Strait Islanders in remote communities', *Issues Analysis,* no. 54, pp. 1–20.

Hunter, B.H. 2009, 'Indigenous social exclusion: insights and challenges for the concept of social inclusion', *Australian Institute of Family Studies,* vol. 82, no. 1, pp. 52–61.

Hunter, B.H. 2010, *Closing the gap: pathways for Indigenous school leavers to undertake training or gain employment,* Australian Institute of Health and Welfare, Canberra, Australia.

Hunter, B. H. 2013, 'Recent growth in Indigenous self-employed and entrepreneurs', *CAEPR Working Paper*, no. 91, Centre for Aboriginal Economic Policy Research, The Australian National University, Canberra, Australia.

Hunter, B. H. and Gray, M. 2012, 'Indigenous labour supply following a period of strong economic growth', *Australian Journal of Labour Economics*, vol. 15, no. 2, pp. 141–159.

Indigenous Business Review 2003, *Report on support for Indigenous business*, Australian Government, Canberra, Australia.

Ivory, B. 1999, 'Enterprise development: a model for Aboriginal entrepreneurs', *South Pacific Journal of Psychology*, vol.11, no. 2, pp. 62–71.

Johns, G. 2011, *Aboriginal self-determination: the whiteman's dream*, Connor Court Publishing, Ballan, Victoria, Australia.

Jones, M. 2007, *Unpacking social enterprise: a discussion paper presenting an Australian perspective*, Social Alchemy Pty Ltd, Paddington, New South Wales, Australia.

Jordan, K. and Mavec, D. 2010, 'Corporate initiatives in Indigenous employment: the Australian employment covenant two years on', *CAEPR Working Paper*, no. 74, Centre for Aboriginal Economic Policy Research, The Australian National University, Canberra, Australia.

Kolig, E. 1987, 'The Noonkanbah story', *The Journal of Polynesian Society*, vol. 96, no. 4, pp. 508–510.

Kukoc, K. and Regan, D. 2008, *Measuring entrepreneurship*, the Australian Treasury, Canberra, Australia, viewed 18 October 2009, <www.treasury.gov.au/documents/1352/PDF/02_Entrepreneurship.pdf>

Maddison, S. 2008, 'Indigenous autonomy matters: what's wrong with the Australian government's "intervention" in Aboriginal communities', *Australian Journal of Human Rights*, vol. 14, no. 1, pp. 41–61.

McDonnell, S. 1999, 'The Grameen Bank micro-credit model: lessons for Australian Indigenous economic policy', *CAEPR Discussion Paper*, no. 178, Centre for Aboriginal Economic Policy Research, The Australian National University, Canberra, Australia.

McKenzie, M. 1976, *Mission to Arnhem Land*, Rigby, Adelaide, Australia.

Muir, S. 2011, 'Australian alternative spiritualities and a feeling for land', *The Australian Journal of Anthropology*, vol. 22, no. 3, pp. 370–387.

O'Lincoln, T. 1993, *Years of rage: social conflicts in the Fraser Era*, Bookmarks Australia, Melbourne, Australia.

The Parliament of the Commonwealth of Australia 2008, *Open for business: developing Indigenous enterprises in Australia*, Commonwealth Printing and Publishing Office, Canberra, Australia.

Pearson, C.A.L. 2012a, 'Australian councils unelected by the citizens in an Indigenous settings: the case of Nhulunbuy in the Northern Territory', *Australian Journal of Public Administration*, vol. 71, no. 3, pp. 278–289.

Pearson, C.A.L. 2012b, 'Recruitment of Indigenous Australians with linguistic and numeric disadvantages', *Research and Practice in Human Resource Management*, vol. 20, no. 1, pp. 66–80.

Pearson, C.A.L. and Daff, S. 2008, 'Recruitment challenges of Yolngu Aboriginal groups from remote communities in Australia: a case study of the Rio Tinto Alcan Gove initiative at Nhulunbuy', *Journal of Australian Indigenous Issues*, vol. 11, no. 3, pp. 19–36.

Pearson, C.A.L. and Daff, S. 2011, 'Collective delivery of work – integrated learning to Indigenous Australians in a remote community', *Asia-Pacific Journal of Cooperative Education*, vol.12, no. 2, pp. 125–145.

Pearson, C.A.L. and Daff, S. 2013, 'Indigenous workforce participation at a mining operaiton in northern Australia', *Australian Bulletin of Labour*, vol. 39, no. 1, pp. 42–63.

Pearson, C.A.L. and Helms, K. 2010a, 'Releasing Indigenous entrepreneurial capacity: a case study of the Yolngu clan in a remote region of northern Australia', *Global Business and Economic Review, Special Issue*, vol. 12, no. 1/2, pp. 72–84.

Pearson, C.A.L. and Helms, K. 2010b, 'Building social entrepreneurship in a remote Australian Indigenous community: the east Arnhem Land housing construction case', *Journal of Australian Indigenous Issues*, vol. 13, no. 4, pp. 2–18.

Pearson, C.A.L. and Helms, K. 2011, 'Indigenous entrepreneurship in timber furniture manufacturing: the Gumatj venture in northern Australia', *Information Management and Business Review*, vol. 2, no. 1, pp. 1–11.

Pearson, C.A.L. and Helms, K. 2012a, 'A chronicle of the timber industry in east Arnhem Land, Australia', in R.S. Adisa (eds.), *Rural development: contemporary issues and practices*, Intech, Rijeka, Croatia, pp. 393–408.

Pearson, C.A.L. and Helms, K. 2012b, 'A hybrid social governance Indigenous entrepreneurship model for sustainable development: the Gumatj Clan innovation', *Journal of Australian Indigenous Issues*, vol. 15, no. 1, pp. 76–94.

Pearson, C.A.L. and Helms, K. 2013, 'Indigenous social entrepreneurship: the Gumatj clan enterprise in east Arnhem Land', *The Journal of Entrepreneurship*, vol. 22, no. 1, pp. 43–70.

Pearson, C.A.L., Helms, K. and Daff, S. 2014, 'An education programme with Indigenous voice and vision: the Ralpa scheme in northern Australia', *Journal of Australian Indigenous Issues*, vol. 17, no. 1, pp. 45–61.

Peredo, A.M. and Chrisman J.J. 2006, 'Toward a theory of community – based enterprise', *Academy of Management Journal*, vol. 31, no. 2, pp. 309–328.

Pholi, K., Black, D. and Richards, C. 2009, 'Is 'close the gap' a useful approach to improving the health and wellbeing of Indigenous Australians?', *Australian Review of Public Affairs*, vol. 9, no. 2, pp. 1–13.

Pretty, B. n.d., *Eldo and after*, Typed report held in the Special Closed Reserve of the Nhulunbuy Library, Nhulunbuy, Australia.

Raggatt, H.G. 1968, *Mountains of ore*, Landsdowne Press, Melbourne, Australia.

Rose, F.G.G. 1987, *The traditional model of production of the Australian Aborigines*, Angus and Robertson, Sydney, Australia.

Russell, D. 2004, 'Aboriginal-Makassan interactions in the eighteenth and nineteenth centuries in northern Australia and contemporary sea rights claims', *Australia Aboriginal Studies*, vol.1, pp. 3–17.

Russell-Mundine, G. 2007, 'Key factors for the successful development of Australian Indigenous entrepreneurship', *Tourism Preliminary Communication*, vol. 55, no. 4, pp. 417–429.

Shearer, E., Cheshire and Apps, R. 1975, 'A restandardisation of the Burt-Vernon and Schonell graded word reading tests', *Educational Research*, vol. 18, no. 1, pp. 63–73.

Shepherdson, E. 1981, *Half a century in Arnhem Land*, Pan Print, Torrens Park, Australia.

Smith, A. 2006, 'Indigenous development – without community, without commerce', *Australian Review of Public Affairs*, vol. 4, pp. 1–7.

Stanner, W.E.H. 1979, *White man got no dreaming*, Australian National University Press, Canberra, Australia.

Suter, K. 2003, 'Australia – one land: two peoples', *Contemporary Review*, vol. 283, no. 1651, pp. 84–90.

Territory 2008, 'Indigenousbizness: creating jobs on the homeland', *Territory Quarterly*, vol. Third Quarter, pp. 40–43.

Thomson, D. 2010, *Donald Thomson in Arnhem Land*, The Miegunyah Press, Carlton, Victoria, Australia.

Thomson, H. 1983, 'Kimberly landrights and resources', *Australian Left Review*, vol. Spring, pp. 38–44.

Trudgen, R. 2000, *Why warriors lie down and die*, Aboriginal Resources and Development Services, Darwin, Australia.

Uniting Justice 2011, *Submission to the independent inquiry on insecure work in Australia*, Uniting Justice Australia, Sydney, Australia.

Wood, G. J. and Davidson, M. J. 2011, 'A review of male and female Australian Indigenous entrepreneur', *Gender in Management: An International Journal*, vol. 26, no. 4, pp. 311–326.

Worsley, P. M. 1955, 'Early Asian contacts with Australia', *Past and Present*, vol. 7, pp. 1–11.

Yunupingu, G. 2009, 'Tradition, truth and tomorrow', *The Monthly*, December 2008–January 2009, pp. 32–40.

Yunupingu, G. 2014, 'Teach our young people to look up: one Arnhem Land community's goal to anchor its future in jobs', *The Weekend Australian*, August 2–3, vol. Inquirer, pp. 32–40.

10 Breaking the poverty cycle through linking farmers to markets in Timor Leste: the World Vision income generation project

Vicente de Paulo Correia and
Maria Fay Rola-Rubzen

Introduction

Timor Leste is a newly independent country. The country has a long history of colonisation, having been first colonised by the Portuguese for around 350 years and then by Indonesia for 25 years. After the 1999 referendum, 78 per cent of the population chose independence from Indonesia for the country, and in May 2002, Timor Leste was formally recognised by the United Nations as an independent country with the official name of República Democrática de Timor Leste (RDTL). Timor Leste's territory is comprised of, not only the eastern side of the island, but also the enclave of Oecusse in the western half of Timor, Atauro Island, and Jaco Islet, totalling around 15 000 km². Administratively, Timor Leste constitutes13 districts, 65 sub-districts and 442 villages. Topographically, one-third of the country, particularly in the west, is composed of mountains, and about one-third of the region is hilly (Ministry of Agriculture, Forestry and Fisheries [MAFF] 2004).

According to the República Democrática de Timor Leste (2011), 'the total population of Timor Leste is around 1.1 million people with 70.4 per cent classified as living in rural areas. The annual population growth rate is 2.4 per cent, and population density is 71.5 persons per km². The current literacy rate is estimated to be 50 per cent (Lundahl and Sjohlm 2005; Rahim 2007).The economy is mainly agricultural, with the agricultural sector 'contributing the largest share to GDP, employing almost three-quarters of the workforce, providing over 70 per cent of the population with their main sources of livelihood and offering the largest potential exports and trade' (MAFF 2004; Saldanha and Costa 1999: 35).

Timor Leste is amongst the poorest countries in East Asia, ranking 142 out of 177 countries worldwide in 2006 (República Democrática de Timor Leste and United Nations Development Programme 2009). The 2010 Global Human Development Report places Timor Leste into the medium human development category, with a ranking of 120 out of 169 countries (United Nations Development Programme 2011). About 44 per cent of the general population live below the poverty line as compared with 25 per cent of urban dwellers. The poverty incidence is about 30 per cent in the eastern region and 46 per cent in the west (World Bank 2003). According to Soges S.p.a. (2009), among rural households, poverty tends to be worse in the highlands, which explains why poverty and other indicators of well-being are worse in the mountainous central and western regions than in the less mountainous east. In addition, most of the population earn less than one US dollar per day, and two-fifths of the population are unable to access basic necessities of living (Hill and Saldanha 2001).

A report from the International Monetary Fund (2007) showed that the percentage of poverty increased from 39.5 per cent in 2001 to 41.5 per cent in 2004. The percentage of the population who lived on only one dollar per day also rose from 20 per cent to 21.5 per cent in 2001 and 2004, respectively. However, recent statistics from the Government of Timor Leste (GoTL) (2011) showed that, from 2007 to 2009, a total of 96,000 people or 9 per cent of the population moved out of extreme poverty.

East Timor is rich in natural resources, with two-thirds of its GDP coming from petroleum income. Although a resource-rich country, according to Soges S.p.a. (2009), unless measures are taken to stimulate growth outside the petroleum sector, non-oil GDP growth will at best keep up with population growth, seriously limiting Timor Leste's chances to achieve the poverty reduction target as set by the Millennium Development Goals (MDGs) by 2015. The target of the MDG goals for Timor Leste is in line with its National Development Goals, which is to improve the political development, reduce poverty and promote rural development, improve social and human development, promote agriculture and industry, improve infrastructure and manage natural resources (República Democrática de Timor Leste and UNDP 2009).

Rural poverty in Timor Leste is linked to the low production and productivity of most agricultural crops, the lack of market opportunities, high rate of illiteracy and unemployment in the country. As most of the population live in rural areas and the majority of them are small farmers, Timor Leste farmers are amongst the poorest of the poor.

Research problem

The majority of farmers practice subsistence farming. This in turn results in low production and low productivity. A large capital investment programme had been introduced in the country since its independence to increase agricultural production and productivity. However, subsistence agriculture in Timor Leste is still likely to persist for the foreseeable future because, while most of the interventions concentrate on how to increase crop production to fulfil food security goals, there is a dearth of activity or programmes that focus on marketing produce. As a result, farmers continue to grow conventional crops to fulfil their family necessities rather than producing for the market. This perhaps partly explains why poverty proliferates in rural areas. Indeed, as concluded by the poverty assessment conducted by the World Bank (World Bank 2003), households who are better linked to the market have lower poverty rates.

A case can therefore be made that to reduce poverty and unemployment farm-ers need to be more market-oriented, changing from subsistence farming to semi-commercial or commercial farming. This means further focus on both pro-duction and marketing. The main problem, however, is that while farmers have resources, primarily land and labour, they lack inputs, capital, technical knowl-edge and access to markets, and they are also constrained by the lack of infrastruc-ture such as rural roads and transportation (Shepherd 2007; Silva 2005).

To overcome these problems and help farmers move from subsistence to semi-commercial farming, it is important for farmers to link with the markets. This may involve government bodies and the private sector in the implementation of the linkage approach, such as linkages through agribusiness firms, coopera-tives, leading farmers, processors and vertical coordination. By participating in these linkages, farmers are likely to benefit. As empirical studies have shown, linking small-scale farmers to the markets benefits farmers (Berdegue, Bienabe and Peppelenhos 2008; Danielou, Labaste and Voisard 2003; Simmons, Winters and Patrick 2005; Swinnen 2007; Patrick 2004). Benefits include improved avail-ability of inputs and credit, assistance and risk reduction. Furthermore, farmers' production, productivity and the quality of the product also improve as there is an assured market for the products. These, in turn, can make a significant contri-bution to poverty reduction and reduce unemployment (Berdegue, Bienabe and Peppelenhos 2008).

How can farmers effectively link to markets? Linking farmers to markets may not be easy especially when there are problems in information or lack of infra-structure and when the markets are far from production areas. To effectively link farmers to markets, farmers must be able to meet the requirements of the market. So far, little research has been conducted on this topic and on the potential of linking farmers to markets in Timor Leste. Moreover, little is known on what critical factors are needed to successfully link farmers to markets.

Review of the literature

Many of the poor in developing countries still depend on agriculture for their livelihood, both directly and indirectly, and the majority of these are small-scale farmers. The productivity and quality of most of the agricultural products pro-duced by small farmers in these countries are very low. This is due to the low skills of farmers, poor crop management, lack of inputs and lack of access to credit and information. Meanwhile, growing populations in developing countries continue to create demand for agricultural products, in particular, fresh produce and pro-cessed horticultural products (Asian Productivity Organization [APO] 2006). Meeting market requirements necessitates having assured quality and safety in both domestic and export supply chains (APO 2006).

Given that farmers are rational and generally respond to incentives, linking farmers to markets (LF2M) by engaging them in the supply chain is likely to encourage increased production, improved quality and better safety of the prod-uct with consequent positive impacts on income if they are able to efficaciously engage with the market. As stated by Shepherd (2007), the opportunity for small farmers to increase their incomes relies on their capability to be involved success-fully in the market place. Thus, enhancing farmers' access to markets should be a key part of the strategy to promote rural development and poverty reduction (Fischer and Qaim 2011).

LF2M is one approach to help small-scale farmers participate more effectively in the market place and assist poor producers increase their output. Through the linkage, farmers will benefit in terms of accessibility to the market, access to inputs and access to credit. This in turn will contribute to increasing their income and reducing poverty in rural areas. As stated by the International Fund for Agricultural Development (2003), improved market access is of crucial and immediate importance to small-scale farmers and rural poor households. Studies suggest that improvement in market access can enhance agricultural-based eco-nomic growth and increase rural incomes (International Fund for Agricultural Development 2003; Shepherd 2006; World Bank 2008). In addition, to support an agenda on 'agriculture for development', it is important to enhance small-holder competitiveness, facilitate market entry, improve market access and estab-lish efficient value chains (World Bank 2008). According to Shepherd (2006), the reasons why farmers need to be linked to markets are because the production push focus is no longer viable and because small surpluses for ad hoc sales are not a realistic approach in the long term. Therefore, farmers need to respond to what the market demands.

Linking farmers to markets can be done through several approaches – through cooperatives; contract farming; marketing boards; partnerships with domes-tic traders; linkages with exporters, agro-processors and retailers and linkages through leading farmers.

NGOs have played an active role in linking farmers to markets. NGOs and other organisations recognised that assistance projects that stressed building up farmers' production capacities is not enough to ensure the sustainability of their income (Shepherd 2007). It is recognised that production support activities must be related to market demand and that this must be considered within the context of the whole supply chain. For instance, in linking traders and mandarin orange farmers in Indonesia, training provided by traders was made possible through the intervention of an NGO in organizing the farmers to receive the training (Shepherd 2007). In some cases, contract farming companies have approached NGOs to organise farmer groups to receive inputs and collect outputs for supply to the factory.

One of the features of an LF2M model involving an NGO is the focus of NGOs on capacity building. NGOs recognise that effectively linking farmers to markets is not just a matter of connecting the two end points. In many cases, farmers are unable to reach markets because of the constraints they face. Thus, it is critical to address bottlenecks faced by farmers. Areas identified by NGOs for training have included management, contract negotiation, market research, supply chain analysis, use of basic business documentation such as delivery and consignment notes and farm enterprise decision tools such as crop budgets (Shepherd 2007).

The objective of this study is to examine an NGO model linking farmers to markets in Timor Leste and its impact on poverty reduction. The NGO project to be evaluated is that of the World Vision income generation program. This study explores the critical success factors in developing and operating a successful LF2M model.

The case study: World Vision income generation and rural development project

The World Vision's income generation and rural community project is one of the programmes that facilitate the transfer of farmers produce to the market. World Vision is an international NGO working in Timor Leste, particularly in the districts of Aileu and Bobonaro. World Vision started its work in Timor Leste in 1995. Most World Vision programmes emphasise improving agricultural crop yield, increasing levels of income in rural communities and addressing the issue of children's health and nutrition. The World Vision's project on income generation and rural communities addressed the issue of poverty alleviation via a whole value-chain approach. It focused on developing the agribusiness private sector in Timor Leste by building the capacity of farmers, developing the entrepreneurial skills of the community and establishing mechanisms to link farmer's produce to the market. This, in turn, encouraged communities to expand their production capacity and to generate surplus for sale in markets outside of local communities.

The aim of World Vision was to increase agricultural production and improve marketing through the introduction of new crop seed varieties, new technologies, linking farmers to markets and improving farmer's income through income generation activities. Capacity building provided to farmers included training in enhancing soil fertility, composting, crop rotation, establishing terraces, weeding, marketing and improved animal health. Other important services included distributing agricultural materials and tools, providing farmers with modern seed varieties, facilitating extension workers to assist farmers, establishing mini greenhouses and facilitating transport of farmers produce to markets.

The activities in which World Vision assisted farmers in production and marketing include encouraging farmers to use proven modern seed varieties, organizing farmers into groups by sharing their labour and skills to increase production, facilitating transport of the produce and training in post-harvest handling and quality control. In these ways, it developed local capacity to engage with a wider market and improve farm productivity.

The LF2M model of the World Vision is as follows. Farmers usually bring their products to the Centro Produto Local (CPL), although, in some cases, World Vision staff collect the produce from the farms and deliver them to the CPL. The centre was established by World Vision in 2007, with the aim of helping farmers to sell their produce to the market. All the products that go through CPL are registered and documented in terms of quantity, type of produce and the agreed price. After the produce has been documented, CPL then washes, cleans, sorts and packs the vegetables. Following these activities, the produce

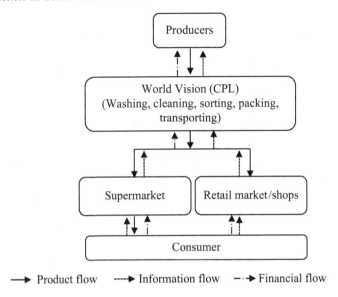

Figure 10.1 World Vision value chain
Source: Correia (2012).

is then transported and delivered to the Dili market using World Vision's own transport as shown in Figure 10.1. Through the centre, farmers save time and money for some marketing activities, such as grading, cleaning, packing and transportation.

The strategy used by World Vision to help farmers in selling their produce is as follows. In the first year, 75 per cent of transport costs are paid by World Vision, and 25 per cent are paid by farmers. In the second year, the cost of transport is split 50:50. In the third year, farmers pay 75 per cent, and World Vision contributes 25 per cent. Finally, in the fourth year and onwards, farmers pay 100 per cent of the transportation costs. This is an important strategy as it involves farmers in organising the transportation of their produce to the market. It is a slow process, but the farmers are clear that by the fourth year they will be responsible for their own transport costs. This is one way to train farmers to collectively organise their produce and share the cost for transporting their produce to the market, as this can reduce the cost of marketing. Furthermore, by involving farmers in sharing the cost of transport progressively, World Vision is showing that their contribution will be withdrawn one day, thus building the capacity of farmers to become independent and stand up on their own. This prepares farmers to take over when it comes to the completion of the project. This means that the sustainability of the programme will be maintained in the future.

The main buyers of World Vision supported products are the retail shops and some supermarkets, and the products on offer are mainly vegetables (e.g. carrots, cabbage, tomato, beans, snow peas and mustard). The percentage of products distributed to supermarkets is about 50 per cent while retail markets/shops take around 50 per cent.

One of the capacity-building activities embedded in this LF2M programme is facilitating the services of extension workers in assisting farmers both in production and marketing. Due to international support and funds from World Vision, farmers benefitted from external extension support that they may not normally have access to. In the current study, this support was considered by farmers as a significant contribution of the World Vision model in helping them increase their vegetable production, improve the quality of their produce and helping them gain access to markets. Compared to other cases on LF2M in Timor Leste (Correia and Rola-Rubzen 2010), this capacity-building element was the distinguishing feature of the World Vision model. As there was a general lack of extension workers in most of the rural areas in Timor Leste, providing farmers with extension support was valuable in assisting farmers improve their production practices and meeting market requirements. As an NGO, World Vision played an important role as the government was unable to make such arrangements to help farmers (Dixie 2005).

Research approach

This study was conducted in the sub-district of Aileu Vila, Timor Leste. Aileu Vila is the capital of Aileu district, and is situated in the northwestern part of Timor Leste, about 47 km from the capital city. It can be reached in one and a half hours by road from Dili.

The research involved mixed methods including a quantitative survey of farmers and in-depth interviews with key informants in the agricultural supply chain. The sample includes farmers, institutional buyers and other downstream buyers such as traders and retailers. For farmers, data was collected through surveys using a random sample of 300 participants. For the NGO LF2M model, 75 farmers were surveyed. Interviews, using complete enumeration, were also conducted with the managers of supermarkets, managers of restaurants/hotels and traders in Dili. In addition, value-chain mapping was conducted to develop a description of the horticulture value chain and identify potential high-value markets. This study is based from the PhD research of one of the authors, Correia (2012). This chapter presents the analysis of the NGO LF2M model.

Results and discussion

Impact of LF2M

How effective was the LF2M model in building farmers' capacity to link to markets and to break the poverty cycle? To determine the impact of the LF2M model, 71 farmers involved in the World Vision programme were surveyed using a questionnaire. An in-depth interview was also conducted with the group leader. The criteria to measure impacts were chosen based on the review of literature as well as findings from the FGDs undertaken as part of the larger study. The criteria included:

1) access to market,
2) access to inputs,
3) crop production,
4) product quality,
5) access to technical advice,
6) risk,
7) profit earned,
8) product price, and
9) access to food for family consumption.

Respondents were requested to score each of these criteria on a five-point Likert scale from 'highly disagree' (1) to 'highly agree' (5). They were also given a chance to provide other criteria to use to measure effectiveness through an open-ended question.

The results of the analysis are presented in Table 10.1 and show that the top five impacts on participant-respondents, based on their perceptions, include

Table 10.1 Mean scores of the impact on farmers of participating in LF2M initiatives

Impact	Highly disagree (%)	Disagree (%)	Neither agree nor disagree (%)	Agree (%)	Highly agree (%)	N/A (%)	Mean
I have better access to markets	0	0	0	28.2	69.0	2.8	4.71
I have lower risk in marketing	0	1.4	1.4	78.9	16.9	1.4	4.13
I have better access to technical advice	0	0	7.0	90.2	1.4	1.4	3.94
My production has increased	0	1.4	11.3	87.3	0	0	3.86
My profit/income has increased	2.8	0	14.1	76.1	1.4	5.6	3.78
I now face lower risk in production	0	0	64.8	35.2	0	0	3.35
I have better access to seeds	0	0	69.0	29.6	1.4	0	3.32
I receive better prices	11.2	35.2	40.8	9.9	1.4	1.5	2.54
My family has better access to food	21.1	0	1.4	14.1	1.4	62.0	2.27
I have better access to fertilisers	4.2	1.4	1.4	1.4	0	91.6	2.00

better access to markets, reduction in marketing risk, better access to technical advice and increase in production and income.

In general, LF2M initiatives have had a positive impact on participants. Most of them generally agreed that, through their participation in the initiative, some of the problems they faced were solved. All of these factors received high mean scores of more than 3.5. For example from the total of 71 respondents, 69 per cent highly agreed that, through their involvement in LF2M initiatives, they were able to better access markets; more than 75 per cent of respondents agreed that their engagement in the initiatives resulted in lowering the risk they faced, improved access to technical advice and increased their production and income. Meanwhile, more than 60 per cent of respondents were not sure whether their engagement in the programme contributed to the reduction of their production risk and led to better access to seeds. The programme also had lesser impact on price, with about 35 per cent and 11 per cent of respondents disagreeing and highly disagreeing that their involvement in the LF2M initiative resulted to them receiving better prices for their produce. Only about 10 per cent of respondents agreed that they received better prices for their product. Despite this, however, some respondents claim that they will still continue to participate in the linkage programme as long as the programme helps them to deliver their produce to the market and provide them with some support and assistance. In addition, through the open-ended question, respondents indicated that other impacts included improvement of farmer skills, enhancement of product quality, adoption of new technology, allowing them to work in a group and better access to information.

Through the case study interviews and discussion with the coordinator and staff of World Vision on the effectiveness of the LF2M initiative, a number of factors have emerged. Table 10.2 summarises the effectiveness of the LF2M initiatives as perceived by the World Vision respondents and farmers.

Table 10.2 World Vision and farmers' perception of the impact of the LF2M initiative

Perceptions	World Vision	Farmers
Improve farmers' skills	√	√
Access to high-end market	√	√
Access to inputs, technical advice and training	√	√
Risk reduced for linkage partner	√	-
Lower cost of marketing	√	√
Profit derived for Zero Star and World Vision	√	-
Assured product supply	√	-
Availability of land and labour	√	-

As shown in Table 10.2, the LF2M initiative contributed to the improvement of farmer's skills, which led to an increase in production and improved quality of the produce. Farmers also gained access to high-end markets and received technical advice and training. Their production and marketing risk were also reduced. Being part of the LF2M initiative also lowered the cost of marketing and improved access to inputs and profits earned from their farm activities. World Vision also benefited in terms of assured product supplies and the availability of land and labour. For example World Vision did not have to rent land and hire labour. The arrangement was for farmers to grow crops on their own land using their own labour. This meant that World Vision did not have to invest in land or spend funds for hired labour. They just provided technical assistance and bought farmers' produce. Through this relationship, farmers were able to ensure regular supply to World Vision and, on the other hand, to guarantee the product to their customers. This result is consistent with the studies done by Shepherd (2006) and Glover (1994), which stated that the benefit stakeholders can gain from their involvement in LF2M initiatives is that the supply of the product is assured without having to make commitments on land and labour resources.

Based on the perception of farmers, the initiative has been effective; they claim that, through their involvement in the linkage program, they were able to access high-end markets and access training; inputs (e.g. seeds) were made available to them, their crop production increased, and marketing cost was reduced. The linkage partners and the farmers had the same perception – the initiative has contributed to better access to markets for farmers, increased crop production, access to inputs and training and reduced marketing cost.

The results of this study are consistent with the literature. For instance, studies have shown that the positive impacts of participation in linking farmers to markets generally are related to income, employment, improved access to credit and assistance (Glover and Kusterer 1990; Grosh 1994; Hayami and Otsuka 1993; Humphrey, McCulloch and Ota 2004;). In addition, linking farmers to markets also improves farmers' skills and knowledge; increases bargaining capacity of farmers, advance payments, access to transport and logistical facilities and transforms the production system from traditional to a more profitable farm enterprise (Glover 1994; Mancero 2007; Rao et al. 2006; Shepherd 2006). These advantages will lead to an increase in production and productivity and an improvement in the quality and availability of the products demanded by the market. This, in turn, will contribute to the increase in farmers' income, employment opportunities and poverty reduction in rural areas.

Challenges

The main challenge faced by this World Vision LF2M model, similar to other NGO-led models, is that the project depends on funding from donors. Therefore, they could not guarantee the continuation of the project in the future. World Vision has tried to address this by putting in place staggered support in marketing, initially shouldering the cost but gradually reducing it so that after a set numbers of years (where farmers' incomes are projected to increase), they are expected to fully cover the costs. This is an integral component of their capacity building.

Another challenge is the lack of modern seed varieties. As most of the seeds grown by farmers are imported and are quite expensive and not available locally, farmers need to spend extra money on transport to get seeds from Dili. A further challenge is the lack of motivation by some farmers to manage the farm. In addition, there are many family events such as funerals and weddings, which dominated most of farmers' time and money that could be used for farm activities. For example, if some of the relatives die, related families need to participate in the ceremony, which sometimes takes weeks. Other challenges are the lack of input suppliers, poor roads and infrastructure, lack of standard measurement and the poor skill level of the farmers (Fritsch et al. 2013; Rola-Rubzen et al. 2010).

Critical success factors

The critical success factors from the World Vision intervention on LF2M programme include external support in terms of funding and assistance, capacity-building support to farmers, the establishment of the CPL, targeting, introduction of new techniques for growing crops and transport facilitation. The external support provided the impetus for World Vision to enhance its activities and improve farmers' capacity in responding to what was demanded by the market. Without this support, World Vision would not have been able to manage its activities in a sustainable way. In addition, building the technical skills of farmers was critical in implementing their LF2M model. In this model, the aim was to support farmers increase their production and improve marketing of their produce through capacity building, technical assistance, provision of critical farm inputs, transport facilitation and buying of farmers' produce. Through these various supporting initiatives, farmers were able to increase their production and have better access to markets. With the support from World Vision, crop production increased; farmers regularly conducted grading, sorting and packing; and used improved packaging and handling materials (e.g. crates). This allowed them access to high-end markets in Dili that was not previously achievable for them.

Another critical success factor is 'targeting'. World Vision limited the area covered only to areas that have potential for the particular products, such as Aileu and Bobonaro. By targeting areas that are known as suitable for certain crops, World Vision was able to reduce their operational risk. Further success factors of the linkage models included the use of new growing techniques to improve yields and the establishment of CPL to market farmers' produce.

Conclusion and implications

The World Vision LF2M model involved developing partnerships between farmers and World Vision who facilitated the linkage with the markets. Through the project local capacity building was developed in production and marketing, thus improving longer term income generation opportunities. One of the key objectives of the partnership is to improve access to existing and emerging growth markets. The key characteristic of this linkage model that differentiated it from other LF2M model in Timor Leste is that World Vision provided capacity-building support and assistance to farmers to increase their crop production and facilitated the transport of the produce to the market. A number of services were delivered to farmers to enable them to participate in the chain, including training and technical assistance, seed distribution, introduction of new technologies and transportation.

The study found that the advantages of linking farmers to markets include enabling farmers' produce to reach new markets, improvements in farmers' knowledge and skills through training, access to technical assistance and improved quantity and quality of the produce. Factors that led to the success of this LF2M model include external support for funding and assistance, innovative marketing strategies applied to gain new markets, specialising with existing products and, in some cases, diversification to increase farmers' income.

The lessons that can be learned from this model are that LF2M programmes need to focus on existing commodities, which have good and reliable markets, as this will lessen the risk faced by farmers. Second, working together as a group can empower farmers' bargaining position in dealing with traders. This will also reduce the cost of transport and transaction cost. Finally, building the capacity of farmers in both production and marketing are critical in ensuring an effective linkage of farmers to markets as farmers need to be able to supply what is required by the market, both quality- and quantity-wise.

This study clearly shows that the contribution of LF2M initiatives as demonstrated by the World Vision model includes increasing farmers' income, providing job opportunities for rural communities and poverty reduction. This result is in line with some previous studies that describe the positive impacts of participation in linking farmers to markets, which include income, employment, improved access to credit and assistance (Glover and Kusterer 1990; Grosh 1994; Hayami and Otsuka 1993; Humphrey, McCulloch and Ota 2004).

The World Vision case presented in the study revealed that small farmers can access high-end markets with appropriate linking mechanisms to markets. However, for the effects to be sustainable in the long run, there is a need for appropriate physical infrastructure, a supportive policy and regulatory environment, as well as an engaged private sector actively contributing to the development. As stressed by Shepherd (2007), Silva (2005) and Simmons (2003), for market linkage to be sustainable and conducive, governments should create a favourable policy environment (e.g. laws and regulations, security) so that any approach or programme related to introducing linkages can function properly and satisfy all parties involved in the linkages, in particular, small and poor farmers. Shepherd (2007) also suggested that, for the private sector to function, governments need to create an environment that enables them to operate in a competitive way.

Thus to improve LF2M initiatives in Timor Leste, there is a need for the government to create a policy environment that is conducive to promote production and improve the marketing system through training, research and provision of extension services, roads and transportation systems and addressing land tenure issues. Likewise, due to the public nature of some potential impacts, the government should set the food quality standards and handle quality certification. The government should promote appropriate policies that can improve the business climate in general and encourage private sector participation. This may include initial assistance in forming marketing groups, support targeting extension and research in the agriculture sector, modification of the system of finance to meet the credit needs of small farmers, enhancing policies on risk management and improving education and training of smallholder farmers (Hazell 2007). The government also needs to provide an enabling environment for investment and encourage private sector participation.

References

Asian Productivity Organization 2006, *Postharvest management of fruit and vegetables in the Asia-Pacific region*, Asian Productivity Organization and Food and Agriculture Organization, Tokyo, Japan.

Berdegue, J.A., Bienabe, E. and Peppelenhos, L. 2008, *Keys to inclusion of small-scale producers in dynamic market*, Innovative Practice in Connecting Small-Scale Producers with Dynamic Market, Sustainable Market Group and IIED, London, UK.

Correia, V.P. 2012, 'Analysis of 'Linking farmers to markets' for carrots, cabbages and snow peas in Aileu Vila, Maubisse and Hatubuilico, Timor Leste', PhD thesis, School of Management, Curtin University, Sydney, Australia, viewed 15 November 2014, <http://link.library.curtin.edu.au/p?cur_digitool_dc199985>.

Correia, V.P. and Rola-Rubzen, M.F. 2010, 'Linking farmers to markets: the case of Zero Star UniPessoal', paper presented to the International Society for Horticultural Sciences, Singapore, 4–8 July 2010, <www.actahort.org/books/895/895_12.htm>.

Danielou, M., Labaste, P. and Voisard, J.M. 2003, 'Linking farmers to markets: exporting Malian mangoes to Europe', *African Region Working Paper*, no. 60, World Bank, Washington, DC.

Dixie, G. 2005, *Horticultural marketing: marketing extension guide 5*, Food and Agriculture Organization, Rome, Italy.

Fischer, E. and Qaim, M. 2011, 'Linking smallholders to markets: determinants and impacts of farmer collective action in Kenya', *World Development*, vol. 20, no. 10, pp. 30–40.

Fritsch, C., Jarvis, P., Brown, A. and Amaral, A. 2013, *Performance evaluation of the USAID/Timor Leste consolidating cooperative and agribusiness recovery (COCAR) project*, USAID, Timor Leste.

Glover, D. 1994, 'Contract farming and commercialization of agriculture in developing countries', in J. von Braun and E.T. Kennedy (eds.), *Agricultural commercialization, economic development and nutrition*, John Hopkins University Press, Baltimore, MD, pp. 166–175.

Glover, D. and Kusterer, K. 1990, *Small farmers, big business: contract farming and rural development*, Macmillan, London, UK.

Government of Timor Leste 2011, *Rural development and poverty reduction the focus for 2010 budget*, media release, viewed 20 January 2011, <www.timor-leste.gov.tl>.

Grosh, B. 1994, 'Contract farming in Africa: an application of the new institutional economics', *Journal of African Economies*, vol. 3, no. 2, pp. 231–261.

Hayami, Y. and Otsuka, K. 1993, *The economics of contract choice*, Oxford University Press, Oxford, UK.

Hazell, P. 2007, 'Transformations in agriculture and their implications for rural development', *Journal of Agricultural and Development Economics – eJADE*, vol. 4, no. 1, pp. 47–65.

Hill, H. and Saldanha, J.M. 2001, *East Timor: development challenges for the world's newest nation*, Asia Pacific Press, Canberra, Australia.

Humphrey, J., McCulloch, N. and Ota, M. 2004, 'The impact of European market changes on employment in the Kenyan horticultural sector', *Journal of International Development*, vol. 16, no. 1, pp. 63–80.

International Fund for Agricultural Development, 2003, *Promoting market access for the rural poor in order to achieve the Millennium Development Goals*, International Fund for Agricultural Development (IFAD), Rome, Italy.

International Monetary Fund 2007, *Democratic Republic of Timor Leste: selected issues and statistical appendix*, International Monetary Fund (IMF) Country Report no. 07/86, Washington, DC.

Lundahl, M. and Sjohlm, F. 2005, *Economic development in Timor Leste 2000–2005*, SIDA Country Economic, no. 4, Stockholm, Sweden.

Ministry of Agriculture, Forestry and Fisheries 2004, *Policy and strategic framework*, Ministry of Agriculture, Forestry and Fisheries, Dili, Timor Leste, viewed 12 October 2014, <http://timor-leste.gov.tl/?lang=pt&s=ministerio+de+agricultura>.

Mancero, L. 2007, *Potato chain study in Ecuador*, Food and Agriculture Organisation of the United Nations and International Potato Center Project, Ecuador, < ftp://ftp.fao.org/es/esa/lisfame/PotatoValueChainEcuador.pdf>.

Patrick, I. 2004, 'Contract farming in Indonesia: smallholders and agribusiness working together', ACIAR *Technical Reports*, no. 54, ACIAR, Canberra, Australia.

Rahim, K.K. 2007, *Market feasibility study for AMCAP*, United Nations Office for Project Services (UNOPS), Bangkok, Thailand.

Rao, P.P., Reddy, K.G.R., Reddy, B.V.S., Gowda, C.L.L. Rao, C.L.N. and Bhavaniprasad, A. 2006, 'Linking producers and processors-sorghum for poultry: a case study from India', proceedings of Regional Consultation on Linking Farmers to Markets: Lessons Learned and Successful Practices, Cairo, Egypt, 29 January–2 February 2006, viewed 5 December 2014, <http://oar.icrisat.org/id/eprint/6855>.

República Democrática de Timor Leste 2011, *Timor Leste strategic development plan 2011–2030*, República Democrática de Timor Leste, Dili. Timor Leste.

República Democrática de Timor Leste and United Nations Development Programme 2009, *The Millennium Development Goals, Timor Leste*, República Democrática de Timor Leste and United Nations Development Programme, Dili. Timor Leste.

Rola-Rubzen, M.F., Janes, J.A., Correia, V.P. and Diaz, F. 2010, 'Challenges and constraints in production and marketing horticultural products in Timor Leste', proceedings of the Third International Symposium on Improving the Performance of Supply Chains in the Transitional Economies, Kuala Lumpur, Malaysia, 4–8

July 2010, viewed 20 November 2014, <www.actahort.org/books/895/895_30.htm>.

Saldanha, J.M. and Costa, H. 1999, 'Economic viability of East Timor revisited, East Timor Study Group', *Working Paper*, no. 01, Timor Institute for Development Studies, Dili, Timor Leste (unpublished paper).

Shepherd, A.W. 2006, 'Strengthening market linkages to farmers through NGOs: lessons from experiences to date', paper presented at the Food and Agriculture Organisation of the United Nations (FAO) and VredesEilanden Country Offices (VECO) Workshop on Enhancing Capacities of NGOs and Farmer Groups to Link Farmers to Markets, Bali, Indonesia, 9–12 May 2006.

Shepherd, A.W. 2007, 'Approaches to linking producers to markets: a view of experience to date', *Occasional Paper*, no. 13, Agricultural Management, Marketing and Finance, Food and Agricultural Organization, Rome, Italy.

Silva, C.A. 2005, *The growing role of contract farming in agri-food systems development: drivers, theory and practice*, Agricultural Management, Marketing and Finance, Food and Agricultural Organization, Rome, Italy.

Simmons, P. 2003, 'Overview of smallholder contract farming in developing countries', *ESA Working Paper*, no. 02–04, Agriculture and Development Economics Division, Food and Agriculture Organization, Rome, Italy.

Simmons, P., Winters, P. and Patrick, I. 2005, 'An analysis of contract farming in East Java, Bali, and Lombok, Indonesia', *Agricultural Economics Journal*, vol. 33, no. 3, pp. 513–525.

Soges S.p.a. 2009, *Sustainable rural development for poverty reduction in Timor Leste*, Final report of the Sustainable Rural Development for Poverty Reduction workshop, 30–31 March 2009, Dili, Timor Leste.

Swinnen, J.F.M. 2007, *Global supply chains, standards and the poor*, Centre for Agriculture and Biosciences International (CABI), Oxford, UK.

United Nations Development Programme 2011, *Developing the non-oil economy in Timor Leste*, United Nations Development Programme (UNDP), Dili, Timor Leste.

World Bank 2003, 'Timor-Leste poverty assessment poverty in a new nation: analysis for action', *Technical Report*, vol. 2, Poverty Reduction and Economic Management Sector Unit, East Asia and Pacific Region, World Bank, Dili, Timor Leste.

World Bank 2008, *World development report 2008: agriculture for development*, World Bank, Washington, DC.

11 Harnessing community capacity to coordinate and integrate natural and behavioural science perspectives

A groundwater management case study from rural India

Basant Maheshwari, John Ward, Maria Estela Varua, Ramesh Chandra Purohit, Hakimuddin Ognawala, Sachin Oza, Yogesh Jadeja and Roger Packham

Introduction

Globally, areas under groundwater irrigation are highest in India (39 million hectares [ha]), followed by China (19 million ha) and the USA (17 million ha), and at present, 204 km³ per year of groundwater is pumped annually in India (Siebert et al. 2010). Several reasons may be attributed to this phenomenon. Access to groundwater has increased since the 1970s, when diesel and electric pumps became affordable to most small landholders (Shah 2008, 2009). The notion of groundwater as a private resource, the rights of which are associated with land rights, has also led to an exploitative extraction regime (Shah 2008). In the case of India, groundwater is the single largest and most productive source of irrigation water (Gangwar 2013); is the primary source of water supply for domestic and many industrial uses; and as a corollary has played a significant role in the status of India's economy, environment and standard of living. The causes of increased groundwater use in India and many other countries are rooted in population growth and economic expansion, and as result, the annual groundwater use is now estimated to exceed the annual rainfall recharge. Furthermore, the adoption of high-yielding crop varieties and increased cropping intensity to meet food demands and for livelihood improvement have resulted in escalated pressure on groundwater resources in most parts of India.

In the recent past, there has been a substantial increase in the dependence on groundwater resources in India due to the scarcity of surface water and the decreasing predictability of the monsoon, particularly in the arid and semi-arid regions (Sakthivadivel 2007). The increase in competition for water from non-agricultural uses, particularly the water supplies for urban population and industries (Lal 2009), has introduced additional stresses to Indian aquifers and groundwater resources. This has led to over-exploitation of groundwater resources resulting in a decline in water tables at an alarming rate particularly in Punjab, Haryana, Gujarat and Rajasthan. Northern India has been reported to be one of the most heavily irrigated regions in the world and this region lost groundwater at the rate of 54 ± 9 km^3/year between April 2002 and June 2008 (Tiwari, Wahr and Swenson 2009).

Water use in semi-arid parts of India is shaped by the annual monsoonal cycle. Changes in this cycle, such as either a delay in rains, reduced monsoon duration or slight declines in rainfall can result in significant reductions in crop yields, are amplified when these changes coincide with critical rainy or *Kharif* season conjunctions. The *Kharif* cropping season is from July–October during the southwest monsoon while the *Rabi* cropping season is from October–March (winter). Managing water shortages is therefore critical to the success of crops. Yield reductions can lower already depressed household incomes, reduce local employment opportunities and, when compounded, extend to aggregate poverty levels in proximate village communities, provinces and the state.

The use of groundwater in agriculture is important in India as it has enabled farmers to manage deficiencies in monsoonal rainfall to minimise crop failures and has allowed dry-season irrigation, thus contributing to poverty alleviation. For this reason, a range of on-ground works to recharge groundwater are being implemented at the village scale throughout India as a part of the Government of India's Mahatma Gandhi National Rural Employment Guarantee Act (MNREGA) to enhance livelihood opportunities while developing a reliable and potentially sustainable groundwater asset base. A significant part of the MNREGA investment programme is assigned to on-ground structures such as check dams, percolation tanks, surface spreading basins, pits and recharge shafts, enhancing long-term, local water security (MNREGA 2014).

Despite historical efforts to improve the sustainability of groundwater in India, the failure of groundwater management to prevent severe aquifer depletion remains, particularly in Rajasthan and Gujarat. In this project, called Managed Aquifer Recharge through Village level Intervention (MARVI), research focussed on developing a suitable participatory approach and associated tools and methodology that will assist in improving both the supply and demand management of groundwater. Another important aspect of the project is the education of and engagement with village communities, local NGOs and government agencies to facilitate coordinated and cooperative endeavours to achieve sustainable groundwater management.

In this chapter, we report on some insights on the capacity-building elements of the MARVI project conducted in five villages in Rajasthan and eleven villages in Gujarat with two main objectives: (i) to describe a set of activities and exercises undertaken by the team on increasing knowledge, skills and ability of the various stakeholders and (ii) to reveal how information and engagement activities can be used by village communities to discover, develop and assess their own viable options for groundwater management, including managed aquifer recharge (MAR) and measures to reduce water demand whilst sustaining livelihoods.

The study watersheds

The work reported here was conducted in the Meghraj watershed in Aravalli district, Gujarat, and the Dharta watershed in Udaipur district, Rajasthan, India (Figure 11.1). Both watersheds have a semi-arid climate, with average annual rainfall in excess of 600 mm, but more than 90 per cent of this rainfall occurs during the monsoon months of June to September. Most farmers in the two watersheds grow maize, black gram, mungbean, guar, soybeans (recently introduced) and vegetables as *Kharif* crops during the rainy season. Wheat, gram and mustard are the main *Rabi* crops grown during the winter season. Farmers who have access to groundwater (and in some instances canal water) grow two crops a year and those who have access to water supplies throughout the year also grow some summer crops such as vegetables and fodder.

The occurrence and distribution of rainfall in both the Meghraj and Dharta watersheds are highly uneven in both time and space. *Kharif* crops are mainly dependent on the vagaries of the monsoon and are often at risk of either complete or partial crop failure due to inadequate rainfall or to rainfall not occurring at a critical stage of crop growth. Therefore, the uneven and erratic distribution of rainfall provides a major challenge to reliable and successful crop production and to sustaining and improving livelihoods. When rainfall does not occur at the right time or in the required amount, supplementary irrigation, also called 'life saving irrigation', using either rainwater stored on the surface or drawn from the underground aquifer systems can be applied to avoid crop failure.

A number of in-situ conservation measures, including farm ponds, percolation ponds and check dams have been constructed in the two watersheds under both the Integrated Watershed Management (IWM) program and MNREGA. The state governments of Gujarat and Rajasthan, along with the central government have previously invested substantial amounts of monetary and extension resources in these two watersheds and continue the construction programmes. However, it is not clear how effective these programmes are in improving groundwater levels and what impacts these investments are having on the security of water access, water availability and water-dependent ecosystems. Figures 11.2 and 11.3 indicate the MAR structures in the Meghraj and Dharta watersheds.

It is important to note that both watersheds are located in groundwater regions described as hard rock, fractured aquifers characterised by low porosity, low connectivity and the movement of groundwater occurs through faults, fissures and fractures. Hence, the aquifers have limited rates of recharge storage, and when stored water is withdrawn by pumps, the emptied pores are not immediately filled

Figure 11.1 The Meghraj and Dharta watersheds

Note: The inset map shows the location of the watersheds in the states of Gujarat and Rajasthan in India.

by flows from adjacent areas. As result of low rain-recharge, and low porosity and low connectivity, the depth to water table fluctuates considerably during the year, and significant water scarcity is often experienced during summer months or drier years.

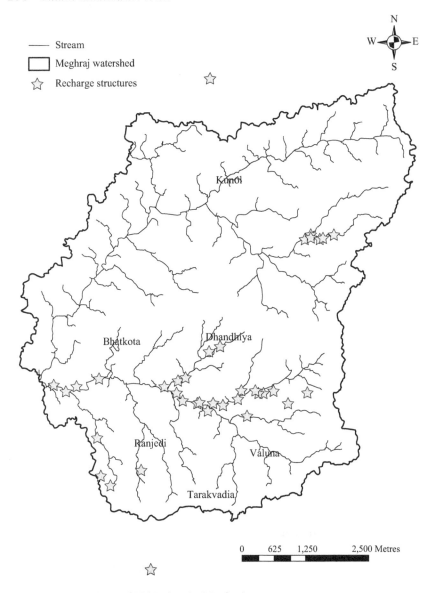

Figure 11.2 Locations of MAR sites in Meghraj

Most farmers in the Meghraj watershed belong to a tribal community, while those in the Dharta watershed are from mainstream groups. The farming practices in the two watersheds are not advanced adequately to cope with declining water supplies. For this reason, the physical and socio-economic conditions in the two watersheds provide a diversity of trans-disciplinary research opportunities and engagement issues around groundwater recharge and management.

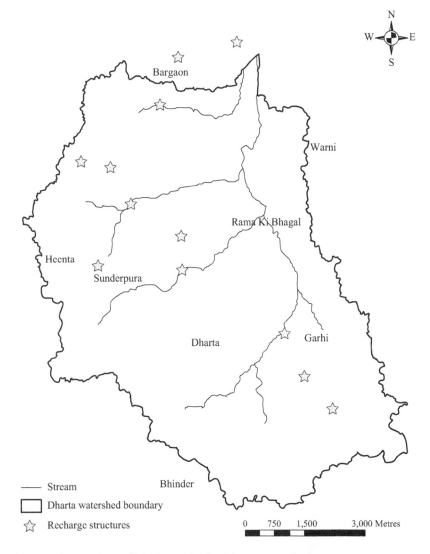

Figure 11.3 Locations of MAR sites in the Dharta watershed

The MARVI approach

The study approach in the MARVI project is underpinned by trans-disciplinary research with a main focus at the 'village scale' to understand the complex inter-relations between rainfall, aquifer recharge, groundwater pumping and liveli-hood opportunities. We define trans-disciplinary research as one in which both researchers from different, unrelated disciplines and non-academic participants, such as farmers and other villagers, work together to realise a common goal

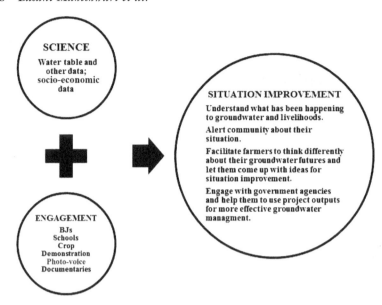

Figure 11.4 Study approach of the MARVI project

and create new knowledge and theory to improve understanding of a complex groundwater/livelihood relationship. Thus, in this project, we recognised the importance of involving local villagers and other stakeholders during the research design and implementation process and engaged them in participatory groundwater monitoring and education to explore options for groundwater sustainability. Figure 11.4 illustrates the application of relevant social and natural sciences research and engagement to improve the field situation.

The main goals of the MARVI project included the following:

- Understand what has been happening to groundwater and livelihoods
- Alert the communities about their groundwater situation
- Facilitate farmers to think differently about their groundwater futures and let them discover ideas for situation improvement
- Engage with government agencies and help groundwater communities use project outputs to coordinate individual water abstractions and craft socially agreed institutions for more effective groundwater management.

With active collaboration with local villagers, the project team collected a range of hydrologic, agronomic, economic, social and cultural data at selected clusters of villages over a two-year period. The engagement of villagers and collected data were then employed to evaluate the status of current groundwater/livelihood interactions and develop bio-physical and socio-economic insights to identify and assess 1) community-based options and strategies and 2) provide a scientific and evidence-based input to enhance watershed development initiatives.

Capacity-building components of MARVI

Although there is now a growing emphasis on the importance of capacity build-ing within the overall scope of water development projects, projects implemented in the 1960s and 1970s were primarily directed towards the provision of physical assets and water infrastructure intended to increase agricultural productivity. His-torically, water has been a resource-intensive sector mostly dominated by engi-neering concerns, focussed on the construction of water distribution networks, treatment plants and irrigation systems.

In a substantial departure from the engineering epoch, there was a growing realisation in the 1980s and 1990s that, in many cases, those development pro-jects had not been successful, and oftentimes, the planned benefits of poverty alle-viation did not manifest. For example irrigation systems were often constructed and handed over without a documented operational manual or without training for the operatives designated to assume operational responsibility (Franks 1999). In the case of the water sector, the first response was the incorporation of training as a component of the project, usually designed for those that were operating or benefiting from the physical asset in order for them to be in a better position to understand and use it effectively.

In recent years, there has been a move away from the provision of physical assets and hardware and a trend to put the primary emphasis of assistance on increasing the knowledge, skills and the ability of the people at the various levels to be more effective in their work (Biswas 1996; Pahl-Wostl et al. 2007). In many cases, the provision of hardware in the project has been almost incidental, and many projects and programmes now are almost entirely directed towards building the capacity of affected communities and individuals rather than physical assets.

The succeeding section discusses the activities and training the MARVI project implemented to increase the capabilities of the various stakeholders to learn and adapt to the changing nature of groundwater.

Capacity assessment and development of shared project vision

The first challenge for the research team was to identify the capability and capac-ity of the groundwater users. Capability refers to the knowledge, skills and atti-tudes of the individual well owners and researchers, or as a community, and their competence to undertake the responsibilities assigned to them. Capacity is the operational dimension of capability, referring to the overall ability and willingness of the individual or community to actually perform assigned responsibilities. It depends not only on the joint capabilities of affected communities and researchers but also on the overall size of the tasks, the resources needed to perform them and the framework within which they are discharged. To undertake research similar to that of MARVI requires a wide range of academic, language, information technol-ogy and managerial skills. To meet this challenge, the first project workshop was organised at Udaipur, Rajasthan, in February 2012 to develop the research team's shared vision for the project objectives, conduct field site visits in Rajasthan and Gujarat to validate the degree of correspondence of research team visions with community objectives and develop a detailed project plan and implementation strategies. The workshop was attended by 32 researchers from the University of Western Sydney (UWS), Development Support Centre (DSC), the International Water Management Institute (IWMI), Maharana Pratap University of Agriculture and Technology (MPUAT) and Vidya Bhawan Krishi Vigyan Kendra (VBKVK).

The three-day workshop was conducted in each district of in-house group work, presentations and discussions and a day-long field trip to the Dharta and Meghraj watersheds. The field trip included a visit to key villages in each district, and the main purpose of this trip was to observe first-hand the situation of the watershed selected for this study; meet with villagers and other stakeholders to explain the purpose of this project; and hear their views about the groundwater conditions, current use and potential management initiatives. The trip was organised by the Watershed Development Unit. The project team met with groups of local farmers, other villagers, school children and teachers and *Sarpanches* (village council mayors) from five *Panchayats* (village councils) in the study watershed. The relationship of groundwater attributes and management and their impact on farming, livelihood opportunities and fluoride in drinking water were discussed and how the MARVI project, communities and the Watershed Development project can coordinate efforts to improve water and livelihoods in the study area. In short, the primary purpose of the joint field trip was to identify and understand the nature of specific problems in the study sites.

A cooperative research team was formed as a principle outcome of the shared vision planning workshop. The group believes that a research team that participates in a well-structured process for creating a shared vision emerges with a compelling sense of purpose that goes much deeper than the written objectives of the research project. Documenting the written narrative is necessary to communicate the vision to others. Within the research group, the vision narrative represents the clear and compelling shared purpose and the values that emerge through a process of facilitated dialog.

When the participants were asked to identify the benefits gained from the various activities during the shared vision planning workshops, the most highly ranked responses were (i) development of team building skills, (ii) gaining of knowledge about empowerment and (iii) building leadership skills. Furthermore, the activities enabled the researchers to recognise and acknowledge alternate disciplinary perspectives, share their expectations for the project and develop trust and support. The process also taught participants to respect individual differences, priorities and capabilities.

Likewise, the workshop was instrumental in collaboratively defining the boundary conditions and research objectives as well as in specifying research questions and success criteria. A research group that engages in a shared vision process emerges as a research team with a strong sense of common purpose with a heightened sense of shared responsibility.

At the end of the workshop, participants agreed that developing capability is an essential component of capacity building. A range of actions aimed at increasing the capabilities of the various stakeholders are discussed in the following section.

Specific project activities

The programme was initiated primarily to improve community knowledge of factors affecting groundwater condition and availability and aquifer connectivity and to assist communities to negotiate and develop rules and sanctions to sustainably manage well operation and placement. The following sub-section describes a set of capacity-building exercises, the formal training of local researchers and field enumerators, participatory school activities, elicitation of women's groundwater perspectives and photo-voice, a photographic narrative technique, to elicit community groundwater attitudes.

Socio-economic surveys and other research trainings

Capacity building begins with a shared and explicit awareness of individual, organisational and institutional strengths and weaknesses in all partner teams and organisations. It is incorrect to assume that every country has substantial groups of fully trained field workers, interviewers and applied statisticians that are ready to operate in the local languages before reporting in English. Early capacity assessment of the research team revealed that this was not the case. Since the research team identified that a baseline social and economic survey needed to be conducted in villages, a survey questionnaire, relying on face-to-face interviews, was designed to address data classes specific to the research agenda. Eight field enumerators from Gujarat and seven from Rajasthan conducted the questionnaire interviews and data compiling.

A three-day enumerator training session was conducted by the Commonwealth Scientific and Industrial Research Organisation (CSIRO) and by DSC in Gujarat and by MPAUT in Rajasthan, intended to brief the enumerators and coordinating socio-economic researchers on ethical protocols, questionnaire rationale, coding and data entry standards and to train enumerators in interview techniques. The survey instrument was revised and refined in response to enumerator comments and expertise. A field visit was made in the second day to pre-test the questionnaire by conducting individual household interviews. The questionnaire was modified based on reported interview times and enumerator and respondent comprehension.

In the second year, the socio-economic study group conducted a workshop on the use of STATA and SPSS to analyse survey data. To get the right people with the right skills in place is more than a managerial or logistical problem. It required a review of the skills needed to achieve the research objectives and an attendant skills audit. Skills deficiencies were identified during the first-year workshop, and a training and development plan was put in place for each research sub-group.

School engagement activities

The MARVI research team is working in close collaboration with five schools in Rajasthan and seven in Gujarat to engage students and teachers through monitoring and education activities. School children and teachers were engaged to record daily rainfall. Total weekly and monthly, as well as seasonal values, of rainfall were displayed on school noticeboard by students to create awareness about rainfall patterns and amounts and general awareness about water issues in their local areas. This collaboration is helping to spread the message to local communities about groundwater quantity and quality issues, and the schools are also providing a local hub for meetings with villagers.

To assess the current level of awareness about water security issues among students, surveys of secondary school students were carried out during February–March 2013 in both Gujarat and Rajasthan study areas. In total, 34 students in Gujarat and 38 students in Rajasthan (mostly year 8 students) participated in the surveys covering both water scarcity and water quality issues, including causes and solutions of these. In both states, a high degree of awareness among students on water scarcity issues was evident, more prominently in Gujarat. Water quality was identified by a lesser number of students as an issue. The survey indicated that water scarcity, especially during summer months, is leading to greater demand on students' time for household activities (especially of girl students to help fetch water), and this may be leading to students getting late to schools or missing school attendance altogether up to 4 days a month.

The school engagement programme of this project is progressing quite well in a number of ways including a poster and painting competition on a range of topics such as drip irrigation, water harvesting, soil testing and climate change. A draft of a 'resource book' has been prepared in consultation with teachers. The book covers eight broad topics, namely, the importance and scarcity of water, the water cycle, groundwater and recharge, agriculture, food and water, sanitation and hygiene, pollution and water quality and water management. The final version of the book is being translated into Gujarati and Hindi, and printed copies will be distributed to schools in 2015.

Photo-voice

Photo-voice is a process by which people can identify, represent and enhance their community through a specific photographic narrative technique. It entrusts cameras to community members to enable them to act as recorders and potential catalysts for change in their own communities. It uses the immediacy of the visual image to furnish evidence and to promote an effective, participatory means of sharing expertise and knowledge (Wang and Burris 1997).

Photo-voice workshops were organised in villages and schools in both watersheds. Students and farmers were trained in photography as most of them had never touched a camera in their lives. The idea of using a camera to express their ideas and thoughts was something new for them, and they actively participated in these workshops. They photographed village characteristics that expressed their past, present and future thoughts about water resources and groundwater as one of the critical factors of livelihood in village communities. The captioned photographs composed by the photo-voice cohort were used to highlight and communicate the realities of the photographers' lives to the public and policy makers to inspire change. Photography provided a cogent medium of individual empowerment without requiring people to stand up and speak in public.

Female participation

A separate survey was also conducted to answer research questions about women's responsibilities regarding water and gendered perceptions of water use, availability and quality and who collects water. Five villages from Gujarat and Rajasthan were selected, and an average of ten women, three men and three members of community associations were interviewed from each village. A random sampling method to select respondents was used. The questionnaire on women was translated in Hindi and Gujarati, and field investigators underwent a training session conducted by the MARVI research team.

During the field visits, women were invited to participate in a number of activities including a forum where women's views on water management, on the impact of groundwater shortage on their children's education and on gender equality. The open forum is recognised as an important process and an opportune time for women to reflect inwardly on how to reshape groundwater management in order to give women greater access to and control over resources.

Field demonstration on farmers' fields and community engagement

Field demonstrations on farmers' fields in the middle and at the end of crop season were conducted on aspects such as water requirements, water conservation practices such as mulching and crop varieties that may be more drought tolerant or may result in improved income for a given water use.

In an effort to engage government agencies, policy makers and researchers from organisations outside this project, a one-day workshop titled 'The Policy Dialogue on Groundwater Governance and Managed Aquifer Recharge' was organised at the DSC, Ahmedabad, on 19 February 2013. The workshop was attended by a total of 40 participants and helped to develop a deeper understanding of groundwater recharge strategies, successes and limitations and identify specific data gaps for effective governance, policy and implementation of groundwater recharge initiatives. The workshop was well covered by state-level newspapers and TV networks.

Furthermore, two community workshops were organised during February 2014 in the Dharta watershed in Rajasthan and the Meghraj watershed in Gujarat. The workshops were attended by about 210 farmers and other stakeholders (120 in the Dharta watershed and 90 the Meghraj watershed).

These workshops indicated that farming and village communities were deeply concerned about groundwater quality and the rapidly declining water tables. Participants were willing to explore options that will help improve water availability for irrigation and drinking purposes but are currently more focused on water availability of their individual wells and did not acknowledge that groundwater needs to be managed at the village and watershed levels and beyond.

A newsletter in Hindi, called 'MARVI Manthan' (the Hindi word *Manthan* meaning 'deep contemplation') was launched in February 2014 to share the project findings with village communities. This newsletter will be published twice a year to coincide with the beginning of *Rabi* and *Kharif* seasons. The target audience of this newsletter are farmers, the general community and other stakeholders, and it is expected that the newsletter will help the project by connecting with local communities and pursuing dialogue with farmers for participatory use and management of local groundwater resources.

Bhujal Jankaars

A total of 25 Bhujal Jankaars (BJs, meaning 'Groundwater Informed' in Hindi) were recruited at the Rajasthan site and 9 BJs at the Gujarat site. During the last 12 months, the BJs were trained on a number of relevant aspects, such as in mapping, Geographic Information System (GIS), the water table and water quality measurements and observations related to geologic aspects. The BJs have now monitored groundwater levels on a weekly basis for over ten months. While BJs are monitoring groundwater, they have also helped to develop effective linkages between this project and local communities and to create awareness about the groundwater issues in the two study areas. The preliminary evaluation of the BJ approach indicated that BJs interact extensively with their communities as they do their measurement tasks on a weekly basis, and they are keen to share project outputs that are written in the local language and tailored to the needs of village communities, particularly sharing some observed water table data to indicate the state of groundwater fluctuations in the area.

There has been some significant progress made in the engagement with the farming community through water table monitoring by Bhujal Jankaars (BJs), targeted community workshops and work with the local schools. The BJ interactions have helped to create community awareness of groundwater as a connected and common resource and to develop the trust and confidence to facilitate future dialogue between the research group and the community to evaluate community options of sustainable use and management of local groundwater resources.

The six-month BJ training programme of eight modules aimed to orient the BJs regarding the MARVI project and to build their understanding about geology, hydrology, watershed management and mapping. While it was comparatively easy to develop an understanding of the depletion of surface water resources, the measures used for water harvesting and groundwater issues are quite complex to comprehend, both for the village communities as well as the project research partner field staff. However, in presenting these module inputs it was realised that, despite the difficulties, it was possible to de-mystify the technical aspects of groundwater management in a language that villagers could understand. It was also recognised that capacity building for the BJs has to be a gradual and continuous process, one that blends theoretical inputs with practical exercises in their own villages in order to help them grasp these complex issues. Convincing people to work on an action research project that does not give them direct benefits requires a lot of effort. In addition, it was observed that coordinated groundwater management is a new concept that is not easily understood by rural communities. Retaining the BJs in the midst of other work opportunities available in and near the villages at a relatively high remuneration was also raised as a concern.

In addition to well monitoring, the BJs also contributed to other key project activities, namely, village-level meetings, field days during and after crop demonstrations and seed and fertiliser distribution. The BJs shared their experiences in a monthly meeting with project community organisers and prepared the plans and strategies for further activities. The BJs also interacted with other village members individually or through various village institutions, for example farmers' clubs, *Sujal Samiti* (water co-operative) and *Gramsabha* (village council). In this way, the BJs worked as a communication bridge between the MARVI project team and villagers.

An emergent aspect of BJs' involvement in this project was that the information collected by BJs made people in the villages curious about MARVI project activities and triggered requests for additional communication. The location of monitoring wells also helped in spreading information as the wells were widely dispersed and every well owner asked why was the BJ taking readings and what would come out of it. These questions assisted in starting communication with the farmers about the current issues of groundwater scarcity. Some of the BJs became capable in preparing charts for displaying current rainfall and well water depth and hung these outside their houses so that more people could see the results. Thus, as a result of the BJs' involvement in the project, most people in the villages came to know that this was a research project, not another project that focussed on on-ground construction works, and that the research data being collected would be helpful for them in the future.

Concluding remarks

A primary focus of the MARVI project was the development of a research community promoting inclusive, equitable and mutually beneficial collective action to manage groundwater at the village level, which acts as a knowledge and learning source for other groundwater-dependent communities. To achieve this, Uphoff and Wijayaratna (2000) have shown the need to develop social capital, which we define as the willingness and capacity of communities to craft effective social compacts and sanctions to resolve the groundwater common pool dilemma. The MARVI project relied on participatory approaches to develop social capital competencies, focussing on training programmes aimed at supporting cognitive aspects of social capital competence. In addition, the project used participatory monitoring for data collection to support this development.

Bhujal Jankaars (BJs) have now become an integral part of the MARVI engagement process and data collection activities in the project in both study areas. There is now an increasing acceptance of BJs in village communities as trusted and reliable sources of information about local rainfall, the extent of water table fluctuations and groundwater quality. They have also become an important link between the project team and the village communities for mobilising farmers for project meetings, field demonstrations and dissemination of research findings from the project.

Given the skills that BJs acquired through training, and subsequent practical experiences, they are able to continue to contribute to various development projects being implemented by local NGOs and government agencies, both in their own and the adjoining villages. Baseline observations at the commencement of the MARVI project revealed limited village-level availability and access to human resources competent in groundwater monitoring. The BJ programme has introduced a village-level source of local groundwater knowledge treated as valid, credible and salient (Cash et al. 2003) that includes well monitoring, data collection experience and a significant impetus to improve groundwater management. Failure to utilise the local water and agriculture knowledge and the skills acquired by BJs means excluding a knowledge source both valued and trusted by the affected groundwater communities. At least one project partner, namely, Arid Community and Technologies, is now considering forming a private limited company of BJs and to engage BJs to work in new natural resources management projects in the two study areas. The emergent BJ-research community–agency coalitions comply with the recent report by the Planning Commission of India highlighting the need to build strong partnerships and collaborations across a broad spectrum of institutions and communities to monitor and implement groundwater management strategies across India (Planning Commission of India 2011).

Capacity building is often couched as a uni-directional process: knowledge and expertise flow or diffuse from a research based knowledge elite to a less knowledgeable rural constituency. Effective capacity building manages to bridge knowledge boundaries and relies on multiple factors, subject to ongoing monitoring and revision. The MARVI project emphasised five capacity-building factors: 1) the research objectives aligned with those of the focal rural communities; 2) knowledge was viewed as salient, credible and legitimate; 3) the project assessed gender-specific knowledge and capacity-building needs; 4) knowledge diffusion relied on schools, BJs, individual households and water management agencies as multiple capacity-building entry points and 5) the complex challenges facing groundwater-dependent communities in Rajasthan and Gujarat necessitated knowledge be introduced as an amalgam of bio-physical, social and economic disciplines.

The visioning workshops held with the research team and validation with the focal communities addressed point 1. The school and BJ programmes, household interviews, consultation with state and community groundwater managers and gender evaluation address points 2, 3 and 4 respectively. Disciplinary integration was initially addressed in the visioning workshop; however, the reinforcement of disciplinary cohesion throughout the duration of the project remained a challenge.

The Bhujal Jankaars played an important and unexpected role in cohering the diverse attitudes and disciplinary methods and objectives of the bio-physical and behavioural science practitioners, thereby improving integrative research capacity. BJs assumed multi-disciplinary roles as groundwater data collectors, well monitors and communicators, introducing science to affected communities and updating the research team of community needs, concerns and aspirations. Monthly BJ consultations and evaluations were reported to all researchers, catalysing ongoing iterations of interdisciplinary dialogue and revision of research efforts in response to BJ insights. Recognition of diverse disciplinary perspectives and the level of integration was therefore an evolving and dynamic process, in contrast to a singular, static event.

We argue that the MARVI project has demonstrated that allowing direct participation of local community, schools and other stakeholders in a research project can lead to joint capacity building of both researchers, groundwater communities and other stakeholders, i.e. bi-directional capacity building, which is quite important in trans-disciplinary research. This kind of bi-directional capacity building represents an advancement in managing the boundaries between rural agricultural research efforts and the community beneficiaries of ongoing research endeavours.

Acknowledgements

Funding for this research was provided by the Australian Centre for International Agricultural Research, Canberra, Australia, and we appreciate the support of Dr Evan Christen, Research Program Manager, Land and Water Resources during this study. Thanks to J. Applebee, Y. Dashora, S. Dave, P. Soni, P. Dillon, T. Shah, P. Singh, S. Prathapar, A. Patel, B. Thaker, R. Kookana, H. Grewal, K. Yadav, H. Mittal, and M. Chew for their assistance during the study.

References

Biswas, A. K. 1996, 'Capacity building for water management: some personal thoughts', *International Journal of Water Resources Development*, vol. 12, no. 4, pp. 399–406.

Cash, D. W., Clark, W. C., Alcock, F., Dickson, N. M., Eckley, N., Guston, D. H., Jäger, J. and Mitchell, R. B. 2003, 'Knowledge systems for sustainable development', *Proceedings of the National Academy of Sciences*, vol. 100, no. 14, pp. 8086–8091.

Franks, T. 1999, 'Capacity building and institutional development: reflections on water', *Public Administration and Development*, vol. 19, no. 1, pp. 51–61.

Gangwar, S. 2013, 'Status, quality and management of groundwater in India', *International Journal of Information and Computational Technology*, vol. 3, no. 7, pp. 717–722.

Lal, R. 2009, 'Soil water management in India', *Journal of Crop Improvement*, vol. 23, no. 1, pp. 55–70.

MNREGA, 2014, *Mahatma Gandhi National Rural Employment Guarantee Act.* Department of Rural Development, Government of Andhra Pradesh, India.

Pahl-Wostl, C., Craps, M., Dewulf, A., Mostert, E., Tabara, D. and Taillieu, T. 2007, 'Social learning and water resources management', *Ecology and Society*, vol. 12, no. 2, pp. 5.

Planning Commission of India 2011, *Faster, Sustainable and more inclusive growth: an approach paper to 12th Five-year Plan (2012–2017)*, Sage Publications India, New Delhi, India.

Sakthivadivel, R. 2007, 'The groundwater recharge movement in India', in M. Giordano and K. G. Villholth (eds.), *The agricultural groundwater revolution: opportunities and threats to development*, International Water Management Institute, Colombo, Sri Lanka, pp. 195–210.

Shah, T., 2008, 'India's groundwater irrigation economy: the challenge of balancing livelihoods and environment', in K. Chopra and V. Dayal (eds.), *2008, Handbook on environmental economics in India*. Oxford University Press, New Delhi, India, pp. 98–120.

Shah, T. 2009, *Taming the anarchy: groundwater governance in South Asia*, Routledge-Resources for the Future Press and International Water Management Institute, Washington, DC.

Siebert, S., Burke, J., Faures, J. M., Frenken, K., Hoogeveen, J., Döll, P. and Portmann, F. T. 2010, 'Groundwater use for irrigation – a global inventory', *Hydrology and Earth System Sciences*, vol. 1, no. 10, pp. 1863–1880.

Tiwari, V. M., Wahr, J. and Swenson, S. 2009, 'Dwindling groundwater resources in northern India, from satellite gravity observations', *Geophysical Research Letters*, vol. 36, no. 18, pp.1–5.

Uphoff, N. and Wijayaratna, C. M. 2000, 'Demonstrated benefits from social capital: the productivity of farmer organisations in Gal Oya, Sri Lanka', *World Development*, vol. 28, no. 11, pp. 1875–1890.

Wang, C. C. and Burris, M. A. 1997, 'Photovoice: concept, methodology and use for participatory needs assessment', *Health Education & Behavior*, vol. 24, no. 3, pp. 369–387.

12 Labour participation and women empowerment

Implications for capacity building of women in potato production in Pakistan

Amjad Khan, Maria Fay Rola-Rubzen and Kantha Dayaram

Introduction

Women occupy a pivotal position in the development discourse. Their importance is not only highlighted by the fact that they constitute more than half of the population but also by virtue of the diverse roles they play in society. Their diversified role ranges from economic contributions of household life to collective societal impact. Women's work is not limited to a particular field or profession. According to research (Food and Agriculture Organization [FAO] 2011; National Commission on the Status of Women 2003; World Bank 2007), in addition to women's family roles as mothers, sisters and wives, their participation can be seen in various professions and the workplace.

Women constitute a substantial proportion of the work force in Oceania (64 per cent), sub-Saharan Africa (62 per cent), Southeast Asia (57 per cent), and South America (59 per cent) (International Labour Organization [ILO] 2009). Because of their significant contribution, women's work needs to be integrated into the human development framework. Policy intervention must recognise their potential as agents of growth, which can prove to be helpful in ensuring food security and achieving better living standards for the rural population. Dheepa and Barani (2009) note that while technology, knowledge and education are indicators of welfare and wellbeing of society, development and advancement are indicators of women's empowerment.

Women's work and contribution are particularly important in developing countries such as Pakistan. Whilst women are essentially a part of the social and economic fabric of society, their work is not fully acknowledged and recognised. This is more so in a country such as Pakistan where the majority of the population live in rural areas with women constituting half of the rural residents. Agriculture and livestock are the mainstays of Pakistan's rural economy. Studies undertaken in Pakistan (Amin, Ali, Ahmad and Zafar 2009; Nosheen 2011) found a significant correlation between women's labour participation rates and rural women in the agricultural sector. While women are found to be an integral part of the agricultural production system, their work was rarely recognised. One of the contributory factors is the lack of accurate workforce data and studies on women's participation and the impact on empowerment. This fact necessitates recognition of women participation and their potential contribution to paid employment, which in turn will affect their income levels and empowerment status, improve living standards and ensure food security for rural masses. Thus, it is critical to gain an understanding of women's labour participation, their levels of development and empowerment in Pakistan. This study examines the participation of women in agriculture in Pakistan and its relationship to empowerment. The following research questions are explored in this chapter:

- What are the areas where Pakistani women farmers' labour participation is most concentrated?
- Is there a correlation between women's labour participation and their empowerment?

This study aims to determine the following objectives:

1) Ascertain the role of women in agricultural activities
2) Measure women's contribution in potato production
3) Ascertain the link between labour participation and women empowerment

Agricultural labour participation

Women's roles may vary from society to society; however, the essence of women's traditional roles remains the same in almost all regions of the world, where men work outside the home and earn money to support their families, while women are bound to the home, maintaining and fulfilling household needs (Pilcher and Whelehan 2004). The World Health Organization acknowledged women's greater participation in society globally, as they were found to perform productive tasks outside the home in addition to their traditional responsibility of traditional work responsibility at home. Women's contribution to the betterment of society is relevant to Pakistani where studies have determined that women perform a dual role both externally and internally (Amin 2010; Nosheen 2011). Their contribution is even more pronounced in rural areas where women share the triple burden of rural, domestic and productive work. Jehan (2000), Rasheed (2004) and Amin (2010) noted women's dual burden in Pakistani society includes domestic roles such as cooking, washing and child rearing, as well as active participation in crop production and in the livestock sector.

In Amin, Ali, Ahmad and Zafar's (2009) study in Tehsil Faisalabad, which analysed the competency and capability levels of men and women in various social, cultural and domestic activities, it was found that women's participation was limited in social, political and community matters. This is largely a result of cultural and societal constraints and the absence of capacity-building measures that support the participation by women in these spheres.

Addressing poverty and the necessity of feeding the family is the main cause behind women's contribution to economic activity. Women have high participation in income-generation activities (Government of Pakistan 2009), and they are able to support their families and share in the work burden of their husbands. Women spent most of their time in domestic and revenue-generation tasks as was found by FAO (1995), although due recognition to their participation has yet to be given.

Agriculture is a key contributor to many developing economies and provides employment and livelihood for majority of the world's rural and poor population. The agricultural sector contributes substantially in poverty eradication in both Asia and sub-Saharan Africa (Rola-Rubzen, Hardaker and Dillon 2001; Lipton 2005; World Bank 2007). It is imperative to analyse gender participation in the agricultural sector for an authentic assessment of the benefits of agriculture in reducing poverty (Birner and Resnick 2010; Bourguignon 2008; Byerlee, de Janvry and Sadoulet 2009; Christiaensen, Demery and Kuhl 2011).

Men and women share the responsibility of agricultural production in most global regions (Amin 2010; FAO 1995; Pradhan, Benda-Beckmann and Benda-Beckmann 2000; Prakash 2003; Satyavathi, Bharadwaj and Brahmanand 2010). This is due to farming processes, which are complex and multi-dimensional and which requires joint collaboration. In some developing countries, agricultural production requires a combination of physical effort through traditional methods of farming such as manual hoeing, weeding and sowing, as well as modern technologies such as hand tractors and other small-scale machineries.

Female labour force participation

The female contribution in the agricultural sector has been mapped globally (Doss 1999; FAO 2003, 1995; Pitcher 1996; Ukpongson and Matthews-Njoku 2003). Female participation rates in the agricultural sector were found to be the highest in South Asia and sub-Saharan Africa (ILO 2012). Antholt and Zijp (1995), Karl (1996), Kaur and Sharma (1991) and Unnevehr and Stanford (1985) also found the contribution by women to be significant in the agricultural sector in Asia. In Turkey, Kazgan (1993) and Ozkan and Ozcatalbas (2003) reported that women contributed to crop production, livestock production, food provision and revenue generation. Abera et al. (2006), Ajuonu (2003), Franklin (2007). Grellier (1995), Ogato, Boon and Subramani (2009) and Olumakaiye and Ajayi (2006) analysed women's participation levels in the agricultural sector in African countries and found that women were participating in most agricultural activities and that they made a significant contribution in the economy.

Women's involvement varies with the nature of the activity. Women are engaged in activities which are more time-consuming but require less physical effort, whereas men are found to undertake activities that require more physical labour (Prakash 2003; Satyavathi, Bharadwaj and Brahmanand 2010). For instance, FAO (1995) noted that women do not participate in fertiliser and pesticide application, whilst ploughing is considered to be a male-dominated activity

(Amin 2010; FAO 1995; Pradhan, Benda-Beckmann and Benda-Beckmann 2000; Prakash 2003; Satyavathi, Bharadwaj and Brahmanand 2010). However, women usually engage in time-consuming activities such as sowing, hoeing, harvesting and picking of agricultural produce, its processing and storage (FAO 1995, 2003; Japan International Cooperation Agency 1999; Olawoye 1985).

Quisumbing's (1995) review of empirical studies on productivity of men and women farmers found that there are no significant differences in the efficiency of male and female farmers. According to Quisumbing, where women farmers' yields are lower, these can usually be attributed to the lower levels of inputs and human capital as compared to men. Timothy and Adeoti (2006) and Mathijs and Vranken (2001) also observed that cultural, social and economic constraints were restricting women in their agricultural activities.

It was observed that women face barriers to effective participation including mobility constraints, absence of skills, education, training and issues such as economic dependency, limited resources and access to extension services in agricultural practices (Ajuonu 2003; Doss 1999; Ezumah and Domenico 1995; Fabiyi et al. 2007; International Fund for Agriculture and Development [IFAD] 1999; Morrison, Raju and Sinha 2007). Unfortunately, there was a lack of due recognition of their significant contribution to the agricultural sector (Agarwal 1998; IFAD 1999; Jiggins, Samanta and Olawoye 1998; Ogunlela and Mukhtar 2009; Zaccaro 2011).

Women's substantial participation in crop production in almost all regions of the world has been well noted (Gawaya 2008; IFAD 1999; Mosavi, Ommani and Allahyari 2011; Van den Ban and Hawkins 1988). Women are involved in various crop production related pre- and post-harvest activities, such as weeding, seeding, harvesting, transportation and crop processing (Ahmed and Hussain 2004; Ezumah and Domenico 1995; Fabiyi et al. 2007; FAO 1995; IFAD 1999; Gawaya 200; Pala 1978; 8). Likewise, women are responsible for growing vegetables and engage in food provision for household consumption (World Bank 1989; FAO 1995; 2003). In Pakistan, women participate in various cropping activities, despite cultural and social hindrances, and continue to make a significant contribution to uplift agricultural development (Amin, Ali, Ahmad and Zafar 2009; Javed, Sadaf and Luqman 2006; Naqvi, Shahnaz and Arif 2002; Nosheen 2011).

Methodology

The study was conducted in Hazara region in Pakistan. The Hazara region is one of the highest potato-producing regions in Pakistan. It is situated in the Khyber Pakhtunkhawa province of Pakistan. The Hazara region is further subdivided into six districts – Haripur, Abbottabad, Manshera, Battagram, Kohistan and Torghar. The Abbottabad and Manshera districts were chosen as the study sites because of the higher concentration of potato farmers in these two districts. From each district, five villages were selected by using stratified sampling. Fifteen respondents were then selected randomly from each district. A total of 75 potato farmers were selected from each district, making up a total of 150 respondents

Table 12.1 Household characteristics of respondents

Characteristic	
Average age	42.3 years
Male average age	44.7 years
Female average age	40.6 years
No. and % of males with primary education	20 (33%)
No. and % of males with secondary education	29 (47%)
No. and % of males with tertiary education	12 (20%)
No. and % of females with primary education	61 (68%)
No. and % of females with secondary education	23 (26%)
No. and % of females with tertiary education	5 (6%)
Farming experience (male)	18.9 years
Farming experience (female)	15.6 years

(89 female and 61 male respondents). The focus of this study is on potato farmers because of the importance of potatoes in Pakistan. Second, potato production has a higher cash return compared to traditional crops such as rice. The characteristics of respondents are summarised in Table 12.1.

The average age of respondents is 42.3 years, with males slightly older on average, at 44.7 years. The average age of females is 40.6 years. Women have lower educational status as compared to men. Men's educational level is also higher than women's educational level – 20 per cent of the men have a tertiary education or have a higher degree, and 47 per cent of male respondents have matriculated in secondary school. On the other hand, only 6 per cent of the women have a tertiary-level education or above, with the majority of women (68 per cent) only having completed primary or have some primary education. The males' farming experience is higher than females' (18.9 years vs. 15.6 years). Overall, the average farming experience for respondents was 16.9 years, with a minimum of 2 and a maximum of 40 years.

Primary data was collected by a survey using a structured questionnaire. The survey was conducted from September to November 2012. Descriptive statistics, frequency distributions, regression analysis, chi-square tests and the phi correlation coefficient were used for data analysis. Regression analysis was used to evaluate the relationship between the level of participation and women empowerment. Statistical Package for Social Sciences (SPSS) was used to analyse the data. The IFPRI Women Empowerment in Agriculture (WEIA) model (Alkire et al. 2012) for measuring women's empowerment in agriculture is utilised in order to calculate women's empowerment status.

WEIA is an innovative model designed by the International Food Policy Research Institute (IFPRI) that measures women empowerment in agriculture.

Table 12.2 Domains, indicators and weights in WEIA

Domain	Indicator	Weight
Production	Input in productive decisions	1/10
	Autonomy in production	1/10
Resources	Ownership of asset	1/15
	Purchase, sale or transfer of assets	1/15
	Access to and decisions about credit	1/15
Income	Control over use of income	1/5
Leadership	Group member	1/10
	Speaking in public	1/10
Time	Workload	1/10
	Leisure	1/10

The IFPRI model calculates women's empowerment across five defined domains, namely, production, resources, income, leadership and time, and provides an insight into women's economic status (Alkire et al. 2012). A total of ten indicators are used to assess and quantify women's empowerment in each domain. Table 12.2 provides details of domains and the indicators used to assess empowerment in the corresponding domain and indicator weightage as developed by IFPRI.

Individual responses to the survey questionnaire are then utilised to give each indicator a value of either 1 or 0. A value of 1 is assigned if the individual is adequate in a particular criterion and 0 if he/she is inadequate. An individual's empowerment score is simply the sum of the weighted averages of the ten indicators. Mathematically, this can be written as:

$$C_i = W_1 I_1 + W_2 I_2 + \ldots \ldots + W_d I_d \qquad (12.1)$$

Where
$I_i = 1$ if the person achieves an adequacy in the indicator I, and $I_i = 0$ if otherwise. W is the corresponding weight given to indicator I with $\sum_{i=1}^{d} W_i = 1$.

An empowerment score of 0.8 and above is considered empowered while an empowerment score of 1 denotes the respondent is completely empowered and an empowerment score of 0 denotes that the respondent is completely non-empowered.

Results and discussion

There are two major parts in analysing the data. The first part calculates women's empowerment, and the second part assesses the relationship of empowerment with labour participation.

The results of empowerment status are shown in Table 12.3. As shown in the table, out of the 89 female respondents who were interviewed during the survey, only 10 (11 per cent) were considered empowered (i.e. achieved an empowerment score greater than or equal to the threshold score of 0.8). For the males, 20 (33 per cent) of male respondents, were empowered, achieving a threshold score of 0.8 and above.

In terms of areas of empowerment, men are more empowered than women in most domains. For instance, 87 per cent of men are considered empowered in input into productive decisions (production), 84 per cent in speaking in public (leadership) and 82 per cent in purchase/sale/transfer decision making (Table 12.4). Meanwhile the area where more women are empowered is in time, with 74 per cent of women considered empowered in terms of available time for work; however, only 40 per cent of women are considered empowered in terms of time for leisure. Notably, few women are considered empowered in access to decisions about credit (20 per cent) and leadership (25 per cent and 30 per cent in group membership and speaking in public, respectively).

Table 12.3 Number and percentage of empowered respondents

Gender	Empowered		Not empowered	
	No.	%	No.	%
Male	20	33	41	67
Female	10	11	79	88

Table 12.4 Gendered empowerment status across five domains and domain indicators

Domains	Indicators	Men %	Women %
Production	Input into productive decisions	87	51
	Autonomy in production	77	40
Resources	Ownership of assets	62	48
	Purchase/sale/transfer decision	82	44
	Access to decision about credit	57	20
Income	Control over use of income	69	38
Leadership	Group member	72	25
	Speaking in public	84	30
Time	Workload	72	74
	Leisure	59	40

To examine the relationship between empowerment and labour participation of women, a regression analysis was conducted. As the survey focused on potato production, farmers' participation in economic activities were disaggregated into participation in potato production (time spent in field), participation in livestock activities, participation in poultry production, participation in other business activities and participation in services. This will allow examination of the effect of participation in potato production alone, as opposed to participation in other economic activities. The results of the analysis are presented in Table 12.5.

The results showed that education, income, access to credit and participation in services were found to be highly significant at 95 per cent level of confidence, while time spent in the field (potato production) and size of farm were found to be significant at 90 per cent level of confidence. In general, labour participation was found to have a positive influence on the empowerment status of Pakistani women. However, not all types of labour participation are significant, only participation in potato production and in services were significant. Labour participation in other activities such as livestock activities and in business activities, although positive, appear not to be significant factors that influence women empowerment.

The results of this study highlight two key things – first, that women potato farmers overall are less empowered in comparison to male farmers. Only 10 per cent women were found to be empowered as against 33 per cent of males.

Table 12.5 Regression results for factors influencing women's empowerment

Variable	Model 1 (0.907)	
	Beta values	P values
Age of respondents	0.000	0.752
Size of farm	0.030	0.061*
Experience	0.001	0.667
Education	0.100	0.000**
Household size	−0.005	0.117
Total income	7.350E–007	0.000**
Time spent in field (potato production)	0.000	0.072*
Access to credit	0.094	0.001**
Other business activities	0.005	0.926
Participation in livestock	0.035	0.202
Participation in services	0.072	0.041**
Participation in poultry	0.036	0.480
R^2	0.907	
F-test (significance)	0.000	

Notes: * significance 10%, ** significance 5%

Furthermore, women empowerment was found to be least in the leadership and resources domains while highest in the time and production domains. Given the low empowerment status of women, more work needs to be done in enhancing the status of women in rural Pakistan.

Second, the study showed that labour participation, particularly in potato production, has a positive significant impact on women's empowerment. This implies that increasing women participation in economic activities will positively impact on their empowerment status. This is because when women contribute to household income they have more say in where income will be spent and in decisions that will affect household welfare.

Empowerment is a multi-dimensional, ongoing phenomenon linked to creating self-sufficiency, self-confidence and the acquisition of strength both at individual and collective levels in cognitive, political, social, spiritual, psychological and economic perspectives (Luttrell and Quiroz 2009; Mosedale 2005; Stromquist 1995). Through empowerment, marginalised and disadvantaged people have the ability to maximise their potential by making choices about their lives (Kabeer 1999; Sen 1999; Swiss Agency for Development and Cooperation 2004). Bharathi and Badiger (2008) and Malhotra, Schuler and Boender (2002) considered economic independence as the major aspect of women's empowerment and noted income as the basic factor for realising this autonomy. This is also strongly supported by Bustamante-Gavino, Rattani and Khan (2011) whose study on women's empowerment in Pakistan acknowledged the concepts of economic stability and social acceptability as leading factors that contributed to women's empowerment within a contextual setting. Women's empowerment is essential to building stronger economies. It also helps in achieving internationally agreed objectives of human development and sustainability, which will improve living standards for all members of society (Amjad 2014).

Conclusion, recommendation and policy implications

This study shows the importance of increasing women's participation in economic activities, particularly in potato production in Pakistan. Women have huge potential if they are provided with the opportunity to participate in economic activities. The first step involves acknowledging women's current participation and then providing them with the opportunity to increase their present levels of participation. Currently, while women are an integral part of rural economy in Pakistan and their present contribution is high, these are mostly unrecognised (Jamali 2009; Javed, Sadaf and Luqman 2006). Capacity building and providing them proper training, knowledge and skills can increase their ability to participate in income-generating economic activities.

Other factors that also have a positive influence on women empowerment include education, income and access to credit. Building women's capacity through proper training in various crop production techniques, new technologies and providing them access to credit so that they can purchase the needed inputs is likely to lead to higher efficiency in farming.

Women have an increased potential to perform and contribute if they are provided with the opportunities to participate in economic activities. Building capacity through mechanisms such as training and development, knowledge and skills can help women improve their participation levels in a more meaningful way. Capacity-building measures at the state level and the incorporation of women into economic growth processes will contribute to further harnessing women's potential.

One way to hasten recognition of women's work and hence build their capacity is through gender mainstreaming. Gender mainstreaming is an innovative transformative strategy (Beveridge and Nott 2002; Elgström 2000; Rangnekar 1998) that is being adopted by most UN member countries. It is aimed at integrating men and women equally in the development process to help bridge the gap between them (Corner 1999; United Nations 1997). The essence of gender mainstreaming is gender equality and equal opportunities in the social, political, cultural and economic spheres of society (United Nations 1997; World Bank 1994). With the implementation of a mainstreaming strategy, legislations and organisational structures would be reviewed for providing capacity building of women in a broader societal perspective (European Commission 2000; Rubery et al. 2002; Thege and Welpe 2002). Gender mainstreaming is key to development and is necessary for women's empowerment. Women must be effectively integrated in the development agenda that can lead to their empowerment (Kabeer 1999; Moser 1989; Taylor 1999). This can be done by providing them with skills training, adequate education and equal opportunities in social, political and economic aspects of life (Razavi and Miller 1995) while overcoming the gender disparities in this regard (Taylor 1999).

Gender mainstreaming also occupies a central position in international donor agencies' criteria, and aid countries are now focusing more on gender-sensitive projects. This is demonstrated by Ransom and Bain's study that analysed funding trends on agriculture-related development projects. Their data showed 'increased trend in number of projects and amounts spent for gender sensitive projects between 1978 to 2003' (Ransom and Bain 2011: 48). Thus, there is a growing need and relevance of gender mainstreaming to the developmental needs of Pakistan.

The present study's limitations are that the research focused only on potato-farming households. To examine the wider applicability in Pakistan, perhaps conducting a similar study across different farming systems will provide wider insights. However, due to the similar socio-economic and cultural factors, the theoretical model could also be used and tested in other South Asian countries. Such a model could provide important insights on factors that would lead to the empowerment of women in rural areas, a critical component of development.

References

Abera, G., Gudeta, H., Belissa, M., Ogato, G.S., Degife, A. and Akassa, B. 2006, *Gender based roles and resource use rights in potato production and marketing system: the case of some districts in Oromia, Ethiopia*, Research report, Oromia Agricultural Research Institute (OARI) and Organization for Social Science Research in Eastern and Southern Africa (OSSREA), Addis Ababa, Ethiopia.

Agarwal, B. 1998, 'Disinherited peasants, disadvantaged workers: a gender perspective on land and livelihood', *Economic and Political Weekly*, vol. 33, no. 13, pp. A2–A14.

Ahmed, N. and Hussain, A. 2004, *Women's role in forestry: Pakistan agriculture*, Agricultural Foundation of Pakistan, Islamabad, Pakistan.

Ajuonu, N. 2003, 'The role and impact of NGOs in gender agricultural commercialization and lives of women in Nigeria', paper presented at the FAO/IITA Workshop on Gender Impacts of Commercialization of Small Holder Agriculture, Ibadan, Nigeria, 14–16 May 2003.

Alkire, S., Meinzen-Dick, R., Peterman, A., Quisumbing, A.R., Seymour, G. and Vaz, A. 2012, 'The women's empowerment in agriculture index', *IFPRI discussion paper*, no. 01240, International Food Policy Research Institute, Washington, DC.

Amin, H. 2010, *Analysis of gender roles in home management and agricultural development: a case study in Faisalabad Tehsil*, University of Agriculture, Faisalabad, India.

Amin, H., Ali, T., Ahmad, M. and Zafar, M.I. 2009, 'Capabilities and competencies of Pakistani rural women in performing household and agricultural tasks: a case study in Tehsil Faisalabad', *Pakistan Journal of Agricultural Sciences*, vol. 46, no. 1, pp. 58–63.

Amjad 2014, 'Does participation lead to empowerment? the case of women potato farmers in Pakistan', Masters of Philosophy (Rural Management) thesis, Business School, Curtin University, Sydney, Australia.

Antholt, C. and Zijp, W. 1995, 'Participation in agricultural extension', *Environment Department Dissemination Notes,* June, no. 24, World Bank, Washington, DC.

Beveridge, F. and Nott, S. 2002, 'Mainstreaming: a case for optimism and cynicism', *Feminist Legal Studies*, vol. 10, no. 3, pp. 299–311.

Bharathi, R. and Badiger, C. 2008, 'Impact of national agricultural technology project on empowerment of women in agriculture through self help groups', *Karnataka Journal of Agricultural Sciences*, vol. 21, no. 4, pp. 561–564.

Birner, R. and Resnick, D. 2010, 'The political economy of policies for smallholder agriculture', *World Development*, vol. 38, no. 10, pp. 1442–1452.

Bourguignon, F. 2008, 'A new agenda for the poor: agriculture for development', *New Perspectives Quarterly*, vol. 25, no. 2, pp. 85–87.

Bustamante-Gavino, M.I., Rattani, S. and Khan, K. 2011, 'Women's empowerment in Pakistan: definitions and enabling and disenabling factors: a secondary data analysis', *Journal of Transcultural Nursing*, vol. 22, no. 2, pp. 174–181.

Byerlee, D., de Janvry, A. and Sadoulet, E. 2009, 'Agriculture for development: toward a new paradigm', *Annual Review of Resource Economics*, vol. 1, no. 1, pp. 15–31.

Christiaensen, L., Demery, L. and Kuhl, J. 2011, 'The (evolving) role of agriculture in poverty reduction: an empirical perspective', *Journal of Development Economics*, vol. 96, no. 2, pp. 239–254.

Corner, L. 1999, 'Capacity building for gender mainstreaming in development', background paper to the High Level Intergovernmental Meeting to Review the Regional Implementation of the Beijing Declaration and the Platform for Action, Bangkok, Thailand.

Dheepa, T. and Barani, G. 2009, 'Emancipation of women through empowerment', *SIES Journal of Management*, vol. 6, no. 2, pp. 92.

Doss, C. 1999, *Twenty-five years of research on women farmers in Africa*, Centro Internacional de Mejoramiento del Maíz y el Trigo, Mexico.

Elgström, O. 2000, 'Norm negotiations: the construction of new norms regarding gender and development in EU foreign aid policy', *Journal of European Public Policy*, vol. 7, no. 3, pp. 457–476.

European Commission 2000, *Women active in rural development: assuring the future of rural Europe*, European Commission Directorate-General for Agriculture, Office for Official Publications of the European Communities, Luxembourg, viewed 4 November 2014, <http://ec.europa.eu/agriculture/publi/women/broch_en.pdf>.

Ezumah, N. N. and Di Domenico, C. M. 1995, 'Enhancing the role of women in crop production: a case study of Igbo women in Nigeria', *World Development*, vol. 23, no. 10, pp. 1731–1744.

Fabiyi, E. F., Danladi, B. B., Akande, K. E. and Mahmood, Y. 2007, 'Role of women in agricultural development and their constraints: a case study of Biliri Local Government area of Gombe State, Nigeria', *Pakistan Journal of Nutrition*, vol. 6, no. 6, pp. 676–680.

Food and Agriculture Organization 1995, *A synthesis report of the Near East region – women, agriculture and rural development*, Food and Agriculture Organization, Rome, Italy, viewed 4 November 2014, <www.fao.org/docrep/X0176E/X0176E00.htm>.

Food and Agriculture Organization 2003, *Gender: key to sustainability and food security, plan of action*, Economic and Social Development Department, Food and Agriculture Organization, Rome, Italy, viewed 4 November 2014, <www.fao.org/docrep/005/y3969e/y3969e00.htm>.

Food and Agriculture Organization 2011, *The state of food and agriculture, 2010–11: women in agriculture – closing the gender gap for development*, Food and Agriculture Organization, Rome, Italy, viewed 4 November 2014, <www.fao.org/docrep/013/i2050e/i2050e.pdf>.

Franklin, S. 2007, *Gender inequality in Nigeria*, Taking IT Global online publication, Toronto, Canada, viewed 4 November 2014, <www.tigweb.org/youth-media/panorama/article.html?ContentID=13667>.

Gawaya, R. 2008, 'Investing in women farmers to eliminate food insecurity in southern Africa: policy-related research from Mozambique', *Gender and Development*, vol. 16, no. 1, pp. 147–159.

Government of Pakistan, 2009, *Pakistan employment trends for women*, Labour Market, Information and Analysis Unit, Ministry of Labour and Manpower, Islamabad, Pakistan.

Grellier, R. 1995, *All in good time: women's agricultural production in sub-Saharan Africa*, Natural Resources Institute, Chatham, UK.

International Fund for Agriculture and Development 1999, *Household food security and gender, memory checks for programme and project design*, International Fund for Agriculture and Development, Rome, Italy.

International Labour Organization 2012, *Global employment trends for women October 2011*, International Labour Organization, Geneva, Switzerland.

International Labour Organization 2009, *Global employment trends for women March 2009*, International Labour Organization, Geneva, Switzerland

Jamali, K. 2009, 'The role of rural women in agriculture and its allied fields: a case study of Pakistan', *European Journal of Social Sciences*, vol. 7, no. 3, pp. 71–77.

Japan International Cooperation Agency 1999, *Country WID profile (Pakistan)*, Planning Department, Islamabad, Pakistan.

Javed, A., Sadaf, S. and Luqman, M. 2006, 'Rural women's participation in crop and livestock production activities in Faisalabad–Pakistan', *Journal of Agriculture and Social Sciences*, vol. 2, no. 3, pp. 150–154.

Jehan, Q. 2000, *Role of women in economic development of Pakistan,* University of Balochistan, Quetta, Pakistan.

Jiggins, J., Samanta, R. and Olawoye, J. 1998, *Improving women farmers' access to extension services: a reference manual,* Food and Agriculture Organization, Rome, Italy.

Kabeer, N. 1999, 'Resources, agency, achievements: reflections on the measurement of women's empowerment', *Development and Change,* vol. 30, no. 3, pp. 435–464.

Karl, M. 1996, *Inseparable: the crucial role of women in food security,* Isis International, Manila, Philippines.

Kaur, M. and Sharma, M. 1991, 'Role of women in rural development', *Journal of Rural Studies,* vol. 7, no. 1–2, pp. 11–16.

Kazgan, G. 1993, *Tarim ve gelisme* [Agriculture and development], Filiz Press, Istanbul, Turkey.

Lipton, M. 2005, 'The family farm in a globalizing world: the role of crop science in alleviating poverty', *Discussion Paper,* no. 40, International Food Policy Research Institute, Washington, DC.

Luttrell, C. and Quiroz, S. 2009, 'Understanding and operationalising empowerment', *Working Paper, no.* 308, Overseas Development Institute, London, UK.

Malhotra, A., Schuler, S. R. and Boender, C. 2002, 'Measuring women's empowerment as a variable in international development', background paper prepared for the World Bank Workshop on Poverty and Gender: New Perspectives, World Bank, Washington, DC.

Mathijs, E. and Vranken, L. 2001, 'Human capital, gender and organisation in transition agriculture: measuring and explaining the technical efficiency of Bulgarian and Hungarian farms', *Post-Communist Economies,* vol. 13, no. 2, pp. 171–187.

Morrison, A., Raju, D. and Sinha, N. 2007, *Gender equality, poverty and economic growth,* World Bank, Washington, DC.

Mosavi, S., Ommani, A. and Allahyari, M. 2011, 'Rural women's attitudes toward their participation in the decision-making process and production of potato crops in Shoushtar, Iran', *Acta Agriculturæ Slovenika,* vol. 97, no. 3, 207–212.

Mosedale, S. 2005, 'Assessing women's empowerment: towards a conceptual framework', *Journal of International Development,* vol. 17, no. 2, pp. 243–257.

Moser, C.O.N. 1989, Gender planning in the Third World: meeting practical and strategic gender needs', *World Development,* vol. 17, no. 11, pp. 1799–1825.

Naqvi, Z. F., Shahnaz, L. and Arif, G. 2002, 'How do women decide to work in Pakistan?', *The Pakistan Development Review,* vol. 41, no. 4, pp. 495–513.

National Commission on the Status of Women 2003, *Inquiry into the status of women in public sector organizations,* Government of Pakistan, Islamabad, Pakistan.

Nosheen, F. 2011, 'Analysis of gender involvement in agricultural decision making and rural development: a case study of District Chakwal', PhD thesis, University of Agriculture, Faisalabad, India.

Ogato, G., Boon, E. and Subramani, J. 2009, 'Gender roles in crop production and management practices: a case study of three rural communities in Ambo District, Ethiopia', *Journal of Human Ecology,* vol. 27, no.1, pp. 1–20.

Ogunlela, Y. I. and Mukhtar, A. A. 2009, 'Gender issues in agriculture and rural development in Nigeria: the role of women', *Humanity and Social Sciences Journal,* vol. 4, no. 1, pp. 19–30.

Olawoye, J. E. 1985, 'Rural women's role in agricultural production: an occupational survey of women from six selected rural communities in Oyo State, Nigeria', *Nigerian Journal of Rural Sociology,* vol. 2, no.1–2, pp. 34–37.

Olumakaiye, M. and Ajayi, A. 2006, 'Women's empowerment for household food security: the place of education', *Journal of Human Ecology*, vol. 19, no. 1, pp. 51–55.

Ozkan, B. and Ozcatalbas, O. 2003, 'The role of women in agriculture and rural development in Turkey', *Asian Journal of Women's Studies*, vol. 9, no. 4, pp. 114–124.

Pala, A.O. 1978, *Women's access to land and their role in agriculture and decision-making on the farm: experiences of the Joluo of Kenya*, Institute for Development Studies, University of Nairobi, Kenya.

Pilcher, J. and Whelehan, I. 2004, *50 Key Concepts in Gender Studies*, Sage Publications, London, UK.

Pitcher, M.A. 1996, 'Conflict and cooperation: gendered roles and responsibilities within cotton households in Northern Mozambique', *African Studies Review*, vol. 39, no. 3, pp. 81–112.

Pradhan, R., Benda-Beckmann, F.V. and Benda-Beckmann, K.V. (eds.) 2000, 'Water, land and law: changing rights to land and water in Nepal', proceedings of a workshop, Kathmandu, Nepal, 18–20 Mar 1998, Legal Research and Development Forum (FREEDEAL), Wageningen Agricultural University (WAU) and Erasmus University Rotterdam (EUR), viewed 4 November 2014, https://www.researchgate.net/publication/264790022_Water_Land__Law._Changing_Rights_to_Land_and_Water_in_Nepal.

Prakash, D. 2003, *Rural women, food security and agricultural cooperatives*, Rural Development and Management Centre, New Delhi, India.

Quisumbing, A.R. 1995, 'Gender differences in agricultural productivity: a survey of empirical evidence', *FCND Discussion Paper*, no.5, International Food Policy Research Institute, Washington, DC.

Rangnekar, S.1998, 'The role of women in small-holder rainfed and mixed farming in India', paper presented at the Women in Agriculture and Modern Communication Technology workshop, Tune Landboskole, Denmark, 30 March–3 April 1998.

Ransom, E. and Bain, C. 2011, 'Gendering agricultural aid: an analysis of whether international development assistance targets women and gender', *Gender and Society*, vol. 25, no. 1, pp. 48–74.

Rasheed, S. 2004, 'Women participation in decision making process regarding agricultural business and family matters: a case study in Tehsil Gojra', Master's thesis, University of Agriculture, Faisalabad, India.

Razavi, S. and Miller, C. 1995, *From WID to GAD: conceptual shifts in the women and development discourse*, United Nations Research Institute for Social Development, United Nations Development Programme, Geneva, Switzerland.

Rola-Rubzen, M.F., Hardaker, J.B. and Dillon, J.L. 2001, 'Agricultural economists and world poverty: progress and prospects', *Australian Journal of Agricultural and Resource Economics*, vol. 45, no. 1, pp. 39–66.

Rubery, J., Ellingsæter, A.L., Gonzalez, M.P., Karamessini, M., Ilmakunnas, S., Plasman, R., Silvera, R., Sjørup, K. and Villa, P. 2002, *Gender mainstreaming in European employment policy*, The European Commission's Group of Experts on Gender and Employment, Manchester, UK.

Satyavathi, C.T., Bharadwaj, C. and Brahmanand, P. 2010, 'Role of farm women in agriculture lessons learned', *Gender, Technology and Development*, vol. 14, no. 3, pp. 441–449.

Sen, A.K. 1999, *Commodities and capabilities*, Oxford University Press, Oxford.

Stromquist, N. 1995, 'The theoretical and practical bases for empowerment', in C. Medel-Añonuevo (eds.), *Women's education and empowerment: pathways towards autonomy,* UNESCO Institute for Education Studies, Hamburg, Germany, pp. 13–22.

Swiss Agency for Development and Cooperation 2004, *Creating the prospect of living a life in dignity: principles guiding the SDC in its commitment to fighting poverty,* Swiss Agency for Development and Cooperation, Berne, Switzerland.

Taylor, V. 1999, *Gender mainstreaming in development planning: a reference manual for governments and other stakeholders,* Commonwealth Secretariat, London, UK.

Thege, B. and Welpe, I. (eds.) 2002, *Gender mainstreaming practices 1: examples from the EU and South Africa,* Institute of Women Research and Gender Studies, Institute for Women's and Gender Studies, University of Pretoria, Pretoria, South Africa.

Timothy, A. T. and Adeoti, A. I. 2006, 'Gender inequalities and economic efficiency: new evidence from cassava-based farm holdings in rural South-western Nigeria', *African Development Review,* vol. 18, no. 3, pp. 428–443.

Ukpongson M. O. and Matthews-Njoku E. C. 2003, 'Women's attitude towards community development in Erema District of Rivers State Nigeria', *Journal of Agriculture Forestry and Social Science,* vol. 1, no. 1, pp. 18–22.

United Nations 1997, *The Report of the Economic and Social Council, General Assembly,* Fifty-second session, A/52/3, United Nations, New York, NY.

Unnevehr, L. and Stanford, M. 1985, 'Technology and the demand for women's labor in Asian rice farming', Proceedings of a conference on Women in rice farming systems, International Rice Research Institute (IRRI), Manila, Philippines, 26–30 September 1983.

Van den Ban, A.W. and Hawkins, H.S. 1988, *Agricultural extension,* Longman, Burnt Mill, Harlow, UK.

World Bank 1989, *Sub-Saharan Africa: from crisis to sustainable growth,* World Bank, Washington, DC.

World Bank 1994, *Fact sheet: women, agriculture* and *rural development–Egypt,* World Bank, Washington, DC.

World Bank 2007, *Agriculture for development: the gender dimensions,* policy brief, World Bank, Washington, DC.

Zaccaro, S. 2011, 'Sustainable agriculture has a woman's face', *Development,* vol. 54, no. 2, pp. 263–264.

13 Can maize (*Zea mays* L) uplift farm economy?

A case study

Kalyan Kanti Das, S. Barman and
Laxmi Thingbaijam

Introduction

Maize (*Zea mays* L) is one of the most widely distributed crops of the world. It represents about 24 per cent of the global cereal production as compared to 27 per cent for wheat and 25 per cent for rice. More than 70 countries (including 15 developed and 58 developing countries) produce maize. Global production of maize is well over 1000 million tonnes, with the United States (USA), the largest producer, producing about 35 per cent of total production (Table 13.1). Other top maize-producing countries include China, Brazil, Mexico, Indonesia, India, France, Argentina and others. In Indian agriculture, maize occupies a prominent position and each part of the maize plant is put to use and nothing goes to waste. Among the cereal crops in India, maize with an annual production of around 23 million tonnes covering about 9.5 million hectares ranks fifth in area being next to rice, wheat, *jower* and *bajra*. *Kharif* maize occupies the lion's share in the cultivation of maize in India. The area under maize is increasing at a steady rate with a simple growth rate of 3.2 per cent per annum (Figure 13.1) in the country. With continued rise in the area under maize, there is an accompanied rise with a simple growth rate of 6.4 per cent per annum (Figure 13.1) in the level of production too.

Capacity is often defined in terms of ability and performance (Kamruzzaman and Takeya 2008), and capacity building refers to assistance that is provided to entities, usually societies in developing countries that need to develop a certain skill or competence or for a general upgrading of performance ability (Waridin 2013). Farmers, in a developing economy, often lack many things. They not only lack in physical resources (which are scarce by nature) but also in knowledge, skills and competence. Agricultural production activities encompass efficient management of land, men (labour) and materials (capital) for improving farming performance, and these factors of production are 'dynamic' in nature. Therefore, the United Nations Development Programme (1991: para. 3) define capacity building as 'the creation of an enabling environment with appropriate policy and legal framework, institutional development, including community participation, human resource development and strengthening of managerial systems'. It is based on the concept of education and training and focuses on a series

Table 13.1 Area, production and productivity of maize around the globe, 2013

Country	Area (million hectares)	Share in global maize area (%)	Production (million tonnes)	Share in global maize production (%)	Productivity (metric tonnes/hectare)
United States	35.478	19.16	353.699	34.74	9.969
China	36.339	19.63	218.623	21.47	6.016
Brazil	15.279	8.25	80.273	7.88	5.254
Mexico	7.096	3.83	22.664	2.23	3.194
Argentina	4.863	2.63	32.119	3.15	6.604
India	9.500	5.13	23.290	2.29	2.451
World Total	163.408	–	1018.112	–	5.499

Sources: Indiastat (2015a, 2015b).

of actions directed at helping participants to increase their knowledge, skills and understandings and to develop the attitudes needed to bring about the desired developmental change (Waridin 2013).

The agrarian economy in this part of Bengal experiences a rather stagnant agricultural growth. (For example the productivity of rice, which is the principal food grain crop, remains at the level of around 2 tonnes per hectare [ha].) This situation is coupled with a steady rise in the population (growth of 1.37 per cent per annum since 2001 to 2011). Farmers are striving for occupational diversification as well as diversification in the cropping system. Many want to come out of the rice-fallow-fallow or rice-fallow-jute cropping system.

The increased adoption of acreage under maize crop in the state (especially, in the northern part) is a result of a desperate search for a profitable cropping venture. With its wide range of utility potential, less water-consumptive behaviour (Singh 2005) and availability of lucrative markets (both for input and output), maize is gaining popularity among farmers. There is a potential to add to the existing 'capacity' and 'performance' of the rural artisans through maize cultivation in this part of Bengal. But there are apprehensions about reaping the fullest potential because weaknesses are multifarious; (i): inherent below-standard educational level, (ii) lack of social mobility, (iii) poor knowledge on cultivation practices, (iv) subsistence attitude towards farming occupation, (v) rather low accessibility towards financial resources and so on. That is why the recent upsurge in maize popularity may be a temporary phenomenon if proper capacity-building development is not undertaken.

West Bengal, with 94,000 hectares under maize cultivation and 364,000 tonnes of production, has 1.09 per cent of area and 1.67 per cent of production (Table 13.2). North Bengal contributes the lion's share in terms of both area (about 81 per cent) and production (88 per cent) of maize in the state.

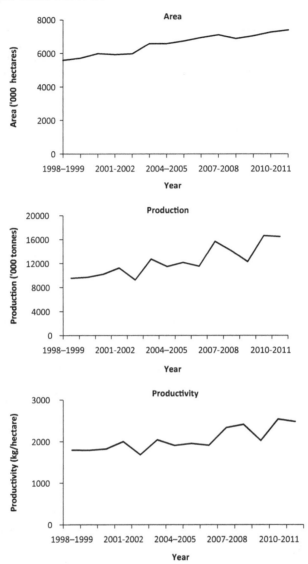

Figure 13.1 Trends in area, production and productivity of maize in India

Darjeeling, Jalpaiguri, Uttar (North) Dinajpur, Malda and Coochbehar are the leading maize-producing districts in the state. But a paradigm shift has occurred in terms of area and production contribution/share of maize within the districts of North Bengal.

Prior to 2000, Darjeeling and Malda used to produce the bulk (about 90 per cent) of production, but production in Uttar (North) Dinajpur and Coochbehar has been increasing in recent years. During 2010–2011, these two districts

Table 13.2 Major maize-producing states in India, 2011–2012

State	Area ('000 hectares)	Share in total maize area (%)	Production ('000 tonnes)	Share in total maize production (%)
Karnataka	1331.00	15.36	4085.00	18.77
Rajasthan	1143.10	13.19	1667.00	7.66
Andhra Pradesh	833.00	9.61	3658.00	16.81
Madhya Pradesh	809.00	9.33	1287.40	5.92
Uttar Pradesh	781.00	9.01	1308.00	6.01
Bihar	594.80	6.86	1610.70	7.40
Tamil Nadu	346.10	3.99	1695.47	7.79
West Bengal	94.10	1.09	364.13	1.67

Sources: Indiastat (2015c; 2015d).

Table 13.3 Major maize-producing districts in West Bengal, 2010–2011

District	Area ('000 hectares)	Share in total maize area (%)	Production ('000 tonnes)	Share in total maize production (%)
Darjeeling	16.10	18.17	40.80	11.58
Malda	8.80	9.93	20.20	5.77
Uttar Dinajpur	25.20	28.44	155.50	44.13
Jalpaiguri	12.90	14.56	41.10	11.67
Coochbehar	9.30	10.50	53.60	15.21
North Bengal	*72.50*	*81.82**	*310.80*	*88.22**

Source: Bureau of Applied Economics and Statistics (BAES, 2012).

* corresponds to percentage share to the West Bengal figure.

contributed about 67 per cent of maize production in the state (Table 13.3), which was only 0.27 per cent during 2000–2001 (Figure 13.3). Meanwhile, the area under maize in Malda is on the decline.

In a rice-dominated cropping system, maize contributes quite a small share (< 1 per cent) in total cereal area and production in the state. But there is a distinct seasonal difference in maize cultivation between the state and the nation; while in the country the crop is cultivated mostly (about 86 per cent) in the *kharif* (July–October) season, it is in the *rabi* (October–November to March–April) season that maize is prevalent (more than 60 per cent) in the state. Also, the state is much ahead in terms of per-unit area production of maize crop.

The relative importance of maize in the production basket of cereals is also increasing. From a traditionally rice-based cropping system, the farmers of Cooch-behar district are gradually shifting towards maize especially during the *rabi* season. Therefore, the share of maize, which was only 0.02 per cent of total cereal area during 2001–2002, reached about 3.15 per cent with 93,000 ha during 2011–2012 (Table 13.4 and Figure 13.2). In all probability, this is at the cost

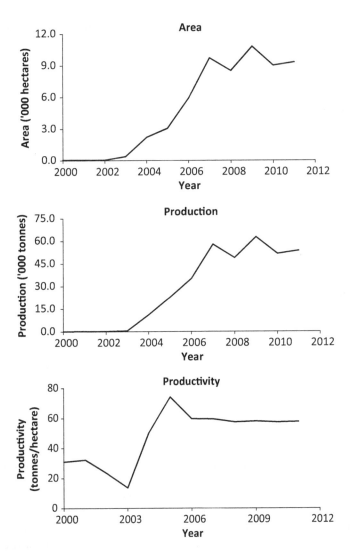

Figure 13.2 Trends in area, production and productivity of maize in Coochbehar

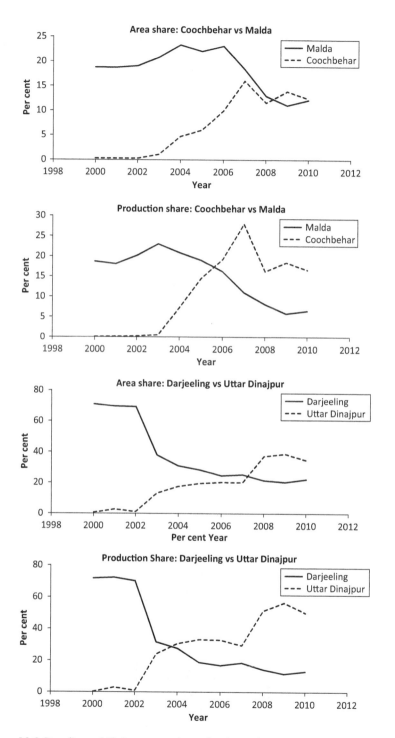

Figure 13.3 Paradigm shift in area and production of maize in the North Bengal District

Table 13.4 Cereal crops: area allocation (%) differential in Coochbehar over the years

Year	Rice			Wheat			Maize		
	Coochbehar	North Bengal	West Bengal	Coochbehar	North Bengal	West Bengal	Coochbehar	North Bengal	West Bengal
2001–02	91.36	87.00	92.55	8.38	10.53	6.62	0.02	1.27	0.51
2005–06	94.05	86.71	92.66	4.70	8.71	5.88	1.02	3.45	1.15
2011–12	93.13	84.47	93.00	3.59	9.14	5.00	3.05	5.23	2.00

Source: BAES (2008; 2012).

of wheat, an erstwhile winter crop in the district. The area allocation pattern of various crops in the district indicates that the percentage share of wheat is on the decline (from 8.38 per cent in 2001–2002 to 3.59 per cent in 2011–2012) in the district. Strong demand for maize in the domestic markets (Bihar, West Bengal), less water consumption, lucrative output price, potential multifarious use, easy availability of quality seed etc. are thought to be responsible for the upsurge in maize area in Coochbehar district in recent years (Barman 2014).The question is: is this upsurge in area coverage under maize in the district of Coochbehar sustainable or not?

It is important to find out whether the crop is really suitable for year-round cropping system and whether it is 'economically' feasible for farmers who have been striving long to improve their plight. Another fact to consider here is that the majority of farming folks belong to marginal (<1 ha) and small (1–2 ha) size category of farmers (BAES 2012). The study undertaken by Kamruzzaman and Takeya (2008) identified that the majority of the marginal and small farmers are well ahead in entering into the second stage (i.e. *Gehilfen* as per German literature) of capacity building compared to medium-sized farmers in Bangladesh, a neighbouring country of India. This study, therefore, examined the economic feasibility of maize cropping and discussed its implications on the status of capacity building in the North Bengal farm economy.

Methodology

The study was undertaken in two of the most promising blocks (in terms of maize area coverage) of Coochbehar district. As shown in the previous section, the district covers one of the rising maize zones in the country, with considerable growth rate in recent years. A household survey of 100 sample maize growers was conducted to gather relevant information. A structured, pre-tested questionnaire was used for the purpose. The ultimate sampling unit (i.e. maize farmers) was randomly selected (following simple random sampling without replacement) from three randomly selected villages for each block. The data gathered pertains to the 2013–2014 agricultural year. Secondary information was derived from various statistical bulletins, by visiting websites and also in consultation with department officials. Tabular methods were applied for assembling the data for meaningful interpretation. Simple statistical tools such as descriptive statistics and t-tests were used to analyse the tabulated data.

Results and discussion

The findings and discussion are divided here into five main themes: (1) the social and demographic characters of maize growers, (2) agricultural land and its pattern of utilisation, (3) the economics of the maize cropping venture, (4) identified constraints in maize cultivation in the area and (5) implications for capacity building of maize farmers.

Social and demographic feature of maize growers

The farming occupation warrants involvement of human labour either from within the family or to be supplemented from outside the family. A larger family size of course increases the potential of supplying more family labour in the venture. The structure of a farm family, thus, gives an idea about the labour supplementing potential of a farm family in an Indian society that was traditionally 'joint' in orientation.

A perusal of Table 13.5 depicts that the average household size of maize farmers in the surveyed areas is small (around 5), in general consisting of an adult male, an adult female and three children. Nowadays, the incidence of joint families is quite negligible, and the study area is no exception. As schooling trend increases, farmers virtually have to depend to a great extent on hired labour to undertake year-round cropping venture.

The district of Coochbehar is traditionally backward caste-oriented and Hindu-dominated, and the latest census shows that the district has about 51 per cent of caste population who are mostly (about 75.5 per cent) of Hindu origin (BAES 2012). Our study area is not an exception; as Table 13.5 indicates, about 86 per cent of the farming folks are of lower caste orientation. Above 80 per cent inhabitants of the district are rural-based, economically poor and live mostly (72 per cent) in *kutcha* houses though their residence is not far away from the main road (Table 13.5).

Table 13.5 Demography of maize growers in the study area

Trait	Sub-trait	Unit	Value
Education of family head		Score	2.16
Age of family head		Yrs.	40.46
Size of farm family		No.	4.95
Farm family education		Score	1.36
Family orientation	Joint	%	7.9
	Nuclear	%	92.1
Caste orientation	Higher	%	13.99
	Lower	%	86.01
Residential status	*Kutcha* house	%	72.00
	Pucca house	%	28.00
Cosmopolitanism		Score	1.54
Source of information	*Krishi Prajukti Sahayak*	Score	2.68
	Fertiliser shop	Score	2.28
	Neighbours	Score	0.70

All the family heads in these two blocks are male. It is interesting to know the age structure of the farm family head as this provides an idea about their potential to respond towards different decision making situations. In this study, the standard of education either of an individual or of the overall farming household is judged through a 'scoring' method whereby the illiterate is assigned the score of 0; up to standard IV (primary level) is 1; standard V to standard X is 2; standard XI to standard XII is 3; and above standard XII is 4. For calculating the score for farm family education, the 'weighted average' method is applied.

It is revealed from Table 13.5 that the family heads are quite young, and their average age is around 40 years. Moreover, their education (score 2.16) is far above their overall family education (score 1.36). The results also show that only 8 per cent of the family heads are illiterate. This, of course, is an encouraging sign from the adoption point of view, as studies have shown that education is positively related to technology adoption (Onphanhdala 2009; Weir 1999).

Almost all the sample farming households in the study area depend mostly on farming for their daily sustainability. Hence, they believe that improvement in farming practices will increase their income situation and standard of living.

Getting or gathering information, especially on latest technological advancements, cropping ventures and prices can also assist in improving their agriculture performance. Hence, in this study, we measured this attribute from two different points of view. One, we tried to understand the source of information, and two, their mobility. In the study, farmers were asked to rank three of their most important sources of information. The source of information ranked first is assigned a score of 3, second as 2, and third as 1. Then the score (for a particular source of information) of all the sample sources is averaged for comparison.

As shown in Table 13.5, farmers in the study rely mostly on government department and officials for information. Fertiliser shops or dealers also form a formidable and trusted media for supplementing information. While interviewing farmers, we found out that information on input price, new/promising variety and fertiliser doses are some of the information they received from these sources.

The trait of cosmopolitanism/mobility was also judged through a scoring method. The respondent farmers were asked to indicate their (farmer or any of his family member) pattern of visit (or interaction) with some social institutes such as the agriculture office, bank, Gram Panchayat/Block Development Office, etc. If the answer was positive, a score of 1 was assigned; otherwise, 0 was assigned.

Two social institutes that the farming folk mostly visited were Gram Panchayet Office and the office of the Assistant Director of Agriculture. These two social institutes are highly relevant for the daily farming life of a farming family. The study found that generally people had negligible visits to other important institutes like financial institutions, farmers club, etc., which is a rather discouraging picture.

Table 13.6 Cropping ventures round the year in Coochbehar

Season	Crop(s) cultivated	Net cultivable area (NCA) (ha)	Area allocated (%)	Yield (qtl/ha)	Seasonal void (%)	Cropping intensity (%)
Kharif	Winter rice	0.63	87.22	27.90	12.78	204.74
Rabi	Maize	0.63	42.57	69.40	14.24	
	Summer rice	0.63	43.19	60.22		
Pre-kharif	Jute	0.63	31.76	20.20	68.24	

Agricultural land and its utilisation pattern

In terms of agricultural land, the study found that farming is mostly marginal (i.e. up to one ha of land holding) in nature; this was also reflected in the randomised selection of sample units (i.e. the farmers). The average landholding (including homestead and pond area) was found to be 0.80 ha of which net cultivable area (NCA) constitutes the major share as expected. Average area of net cultivable area hovers around 0.62–0.63, ha which is distributed among three plots (Table 13.6).

Although the average irrigated area is hovering around 36 per cent of NCA, there was partial problem in the irrigation water in these two areas (BAES, 2012). Water was unavailable towards the end of the *rabi* season and during the pre-*kharif* season. As a result, the land mostly remained void during the pre-*kharif* season, and the cropping intensity hovered around 204 per cent in the study areas (Table 13.6). Major crops in this rice-based cropping system are winter rice (*aman*), maize, summer rice (*boro*) and jute. Rice-maize-fallow, rice-rice-fallow, rice-wheat-jute and rice-potato-jute are the prevailing cropping sequences.

Economic feasibility of maize cultivation

The introduction of maize in the cropping sequence is a rather recent phenomenon in this area (Table 13.7). The average experience in maize cultivation ranges from 1–4 years (mean = 1.74 years). Maize is cultivated as a *rabi* season crop from December to April. Government officials like Krishi Prajukti Sahayak, the office of the ADA, and the university are the perceived sources where farmers got information about maize culture. Of course, good market demand (domestic) from adjoining areas pose as an incentive for farmers to gradually increase the area allocation under maize. Although in most cases, the area under summer rice is replaced, there are instances of replacement of areas under wheat, potato and jute to accommodate maize production.

As maize is cultivated as a *rabi* season crop in this area, land is prepared from end of November to the first week of December after the harvest of *kharif* rice is over. The general level of application of organic manures, chemical fertilisers and chemicals (insecticides, pesticides, herbicides etc.) is low in comparison to

Table 13.7 Primary information on maize cultivation in the study area

Traits	Unit of expression	Magnitude/description
Major season of cultivation	–	*Rabi* (Nov–Dec to April–May)
Average years of introduction in the area	years	1.74
Area under cultivation	hectare	0.23
Size of maize plot	hectare	0.12–0.20
Replaced crop	–	Summer rice, wheat, jute
Source of first information	–	Department of Agriculture & University (*Krishi Vigyan Kendra*)
Perceived advantage	–	Attractive marketing demand

Table 13.8 Item-wise direct cost (prime cost) of maize cultivation

Cost item	Prime cost (Rs/hectare)	Percentage share
Land preparation	5115.38	14.37
Seed sowing	5212.50	14.65
Manure	7350.00	20.66
Fertilisers and micronutrients	2462.21	6.92
Irrigation	5 782.50	16.26
Weeding	2 370.00	6.66
Plant protection (PP) chemicals	51.00	0.14
Harvesting	3 240.00	9.11
Shelling	3 990.00	11.23
Total	3 5570.59	100.00

recommended levels, but human labour is used in sufficient numbers. Expenditure towards wage payment constitutes almost 50 per cent of the farming costs. Operation-wise, the cost break up is depicted in Table 13.8, which shows the percentage share of each operation. An idea about potential in capital investment in maize cultivation can be gleaned from the table. About Rs35,570 may be required as direct/paid-out cost for undertaking maize cultivation in a hectare of field; if taxes, imputed interest, depreciation etc. are taken into account, this would be inflated to Rs37,042. (Cost A_1). Again, when imputed family labour wage is added, cost (Cost C) becomes Rs49,402.

In general, hybrid varieties that have high yield potential are utilised in *rabi* maize cultivation (Badal and Singh 2001). The hybrid varieties like Monsanto 9081, Allrounder and Kaveri are widely cultivated in this area of study, and the yield level varies between 67–73 quintals per hectare. The yield level is good especially in the context of national (40.76 qtls/ha) (www.agriwatch.com) or state (38.27 qtls/ha) averages. Maize growers are mostly cultivating Monsanto 9081, Allrounder and Kaveri, which are high-yield varieties. As there is potential demand from the adjoining markets of Bihar (also Bangladesh), disposal of output is not a problem so far (Chauhan and Chhabra 2005). On average, a farmer can earn a gross sum of Rs 74,460 out of a hectare of maize field. The by-products of maize crop are hardly sold, and thereby, no return accrues (Table 13.9).

After reviewing the cost structure in detail, we now turn towards efficiency measures. Some important net return concepts along with ratio measures are used for judging farm efficiency in maize cultivation (Kahlon and Singh 1992, Thingbaijam 2011). A close perusal of the tables shows that farmers are earning an approximate net sum of about Rs39,000 over prime cost; Rs37,400 over Cost A_1 and Rs25,000 over Cost C. This finding is similar to that of Navadkar et al. (2012).Thus, the output–input ratio is 1.53 (on the basis of Cost C). If only paid-out cost is considered, the output–input ratio becomes 2.16, indicating a relatively better economic prospect of the venture (Table 13.10).

Table 13.9 Cost and return prospect in maize cultivation

Item	Type of cost	Cost/return (Rs./hectare)
Cost	Prime cost	35570.59
	Cost A_1	37042.91
	Cost C	49402.91
Return	Gross return	74460.19
Profitability	Return over prime cost	38889.60
	Return over Cost A_1	37417.28
	Return over Cost C	25057.28

Table 13.10 Farm efficiency measures in maize cultivation in the study areas

Attribute	Unit of expression	Value
Physical yield	Quintals per hectare	69.39
Output–input ratio (on the basis of total cost)	Ratio	1.53
Output–input ratio (on the basis of paid-out cost)	Ratio	2.16
Output per man-day application	Rs. per man-day	463.36

Constraints in maize cultivation

As has been observed both from the secondary as well as the primary information in the previous sections, maize is a lucrative cropping venture, and its area is increasing in both the Coochbehar-I and Coochbehar-II blocks in recent years. Gradually, the crop is gaining importance in the food grain basket. Good market prospects coupled with the multifarious potential utilisation of maize induced farming folks in these areas to replace summer rice, wheat and other crops with *rabi* maize. As such, farmers do not foresee any problem in the cultivation practices, but they voiced apprehension regarding some aspects that may deter their present enthusiasm and cause a slump in the cropping venture. Therefore, an attempt has been made to trace out the constraints perceived by the maize growers in these areas. The results are presented in Table 13.11. Possible problems identified through the pilot survey were listed in the questionnaire, and farmers were then asked to indicate the gravity of the problem. Scores were assigned as absolutely true = 3, partially true = 2, cannot decide = 1 and absolutely not true = 0. Obtained scores were averaged to find out the biggest constraints. As observed from the table, low output price, lack of technical expertise, non-availability of labour, non-availability of high-yielding variety (HYV) seeds, and uncertain climate were perceived as the most important problems in the study area.

Capacity building: intervening issues

Results of the study show that maize cropping venture is highly suitable for farming, particularly for marginal farmers. Maize can provide the role of a 'cash crop'

Table 13.11 Perceived constraints in maize cultivation

Constraints	Obtained score	
	Coochbehar-I	Coochbehar-II
Low output price	3.0	3.0
Lack of knowledge	3.0	3.0
Non-availability of labour	2.0	2.0
Uncertain climate	2.0	2.0
Non-availability of HYV seed	2.0	2.0
Insufficient capital	1.74	2.37
Non availability of irrigation water	1.68	1.79
Lack of market	0.0	0.0
Low productivity	0.0	0.0
Diseases and pests	0.0	0.0
Non availability of other inputs	0.0	0.0

and can be a big boost for uplifting the socio-economic status of a farm family. However, the momentum, so gained, has to be sustained for better capacity building and improving the overall farm economy. Recent enthusiasm in allocating more area under maize by replacing other *rabi* crops can be sustained through institutional/non-institutional measures.

In the constraint analysis, farmers were asked to prioritise the problems they faced, and 'lack of knowledge' about the cultural practices of the crop was opined to be the prime issue (Table 13.11). This is where the role of extension agencies – both government (State Agricultural Extension Department and *Krishi Vigyan Kendras*) and non-government (farmers' clubs, NGOs etc.) – play a catalytic role. The farming community, in general, is 'mis-informed' about the 'package of practices' of maize cultivation, so indiscriminate use of inputs is a recurring phenomenon. Little knowledge about nutrient management may have devastating effects on soil quality too. The yield level, which, at present, is around 7 metric tonnes per ha (mt per ha), may come down to a dismal level (say, 4–4.5 mt per ha, the present average national figure) due to poor soil fertility. This will put at risk the potential for a year-round economically feasible cropping venture. Therefore, regular awareness campaign (especially at the beginning of the season) for new agricultural knowledge and cropping practices is needed, particularly in light of the fast changing technologies in agriculture.

Results of the study showed that farmers do not have problems regarding marketing of their produce/output. But, with the expansion in area (and production) under maize in the coming years, it is likely that the venture may be affected (demand-supply-price tangle). At present, the zone does not have any agro-processing unit to process upcoming increased output. Establishment of a suitable agro-processing unit may solve the potential problem.

Price volatility (Rs. 9,000 to Rs. 12,000 per mt in the current year) of maize output was also considered a problem in the study. In the absence of price-control mechanisms or market regulation, output price is likely to be volatile in future. If the cropping venture has to sustain its present economic potential (benefit–cost ratio = 2.16), price stabilisation measures may need to be considered. This issue needs further investigation.

Finally, farm mechanisation has a role to play as migration of human labour (towards neighbouring states for alternative opportunities) is a recurring and ever rising phenomenon in this area. Apart from field operations, there is also a need for mechanised operations in extraction of grains (shelling) from the cob and various post-harvest operations. Shelling opens up scope for service provision and can well be an opportunity for off-farm enterprise in capacity-building programmes, especially for farm women.

Conclusion

Time series analysis indicated that the district of Coochbehar is gaining importance as a maize-growing area in the Bengal economy, but 'sustainability' was a prime concern. Incorporation of *rabi* maize in the cropping system is indeed an economically worthwhile enterprise in the area under study and can well be thought of as a feasible venture for improving the plight of farming folks. However, while farmers were really enthusiastic in accommodating maize year round, they need to improve their knowledge on modern cropping practices. In particular, areas for better capacity building need to focus on some important issues like awareness/refreshment of knowledge situations, development of market linkages for proper disposal of output and reducing price instability (especially, output price). These are critical to ensure long-term sustainability of maize-cropping systems in the area.

Awareness or refreshment of knowledge is the responsibility of extension officials (government) and the farmers' clubs (private) operating in an area. Improving farmers' knowledge and building their capacity has two advantages: one, the possibility of better cropping practices due to upgraded knowledge of the farmers and, two, better management of existing scarce resource bases leading to better cropping sequence. With continued training programmes, individual farmers can, at least, plan profitable cropping sequence around the year. Training programmes at the beginning of the season are thus beneficial for maize growers.

In the absence of a minimum support price for maize in this part of the country, timely availability of market information may act as possible cushion for distress sale of farm produce. Development of forewarning system through 'messaging' (by cell phone) may be a feasible option in this regard. Therefore, orientation towards strengthening market linkages or increasing the (rather sluggish) farmers' mobility should be a component of capacity-building programmes. The role of non-government organisations or the farmers' clubs is of paramount importance here and is an area for future studies.

References

Bureau of Applied Economics and Statistics 2012, *District statistical handbook: Cooch Behar*, Bureau of Applied Economics and Statistics (BAES), Department of Statistics and Programme Implementation, Government of West Bengal, West Bengal, India, pp. 39–41.

Bureau of Applied Economics and Statistics 2008, *Statistical abstract*, Bureau of Applied Economics and Statistics, Government of West Bengal, West Bengal, India, pp. 117, 135, 153.

Barman, S. 2014, 'Role & contribution of maize (*Zea mays* L) in improving farm economy – a study in Coochbehar district of West Bengal', M.Sc(Ag) thesis, Department of Agricultural Economics, Uttar Banga Krishi Viswavidyalaya, Coochbehar, West Bengal, India, pp. 41–48.

Badal, P.S. and Singh, R.P. 2001, 'Technological change in maize production: a case study of Bihar', *Indian Journal of Agricultural Economics*, vol. 56, no. 2, pp. 211–219.

Chauhan, S.K. and Chhabra, A. 2005, 'Marketable surplus and price-spread for maize in Hamirpur District of Himachal Pradesh', *Agricultural Economics Research Review*, vol. 18, no. 1, pp. 39–49.

Indiastat 2015a, *Statistical information*, Datanet India, New Delhi, India, viewed 22 July 2015, <www.indiastat.com/table/agriculture/2/maize/17199/897928/data.aspx>.

Indiastat 2015b, *Statistical information*, Datanet India, New Delhi, India, viewed 22 July 2015, <www.indiastat.com/table/agriculture/2/maize/17199/897969/data.aspx>.

Indiastat 2015c, *Statistical information*, Datanet India, New Delhi, India, viewed 22 July 2015, <www.indiastat.com/agriculture/2/maize/17199/454876/data.aspx>.

Indiastat 2015d, *Statistical information*, Datanet India, New Delhi, India, viewed 22 July 2015, <www.indiastat.com/agriculture/2/maize/17199/80071/data.aspx>.

Kahlon, A.S. and Singh K. 1992, *Economics of farm management in India: theory and practice*, 2nd ed., Allied Publishers, New Delhi, India.

Kamruzzaman, M. and Takeya, H. 2008, 'Determination of Capacity Building by Life Stage for the farmers in Bangladesh', *Nature and Science*, vol. 6, no.4, pp. 8–15.

Navadkar, D.S., Amale, A.J., Gulave, C.M. and Nannaware, V.M. 2012, 'Economics of production and marketing of Kharif Maize in Ahmednagar District of Maharashtra State', *Agricultural Situation in India*, September, vol. LXIX, no. 6, pp. 309–316.

Onphanhdala, P. 2009, 'Farmer Education and Agricultural Efficiency: Evidence from Lao PDR', *GSICS Working Paper Series*, no. 20, Kobe University, Japan.

Singh, S.S. 2005, *Crop management*, Kalyani Publishers, New Delhi, India.

Thingbaijam, L. 2011, 'Economics of production and marketing of pineapple in Thoubal District of Manipur', M.Sc (Ag) thesis, Department of Agricultural Economics, College of Agriculture, Central Agricultural University, Imphal, Manipur, India.

United Nations Development Programme 1991, 'Defining Capacity Building', briefing paper for the A Strategy for Water Sector Capacity Building symposium, UNDP and International Institute for Hydraulic and Environmental Engineering, Delft, Netherlands, viewed 20 July 2015, <www.gdrc.org/uem/capacity-define.html>.

Waridin 2013, 'Capacity building on food-crop farming to improve food production and food security in Central Java, Indonesia', *Asian Journal of Agriculture and Rural Development*, vol. 3, no. 3, pp. 108–114.

Weir, S. 1999, 'The effect of education on farmer productivity in rural Ethiopia', *Working Paper*, no. 99–97, Centre for the Study of African Economies, University of Oxford, Oxford, UK.

14 Concluding thoughts

Maria Fay Rola-Rubzen, John Burgess and Yue Liu

Capacity building is now widely recognised by governments and international development organisations as a critical and essential part of sustainable development. As such, many governments, particularly in developing countries have made capacity building one of the cornerstones of their development strategies. Capacity building is recognised to be important in creating self-sustaining societies where people can better enjoy their rights as well as participate in the economy.

The volume demonstrated the many different processes and programmes linked to capacity building across the Asia-Pacific region. Capacity building is linked to community development, and there are strong similarities between the rationale and design of capacity building in a developmental context to community development programmes in deprived urban regions of developed economies (Craig 2005). The key is community engagement and participation in programmes and an ongoing process of development. In this volume, the examples of capacity building demonstrated that capacity building applies to both poor and developed economies; it incorporates infrastructure and capital investment, and ideas and opportunity. It is about empowerment and providing access to skills, information, training and knowledge that can assist in opening up opportunities and improving local living conditions. Also, it is not about immediate gains in production, employment or investment; it incorporates less visible gains such as opportunities, access, participation, health, skills and know-how. The United Nations Human Development Report for 2014 (United Nations Development Programme 2014: 1) captured these issues when it stated that:

> Real progress on human development, then, is not only a matter of enlarging people's critical choices and their ability to be educated, be healthy, have a reasonable standard of living and feel safe. It is also a matter of how secure these achievements are and whether conditions are sufficient for sustained human development.

All of these issues come through the chapters that are included in the volume. The case studies presented in this book demonstrate the multi-faceted nature of capacity building which can occur at individual, organisational, local, regional, state and national levels. As experience has shown, the impact of capacity build-ing cannot be overlooked. Capacity building is an important way to invest in the future. As the case studies in this volume suggest, capacity building can empower people and can transform organisations and communities.

What is needed for capacity building to work? It is evident that, for capac-ity building to be effective, it is important that the needs and initial capacities are first identified and that the objectives or goals of the capacity-building activity(ies) are clear. Identifying the appropriate method of capacity build-ing is also important, including the way capacity building is employed, the use of resources, and the delivery of capacity-building programmes. Capacity-building programmes often also need resources (financial, human, informa-tion, decision-making tools and physical resources). Strong leadership and partnerships are also important whether they be with governments, NGOs, educational and research institutions and other parties that can contribute to capacity building.

Although capacity building is important, there are also a number of challenges. The key challenges for capacity building often include the lack of resources to support capacity-building activities, it may not be easily transferable, and there is a lack of evaluation of the effectiveness of capacity building. Funding can be a limiting factor. Project-based, capacity-building activities, for instance, often face the issue of sustainability, i.e. of how to continue successful capacity-building programmes when the project funds run out. It is difficult to adopt capacity building to improve institutions in countries with limited resources.

Capacity building is also not a one-size-fits-all state of affair. A specific capacity-building programme in an urban area, for example may not resolve the problem in a rural area (Katsuhama 2010) or in another urban area. Hence, understanding the specific needs of the focal individuals or organisations or groups is important in designing appropriate capacity-building programmes.

Furthermore, although there are numerous frameworks for capacity building, the situation varies across sectors. There is still a lack of policy and monitoring frameworks in some sectors (e.g. see Alaerts, Blair and Hartvelt [1991] on the water sector). Moreover, there is not enough managerial skill in some institutions to help with capacity-building projects.

In its call for a concerted attack on reducing inequality in Asia, Oxfam (2015) suggested that an effective programme for change rests on five pillars: people empowerment, access to essential services, access to land and produc-tive resources, fair wages and fair taxation. Local capacity building is important across all these pillars. Opening up opportunities for marginalised groups such as women enhances both economic and political capability. Local access to key ser-vices such as health and education also improves earnings potential through skill improvements and ongoing workforce participation. Access to other productive services such as energy, transport and communications can also make a difference to long-term living standards. Delivering core public services includes a legal system that is operational across the community and a taxation system that is fair and equitable and can finance local development.

The UK Department for International Development (Department for International Development [DFID] 2013: 15) in its review of its own community and capacity-building projects suggested that the following lessons (among many that were listed) were important:

- Examining the relative strengths and weaknesses of community development interventions with different forms of partnership, and over different time-frames, in order to identify the variables that bring about significant and positive change in power relations, equity and voice, as well as other benefits.
- Supporting pilot community development initiatives that take a systemic approach in different contexts . . . in order to identify more clearly which variables have critical impact on CD effectiveness.
- Supporting the development of innovative strategies for evaluation of CD and change processes from a systems and learning perspective – paying particular attention to comparative analysis of existing capacity and resulting needs, and processes by which CD interventions are then established through collaboration of different stakeholders.
- Engaging with international and regional networks that are problematising and addressing CD challenges, and providing support to those institutions.

The report went on to emphasise the importance of empowerment, fostering R&D processes in developing countries and supporting researchers and local research in those countries.

In this book, we have seen a variety of capacity development programmes that include women in leadership (Myanmar), rural public works programmes (Indonesia), local training programmes (Australia), improved water management programmes (India), improved crop management programmes (India), improved access to markets for agricultural produce (Timor Leste) and addressing corruption in public sector organisations (India).

The preceding chapters demonstrate the multifaceted process of capacity building and the range of capacity-building programmes that have been developed across Asia and the Pacific. What we can learn from the research is as follows. First, capacity building supports local community development, and it is linked to local community aspirations. This involves both ownership and participation in programme development at the local level. Second, capacity building does not necessarily involve large-scale investments. Simple programmes that provide training, support and knowledge can be effective in assisting local development. Third, capacity building extends beyond physical capital and infrastructure; many of the programmes discussed were about developing human skills and capacity in terms of leadership, participation and accessing knowledge. Fourth, there remains a role for external donors in providing capital, communications infrastructure, skills, expertise, training, knowledge, seed varieties and market access. Many of the programmes outlined were supported by and dependent on external donors, and donors continue to have an ongoing and key role to play in capacity building. Fifth, ongoing development challenges in terms of including groups that are marginalised from labour markets, training, paid employment and governance systems and alleviating individual and community risks linked to natural disasters, public health and political instability remain priorities. One of the biggest challenges remains that of supporting and facilitating excluded and marginalised groups, especially women and those in remote communities, into the formal economy and into decision making and governance processes.

There are opportunities for conducting research into capacity building at a number of levels. At the theoretical level, there is the opportunity to incorporate the emerging literature in such areas as leadership development, entrepreneurial capabilities, sustainable development, the knowledge economy, skills and competency development and diversity management. Across the globe, including advanced economies, remote regions with low average incomes and without the infrastructure to support development have always been a challenge in terms of development assistance, service access and infrastructure development (Queensland Government 2008). New technologies, new theoretical insights and new conceptualisations of the development process offer the opportunity to experiment and develop programmes that are accessible and cost effective and have a positive impact on local communities (DFID 2013; United Nations Environmental Program 2006). Many of the cases cited in this volume serve as examples of where this has happened. It is also important to not only re-conceptualise and experiment; it is also important to document cases and establish the determinants of effectiveness and learn from those cases that did not succeed. Many NGOs are developing extensive case files and guides to programme development, implementation and evaluation (DFID 2013). This highlights the importance of examining all phases of capacity programmes from their design to their implementation and governance mechanisms, through to their immediate and long-term effects.

Finally, the process is ongoing and covers all aspects of community and economic development. While capacity building is a broad-ranging agenda, it does not mean that capacity building should be devoid of systematic and thorough evaluation. The effectiveness of capacity-building programmes needs to be examined. Given the importance of capacity building in sustainable development and poverty alleviation, understanding the impacts of various programmes, the delivery models, the frameworks and the factors influencing success is vital. Development practitioners and governments need to know the barriers and constraints affecting capacity-building activities and programmes. Even information on unsuccessful programmes is vital in providing insights of what works and what does not work and thus contribute in development of better and more effective capacity-building programmes. What works and what does not may in many cases be defined by local cultural and political conditions, but there still remains a need to document and evaluate all programmes. This book has contributed to this process by setting out a diverse range of cases where capacity-building challenges have been identified and addressed to different degrees.

References

Alaerts, G. J., Blair, T. L., and Hartvelt, F.J.A. 1991, 'A strategy for water sector capacity building', proceedings of the UNDP Symposium, Delft, Netherlands, 3–5 June, 1991. International Institute for Hydraulic and Environmental Engineering and United Nations Development Programme, viewed 20 November 2015, <www.ircwash.org/sites/default/files/202.2-91ST-9224.pdf>.

Craig, G. 2005, *Community capacity-building: definitions, scope, measurements and critiques,* Organisation for Economic Co-operation and Development (OECD) Publishing, Prague, Czech Republic.

Department for International Development 2013, *DFID research strategy 2008–2013: working paper series: capacity building,* Department for International Development (DFID), London, UK.

Katsuhama, Y. 2010, 'Capacity building for flood management in developing countries under climate change', PhD thesis, Department of Civil and Environmental Engineering, Colorado State University, Fort Collins, CO. ProQuest Dissertations & Theses Full Text; ProQuest Dissertations & Theses Global database.

Oxfam 2015, *Asia at the crossroads: why the region must address inequality,* Oxfam, Oxford, UK.

Queensland Government 2008, *Community capacity toolkit for regional and remote communities,* Department of Communities, Brisbane, Australia.

United Nations Development Programme 2014, *Human development report 2014,* United Nations, New York, NY.

United Nations Environmental Program 2006, *Ways to increase the effectiveness of capacity building for sustainable development,* United Nations Environmental Program, Stavenger, Norway.

Index

Page numbers in *italics* refer to figures and tables.